THE
RADICAL DURKHEIM

TITLES OF RELATED INTEREST

*The Elementary Forms of the Religious Life**
Emile Durkheim

The Protestant Ethic and the Spirit of Capitalism
Max Weber

Max Weber, Rationality and Modernity
Sam Whimster and Scott Lash (eds)

Max Weber and his Contemporaries
Wolfgang Mommsen and Jürgen Osterhammel (eds)

Max Weber and Karl Marx
Karl Löwith

Max Weber: Essays in Reconstruction
Wilhelm Hennis

Max Weber's 'Science as a Vocation'
Peter Lassman and Irving Velody, with Herminio Martins

Law, Socialism and Democracy
Paul Q. Hirst

Marxism, Class Analysis and Socialist Pluralism
Les Johnston

*Not available from Unwin Hyman Inc in the USA

THE RADICAL DURKHEIM

Frank Pearce

London
UNWIN HYMAN
Boston   Sydney   Wellington

Published by the Academic Division of
Unwin Hyman Ltd
15/17 Broadwick Street, London W1V 1FP, UK

Unwin Hyman Inc.,
8 Winchester Place, Winchester, Mass. 01890, USA

Allen & Unwin (Australia) Ltd,
8 Napier Street, North Sydney, NSW 2060, Australia

Allen & Unwin (New Zealand) Ltd in association with the
Port Nicholson Press Ltd,
Compusales Building, 75 Ghuznee Street, Wellington, New Zealand

First published in 1989

British Library Cataloguing in Publication Data
Pearce, Frank
   The radical Durkheim
   1. Sociology, Theories of Durkheim, Emile
   I. Title
   301'.092'4

   ISBN 0–04–445269–1
        0–04–445270–5 Pbk

Library of Congress Cataloging-in-Publication Data
Pearce, Frank.
   The radical Durkheim/Frank Pearce.
      p.   cm.
   Bibliography: p.
   Includes index.
   ISBN 0–04–445269–1 (alk. paper). – ISBN 0–04–445270–5 (pbk.:
alk. paper)
      1. Durkheim, Emile, 1858–1917. 2. Sociology–France–History.
   I. Title.
   HM22.F8D869 1989   88–31366
   301'.092'4–dc19   CIP

Typeset in 10/11 point Bembo by Columns Typesetters of Reading and
printed in Great Britain by Billing and Son, London and Worcester

**Dedicated to
Elaine, Rory and Blake**

Displacement is the opposite of citation, of the theoretical authority which is always falsified by the mere fact of becoming a citation; a fragment torn out of its context, its movement, and finally its epoch as a general reference and as a precise choice which it was within this reference, exactly recognized or erroneous. Displacement is the fluid language of anti-ideology. It appears within communication which knows that it cannot pretend to hold any guarantee in itself and definitively. It is, at its highest point, the language which cannot be confirmed by any ancient and supra-critical reference. On the contrary, it is its own coherence, within itself and with practicable facts, which can confirm the ancient grain of truth which it brings out. Displacement has not grounded its cause on anything external to its own truth as present critique.

(**Guy Debord,** *Society of the Spectacle*)

Contents

Preface

In this book I want to look at some of the writings of Durkheim, not to point to their shortcomings, but rather to show how his more fruitful arguments can be developed to extend our understanding of social and political change. In the opening chapter I discuss the problem of reading theory creatively – an important one if we are to learn to recognize and unravel the different discourses and chains of meaning that lie embedded in any piece of theoretical writing and learn to put theory to good use, rather than simply accepting or rejecting it. My main aim is to reveal and retheorize the concepts that inform Durkheim's work, and out of this exploration to generate and develop new and, I believe, important theoretical analyses. This rereading, indeed any rereading, is determined and informed by the concerns of the reader. My theoretical and political concerns therefore affect both the way I read and the kinds of reformulation I seeks to undertake. This is the nature of intertextuality, or what Dominick LaCapra has called the transferential relationship: the conscious and, at times, unconscious dialogue between a writer and a reader, where the reader finds his own symptoms in the text alongside the manifest concerns of the writer, and seeks answers to his own questions, which may be different from those posed by the writer. Writer and reader leave their marks, or traces, on one another, and this process is reproduced when the reader commits his thought to writing, thus opening the way for greater textual richness and dialogue with other readers.

Why should we return to Durkheim's work yet again? First because, contrary to the almost universal consensus amongst sociologists, in Durkheim's texts neither the dominant discourses nor those present only as partially suppressed fragments can be construed as inherently conservative or positivistic. His *oeuvre* is complex, multifaceted, often characterized by a ruthlessly anti-Utopian logic and with an extraordinary potential fruitfulness. Then, to put it simply, it is because as a committed socialist and social scientist I believe that whilst Marxism is the most fruitful of all socialist and sociological discourses it needs the aid of Durkheim's concepts to rid itself of both its Utopianism and its anthropocentrism. Marxism's claim is that it has the necessary tools to analyse the nature and bases of class societies, to specify feasible alternative non-exploitative social orders and to identify the agents and mechanisms by which there will be movement from one to the other. The contemporary crisis of Marxism shows how problematic these claims are. However, this crisis has not, as only too many self-styled 'post-Marxists' seem to imagine, signified the exhaustion of Marxism, but rather provided the task and opportunity of ruthlessly pruning Marxism of its errors and incoherences and of inhibiting its overextension. Thanks to the critical theoretical work of Althusser and others in the structuralist tradition there is now a much slimmed down version of Marxism, within which some key concepts, such as the relations of production, have been retained and others, such as ideology, have been displaced. In this new system of concepts inevitably there are lacunae, which can only be remedied by a selective borrowing from kindred traditions such as a retheorized Durkheimism. To be more accurate, fruitful theory can be developed by a transferential and countertransferential relationship between the slimmed down versions of both traditions.

The goal of this book, then, is both to engage in an immanent critique of Durkheim's *oeuvre* and then, through a dialogue with a non-humanistic Marxism, to retain, develop and modify certain of his conceptualizations. This reconstituted Du.kheimism will in turn be used to critique certain aspects of Marxism. The early chapters involve a somewhat structuralist and realist interrogation of Durkheim's work followed by a reconstitution of certain of his concepts and a reformulation of his arguments. Since a major concern of the book is to develop a more adequate picture of the parameters within which a *feasible socialist society* could operate, there is continual reference to the manifest and latent socialist elements of Durkheim's thought. In Chapters 3–7 Durkheim's work is interrogated and reworked in relationship to these concerns. Thus attention is particularly paid to *The Rules of Sociological Method*, *The Division of Labour in Society*, *Suicide*, and *The Elementary Forms of the Religious Life*, although many other texts are also utilized.

In Chapter 8 this reconstituted Durkheimism is used in turn to interrogate Marxism. Whilst Marx was scathing about Utopian socialism he was by no means immune to its dangers and this was particularly true of his image of communism and of its relationship to socialism. Durkheim helps provide a critique of Marx's concept of communism, and forces socialists to be somewhat less sanguine about the presence and role of the state and law in socialist societies. In Chapter 9 it is shown that, whilst there are significant discontinuities between capitalist and socialist societies, there are also continuities – in relationship to their forms of order and their likely sources of disorder. This could help socialists produce less moralistic critiques of capitalism and develop more realistic, hence modest but also realizable, political programmes. This interrogative dialogue between a reconstituted Durkheimism and a slimmed down Marxism, which is summarized in the concluding chapter, has, then, both a theoretical and practical import. Reading/rereading theory is never a disinterested act and it may therefore be limited by the designation of only certain problems as worthy of exploration; yet for all that it can produce unexpected conclusions – the conclusions of this work were only in part anticipated – and this provides both some of its excitement and, by suggesting that it is not merely a rationalizing activity, some warrant of its authenticity.

This book has grown out of more than twenty years' struggle with sociological theory and particularly with the works of Marx, Weber and Durkheim. Needless to say I have read and reread their major texts many times, and, if such rereadings have been different, it is because I have also been involved in trying to understand and evaluate other more contemporary schools of thought. My own preferences are relatively clear, but it seems to me axiomatic that no one theoretical discourse monopolizes knowledge and equally that any serious school of thought always produces some valuable insights. I also believe that it is only if one is rigorous in exegesis and criticism that one treats such schools with respect. I would underline the need to respect the integrity both of other theorists as people themselves struggling with difficult problems and of the discourses that they produce in the course of that work. I hope I have succeeded in relating to the work of Durkheim (and others) in that spirit. If I have it is in large part due to the help of a number of people over many years. This book is based upon a PhD thesis successfully submitted at the University of Essex. I am grateful to Ian Craib who was the most collegial of supervisors and whose pointed questions and timely silences gave me the space to discover what it was that I was doing. I thank Ted Benton and Mike Gane, the internal and external examiners, for making my PhD *viva* a rich and creative experience. Mike Gane's comments on different drafts of this book have undoubtedly helped to make the arguments clearer and I hope more rigorous. Paul Hirst, James Dickinson, Michael Bodemann and Julia Casterton have also commented on earlier drafts of this book. The whole enterprise would have been far more difficult without the invaluable help of John Knockles, librarian at Wolverhampton Polytechnic. Andy Roberts first showed me the absurdity of the conventional dismissals of Durkheim as a positivist and a reactionary, not least by his own creative use of the concept of the *conscience collective*. Jerry Palmer has been an invaluable guide through the vagaries of literary theory. My vigorous discussions with Jock Young have been and remain a source of great intellectual stimulation. The same is true of my many dialogues with both John Lea and Roger Matthews. For many years Tony Woodiwiss has shared with me his understanding of the sociological classics, structuralism and post-structuralism and much else besides. These discussions and his own work have been a continuous inspiration. To all of these I owe my heartfelt thanks. Finally I am particularly grateful to Elaine. In the context of our bringing up Rory and Blake, our two wonderful, if sometimes infuriating, children she has not only tolerated my distracted air but has encouraged it. By sharing with me her knowledge of French political theory she has forced me to acknowledge the power of 'humanism' even if I have put it 'to work' in a different discourse. Needless to say, neither she nor anyone else is responsible for any errors or weaknesses in what I have finally written.

THE
RADICAL DURKHEIM

1 *Introduction*

Introduction

Why, if at all, should we return yet again to Durkheim? Since his theories have been explored with a superabundance of exegeses and commentaries, of critiques, corrections and comparisons, is it possible in reading his work to discover anything new? Perhaps more importantly, why should contemporary radicals, particularly socialists and Marxists, bother to read such a positivistic, conservative thinker? And yet recently at least three radical commentators – Gane (1983a,b, 1984), Hirst (1975, 1986, 1987) and Therborn (1980) – have praised many of his arguments and conceptualizations and made significant and innovative use of them. This suggests that his work been inadequately analysed, that the full range of his concepts has not been grasped.

The major argument of this book is that, with few exceptions, Durkheim's concepts have been accepted or rejected in a somewhat dogmatic and unimaginative way and that too little attention has been paid to the possibility of *developing* them fruitfully. The corpus of his work needs to be carefully examined and then retheorized – a task that needs theorizing itself. Neither Durkheim himself nor his disciples have exhausted the potential of his concepts, either for exploring general issues – the nature of 'social order' and how the human subject is socially constituted, for example – or for confronting and, in part, resolving Marxism's current crisis. Economism and anthropocentrism still undermine Marxism's attempts to theorize the bases of social order and social change, i.e. to address the meaning of 'mode of production' and 'social formation'; the nature of the state; the role of class relations in constituting social groupings; the place of ideology; the variety and forms of oppression and resistance; how to identify the diverse agents of progressive social change and specify the kinds of strategies needed to unify them around a socialist programme. There remains no less of a problem about the nature of a socialist social order and which 'social problems' could, or could not, be

1

eliminated or displaced by its realization.

Reading theory is not a simple, self-evident task – intellectual activity is never presuppositionless. Whilst within critical social science the recognition of the importance of the epistemological, political and moral assumptions that lurk within allegedly objective sociological analyses has a long and useful history, there remains the problem of the appropriate stance to take towards 'flawed' work. In recent years the problem of the interpretation, assessment and use of theoretical discourses has been usefully raised for literary theory and cultural studies as well as the social sciences by the 'structuralist' and 'post-structuralist' schools. An important implication of such work is that the specification of the inadequate political and epistemological assumptions within a text does not simply discredit it; it still may be an advance in its specific field, and it may be possible to reformulate it so that it is more coherent and productive. This chapter will briefly address this question of 'reading'. First, I shall briefly discuss the conventional modes of viewing Durkheim's work.

The political evaluation of Durkheim

One reason for the underdevelopment of Durkheimian theory is the generally hostile relationship between sociology and Marxism. Sociologists either ignored Marxism – engaging in what Appleman Williams (1964) described in the context of history as 'the great evasion' – or parodied it and then dismissed it as an ideology.[1] Some, like the more humanistic of American sociologists, have used the works of Marx selectively, borrowing from his early writings to give more substance to their less technocratic 'alternative' sociology. Yet others have developed a neo-Weberian interpretation of his work, thereby missing many of its strengths and rendering it more vulnerable to their criticisms. Sociology's hostility towards Marxism has been matched by Marxism's own attitude to sociology.[2] Many Marxists have argued that there is a fundamental opposition between the two discourses. Some Marxists, for example Nizan and Llobera, and some 'radical sociologists', such as Zeitlin and Coser, have singled out Durkheim's work for criticism – because of 'its inherent conservatism'. Sorel (1895a), however, whilst critical of his work, early recognized its potential and, more recently, Taylor, Walton and Young have claimed that his concept of anomie and his desire to abolish inherited wealth made Durkheim a radical critic of capitalism (1973, pp. 87–8). Hunt (1978) and Lukes (1975) have a more complex and adequate position than most of these since they capture the ambiguities in Durkheim's work produced by the presence of a number of different political discourses within it.

If one contextualizes Durkheim's arguments,[3] and particularly if one recognizes quite how 'adventurist' much nineteenth-century revolutionary socialism was, then even Durkheim's negative comments about syndicalism and Marxism cannot simply be read as inherently conservative. In fact, many of the specific practical political demands Durkheim supported did not differ that much from those of *The Manifesto of the Communist Party* (Marx and Engels, 1948). His analysis of religion is similar to that of Marx, at least in his Feuerbachian phase, and, in part, overlaps with Althusser's theory of ideology (Strawbridge, 1982). Indeed French neo-structuralists from Lévi-Strauss through to Althusser and, whatever he might usually have claimed, Foucault are indebted to *both* Durkheim *and* Marx. Durkheim's unique sense of the power and irreduceability of the 'social', of the indispensable and creative nature of the 'ideological community', can be developed and synthesized with a rigorous version of Marxism to produce a more complex understanding of the social realm.

Durkheim and science

Durkheim's work is somewhat confused, often contradictory, assertive and prescriptive so it is not surprising that there have been very different evaluations and uses made of it. Some of those sympathetic to Durkheim have attempted to systematize and clarify his work in order to make it more scientific, i.e. objective and empirical. Alpert (1939, 1965), for example, has claimed that Durkheim's analysis of both law and religion can then be shown to be sound. Selvin (1965) and Merton (1965) have endorsed much of his theory and methodology but believed it needs to be formalized and subject to more adequate empirical control. Parsons congratulated Durkheim for also being preoccupied with 'the problem of the integration of the social system', but then claimed to show how 'it has been both necessary and possible to go beyond the stage at which he left them' (Parsons, 1960, p. 118). Parsons' earlier position in his *The Structure of Social Action* was much more complex. Durkheim's thought, he argued, passed through four phases and although each confronted important problems none of them provided a satisfactory solution – indeed ultimately 'in escaping from the toils of positivism' he shot 'clean over into idealism' (Parsons, 1949, p. 445). Parsons' own theory of social action neither adequately synthesized the valid elements of the classical sociological theories (Wrong, 1961; Hindess, 1977b; Savage, 1981) nor solved the problems that had defeated Durkheim amongst others. Berger and Luckman (1967) produced a somewhat different synthesis of elements of the thought of Weber and Durkheim, although this time stirring the young Marx into their cocktail – but a Weber minus his analysis of power, a Marx with no theory of exploitation and, of most interest here, a Durkheim with an undynamic, indeed lifeless sense of the social (Lichtman, 1971; Geras, 1971; Filmer et al, 1972). Such theorists do not adequately respect the complexity, integrity and uncomfortable implications of theoretical discourses – they are willing to raid them, dismantle them and borrow from them to give authority and flesh to what they already believe or to generate syncretic syntheses. Yet other commentators have questioned Durkheim's scientific pretensions. For Douglas (1967) his substantive work is irrelevant since his methodology is inappropriate for the analysis of human behaviour, and his theory is unscientific because it is tautological. For Nisbet (1963), Durkheim's lack of objectivity, i.e. his conservatism, is a strength since the search for an absolutely objective social science is an illusion.

Thus on the one hand there are many critics who wish to render Durkheim more 'scientific', by tidying him up or by eliminating distortions due to the intrusion of value bias, so that his work fits the procrustean bed of a positivistic hypothetico–deductive science. On the other hand there are those who reject the relevance of science for the analysis of human behaviour and advocate instead one or other form of idealism. Much recent writing has demonstrated that these are false alternatives not least because the positivist model does not even fit the natural sciences (Keat and Urry, 1975; Bhaskar 1978); furthermore Durkheim's 'scientific rationalism' is not a simple variant of positivism. Of major interest is that, whether correcting or dismissing it, both positions share a dogmatic approach to Durkheim's work – judging it by some already constituted theoretical discourse.

Rereading theory

The characteristics and limitations of such an approach to theory were explored by Althusser in his discussion of the two different ways in which Marx read classical political economy. In a dogmatic reading the earlier text is reduced to the status of an anticipation (or ramification) of the later discourse and its study will therefore yield little of interest. In contrast to this he advocates a 'symptomatic reading' by which one can identify 'the combined existence of sightings and oversights which in an author "poses a problem, the problem of their combination".' This helps one to search for examples of 'the correct answer to a question . . . that was never posed' (Althusser and Balibar, 1970, pp. 19–22) and to recognize the presence of more than one discourse in a text, to separate them out and to discover if they complement, suppress or displace each other thereby truncating each other's development. The symptomatic reading will be effective

> in so far as it divulges the undivulged event in the text it reads, and in the same moment relates it to a different text, present as a necessary absence in the first . . . the second text is articulated with lapses in the first.
>
> (Althusser and Balibar 1970, p. 28)

In practice Althusser distinguishes between two different kinds of texts, one of which can indeed be assessed dogmatically, as having nothing to say – although it may be internally consistent to the point that it only ever poses questions that it has already answered – whereas the other is not so much ideological as pre-scientific.[4] The latter are read symptomatically from a position grounded in an already constituted scientific discourse. This helps to identify its useful parts and to discover symptoms (of incoherence) and to assess whether these merely indicate inadequacies or a point at which discourses intersect. Hirst's *Durkheim, Bernard and Epistemology* (1975) is such a reading of Durkheim. He stresses the power of Durkheim's critique of social contract theories, applauds his consistent anti-humanist stance, his anti-subjectivism and his assertion of the irreduceable nature of the social, but criticizes him for misrepresenting Bernard and for succumbing to a form of metaphysical essentialism. Thus Durkheim is congratulated for anticipating structuralism and for implicitly answering questions not put in his texts. His work is useful in so far as it agrees with or anticipates structuralism. The rest is confined to silence, or better is repressed, perhaps with the danger that it might re-emerge unbidden in the critic's own discourse.

Fundamental to these arguments of Althusser and Hirst is the belief that there exists a realm of scientific discourses that can be used to judge others, demanding compatibility in so far as they overlap. The mode of reading may be more sophisticated but it is still undoubtedly dogmatic.[5] Hindess has argued that we must abandon any dogmatic distinction between science and ideology.

> If theoretical discourses are to be criticised it can no longer be because they are alleged to be derived from some empiricist process or from epistemology but only because of an inadequacy at the level of their concepts and the relations between these concepts.
>
> (Hindess, 1977a, pp. 223–7)

Such analyses help us to specify what is worth retaining within a discourse and to locate where it has become incoherent and thus how to rework it to generate more valid arguments. Hindess here acknowledges the potential incompatibility of internally coherent discourses but implies that the analysis of discourses is an activity of discovery – of stumbling upon, or unveiling what is already latent in the texts, thereby underplaying the intertextual nature of reading.

Reading is intertextual in that discourses are often identified only through the examination of more than one of an author's texts and a serious reading will involve examining a wide range of these. We must ask whether everything an author 'wrote, said or left behind is part of his work?' (Foucault, 1986, p. 103). In Durkheim's case these might include his 'marginal' writings on law, for example his somewhat Hobbesian 'La Science positive de la morale en Allemagne' or his wartime articles on Germany, where he pointed out that legal formalism could contribute to an unjust, aggressive social order (LaCapra, 1972). The texts that constitute an *oeuvre* are inevitably a selection. In this book an attempt is made to identify the discourses that traverse Durkheim's texts, to disarticulate and evaluate them and to show how the development of some of the more fruitful is truncated by the presence of others that are less coherent. The main focus is on *The Division of Labour in Society, Suicide, The Elementary Forms of the Religious Life, Moral Education, Professional Ethics and Civic Morals, The Rules of Sociological Method* and *Socialism*. Reference is made to many of his other works and much of his other published work has been consulted. Since this book does not aim to be an *exhaustive reading* this selectivity does not affect the substance of its argument.

Texts are also intertextual in that those who read them are always themselves already positioned by other texts and by the relations between discourses, discursive practices and the forms of subjectivity thereby constituted. Social practices work in part through the interpellation of subjects and this is as true of reading subjects as speaking/writing subjects or acting/feeling subjects.

> A meaning effect does not pre-exist the discursive formation in which it is constituted. The production of meaning is an integral part of the interpellation of the individual as a subject; in so far as, amongst other determinatons the subject is 'produced as cause of himself' in the subject form of discourse, under the influence of interdiscourse.
>
> (Pecheux, 1982, p. 187)

The practice of reading, then, is always one produced by an interdiscourse. Thus, for example, whilst Nisbet (1963) is correct that the conservative elements of Durkheim's work form 'one of the coherent systems of his thought', he seems blind to the fact that, as Hunt (1978) and Lukes (1975) have argued, it is only one such system in a complexus of political discourses – socialism, radicalism, conservativism – that traverse his work. All three commentators, however, can be criticized for not attempting to specify from 'where' they themselves engage in such readings – to read a text is to be positioned by it, by the other texts with which it is articulated, and by the other discursive formations within which one is imbricated. These relationships determine why these particular texts are read and affect the process by which the presence of particular discourses (and signifying chains) within them is detected and ultimately what strategies are used to systematize, clarify, elaborate, disentangle and criticize them. They make it possible to isolate and assess the epistemologies, methodologies, political ideologies and problematics present – and, indeed, often at stake – within them.

Dominick LaCapra's discussion of the 'transferential' relationship between the critical historian and *both* historical documents and the writings of other historians help clarify this issue.

> . . . the desirable but elusive objective of an exchange with an 'other' is to work through transferential displacement in a manner that does not blindly replicate debilitating aspects of the

past. Transference . . . is as much denied by an assertion of the total difference of the past as by its total identification with one's own 'self' or 'culture'.

The difficulty is to develop an exchange with the 'other' that is both sensitive to transferential displacement and open to the challenge of the other's 'voice'. In this sense it is a useful critical fiction to believe that texts or phenomena to be interpreted may answer one back and even be convincing enough to lead one to change one's mind.

(LaCapra, 1987, pp. 72–3)

Thus such a textual analysis must not simply be negative but must also help the 'liberated' concepts to be put to work in a new manner. Needless to say any new texts generated by a 'reformulation' of a deep structure of concepts will not represent a mere tidying up or correction of the old texts. The original texts will be displaced by the theoretical work expended upon them producing conceptual systems with significantly different substantive implications. Once different discourses (signifying chains) have been identified and their relationship to each other specified it is possible to discard those aspects of each that are fundamentally incoherent, and retain and synthesize those that are coherent and compatible with each other, supplementing this at times somewhat fragmentary conceptual system with other (equally compatible) concepts drawn from elsewhere – thereby achieving a non-syncretic synthesis. It is important to note that to utilize a signifying chain or set of concepts is also to be constrained by its logic – one is not free simply to pick and choose when to use which element of which argument. *Rigorous retheorizing constrains the theorist, forcing him or her to think through the general implications of 'regional' analyses.*

Conclusion: The radical Durkheim

Marx and Freud as founders of discursivity . . . made possible not only a certain number of analogies, but also (and equally important) a certain number of differences. They have created a possibility for something other than their discourse, yet something belonging to what they have founded. . . .

(Foucault, 1986, p. 114)

A major goal of this book is to show that Durkheim was also a 'founder of discursivity'. It will be argued that his texts are traversed by a series of discourses which vary in their coherence, systemacity and completeness. Some discourses are relatively systematic but incoherent, others coherent but underdeveloped. The texts are explored to identify and analyse the discourses (and signifying chains) and hierarchies of concepts that constitute and are constituted by them. Where the lower level of concepts are found to be contradictory and confused then, in order to produce a more coherent theory, it is necessary to try to generate new concepts at this lower level. Such concepts generate models of a variety of social forms some of which may already exist and others that could exist. A major aim of the book is to theorize elements of one of these in particular, namely an egalitarian socialist system.

In the next chapter I start my analysis with a brief exegesis and assessment of Durkheim's epistemology and sociological concepts, showing how these can be reworked to produce truly social and dynamic analyses of the social order. This is exemplified by a social explanation of the phenomenon of 'charisma'. In Chapter 3 I explore in some detail the different political discourses within Durkheim's work. In the next chapter, the fourth, I turn to the conceptual structure of his *The Division of Labour in Society*. This is shown to be incoherent but its potential fruitfulness is demonstrated by an elaboration of Durkheim's underdeveloped radical socialist analysis of the relationship between the 'forced division of labour' and unjust advantage. In Chapter 5, with the aid of one of his earliest articles, 'La Science positive de la morale en Allemagne', his conception of law is worked upon and reformulated. Then, in Chapter 6 and 7, *Suicide* is transformed from an analysis of a social problem to an exploration of some forms of rational and irrational social orders and of the social conditions of existence of rational subjectivities. In many of the earlier chapters Marxism is drawn upon to critique and reformulate Durkheim's work; in the eighth chapter some of Durkheim's arguments (mainly to be found in his *Socialism*) are used to interrogate and then in turn *retheorize* Marxism. This dialogue between Durkheim and Marx is used to produce a non-syncretic fusion of a reconstituted Durkheimism with a significantly modified Marxism, making it possible in Chapter 9 to retheorize the nature and bases of social order, the ways in which the individual is socially constituted and the different role that the state, politics, the law, the juridical relation and deviant behaviour can play. In the concluding chapter the major theme of the book, that the development of many of Durkheim's concepts can be used to help specify a realistic set of socialist goals, will be restated in a summary form. I shall thus develop *a more rigorous specification of many of the features of a feasible democratic socialist society*. The development of a self-conscious method of reading/rereading theory thus will be shown, I believe, to be of both theoretical and practical (political) interest.

Notes

1 Anglo-American sociology in the early 1960s was based upon empiricist research methods, made use of concepts derived from a liberal–conservative tradition of political theory and social analysis unsympathetic to Marxism, and advocated a somewhat reformist politics.
2 True some Marxists – the Austro-Marxists, the early Frankfurt School, for example – attempted to develop a distinctive Marxist sociology (Bottomore and Nisbet, 1978, pp. 118–48; Bottomore and Goode, 1978), but only too many Marxists have subscribed to the view that there is an essential conflict between Marxism and sociology, which perhaps explains why their own work is increasingly in the realms of philosophy, political economy or politics. This is somewhat ironic since the totality of the concepts of neither Weber nor Durkheim are inherently antithetical to those of Marxism. Weber's *Ancient Judaism* (1967), *The Agrarian Sociology of Ancient Civilisations* (1976; Wiener, 1982), much of *Economy and Society* (1978) and many of his political writings are remarkably compatible with Marxian analysis (Beetham, 1974) – it is no accident that the Frankfurt School has long been locked in an antagonistic/synthetic relationship with his work (e.g. Habermas, 1971).
3 In his introduction to Durkheim's *Socialism* (1962), Gouldner refuted Parsons' interpretation of Durkheim and recognized both Durkheim's radical impulses and his failure to realize them by adequately developing appropriate concepts. Both Giddens (1971b) and Fenton (1984) contextualize Durkheim's work and provide trenchant criticisms of the Nisbet thesis.
4 For Althusser sciences like Marxism only require a purification process so that the science 'will out'. Thus Althusser disingenuously claims that in any of Marx's scientific texts, when answers are discovered to be unanchored in corresponding questions, such questions will be found elsewhere in the text. Althusser does acknowledge an exception to this – 'the concept of the effectivity of a structure on its elements' was one that the age in which Marx lived could not provide for him. But here Althusser claims to provide the question (as if it is a coherent concept) whilst failing to demonstrate the presence of the answer in Marx's texts

(Althusser and Balibar, 1970, p. 29; Bennett, 1979, pp. 111–20; Benton, 1984, pp. 35–51). Althusser later criticized his earlier position on science and ideology as overly 'theoreticist' (cf. Althusser, 1971, p. 23). Hirst dramatically modified his position also (cf. Hirst and Woolley, 1982).

5 Nevertheless it is possible to adapt Althusser's distinction between science and ideology. Scientific discourses, he argues, have their own autonomous problematics and are thus open-ended, guiding, but not determining, the results and significance of research. Whereas in ideologies

> the formulation of a *problem* is merely the theoretical expression of the conditions which allows a solution already produced outside the process of knowledge because imposed by extra-theoretical instances and exigencies (by religious, ethical, political or other 'interests') *to recognise itself* in an artificial problem manufactured to serve it both as a theoretical mirror and as a practical justification.
>
> (Althusser and Balibar, 1970, p. 52)

Now if we examine many of Marx's political writings, for example *The Manifesto of the Communist Party*, we find an interpretation of historical development that suggests that society will increasingly polarize into two classes, the bourgeoisie and the proleteriat, that there will be an increasing homogenization and (often absolute) immiserization of the latter and that these processes are generated by the development of and inherent contradictions within capitalism, particularly the tendency of the rate of profit to fall. These political writings are thus supported by a particular *interpretation* of the labour theory of value.

Given the nature of economic and social development since Marx's time there is clearly a problem about such an analysis. The problem, however, lies in the fact that within Marxism a political *ideology* (in the sense defined by Althusser above) has led to a misapplication of the labour theory of value. Marx and Engels' polemical attacks on Utopianism and Reformism led them to oversimplify their own position. But as Marx himself made clear elsewhere, in *Wage Labour and Capital* for example, the worker suffers a relative not necessarily an absolute impoverishment under capitalism (McLellan, 1977, p. 259). Furthermore a consideration of the nature of capitalism would suggest that there will always be within it contradictory class positions (charge hands, foremen, etc.), that its conditions of existence include a state whose administrative, legal, police and military functionaries are not assignable to any specific class and that, if the workings of the market are not themselves adequate to produce a healthy, skilled and loyal working class, state institutions and *personnel* who again are not assignable to any class will be required. Furthermore there is little analytic reason to endorse Marx's view that the tendency of the rate of profit to fall is the dominant tendency within capitalism since the counter-tendencies to this (he mentions five including the possibility that technological innovation can diminish the relative value of constant capital for example) and the combative power of the working class are equally ever-present. The value of labour power is not a given; it depends upon the aspirations of the working class (Marx, 1965, p. 171) and its capacity to realize them, and this in turn depends upon the regional *and* international level of class struggle at any particular time. Thus the problem of much of the political analysis and predictions of Marxism is due not, as Laclau and Mouffe (1985) and Foucault (1970, 1980a) have argued, to the *fundamental* inadequacies of Marxist theory but rather to its misapplication (Geras, 1987; Woodiwiss, 1987b; Pearce, 1988). The ideological discourse to be found within Marx's texts does not invalidate Marx's conceptual schema because it is possible to develop this differently to produce more fruitful concepts by acknowledging where it is incoherent, inadequate, underdeveloped and overextended. The recent work of Wolpe (1980) and Rattansi (1985) is, in this respect, exemplary.

2 Durkheim's epistemology and sociology

Durkheim and epistemology

> At the same time that it is teleological, the method of explanation generally followed by sociologists is essentially psychological. These two tendencies are interconnected with one another. In fact, if society is only a system of means instituted by men to attain certain ends, these ends can only be individual, for only individuals could have existed before society. From the individual, then, have emanated the needs and desires determining the formation of societies, and it is from him that all comes, it is necessarily by him that all must be explained. Moreover, there are in societies only individual consciousnesses; in these, then, is found the source of all social evolution.
>
> (Durkheim, 1938, pp. 97–8)

This chapter identifies some of the major strengths and weaknesses of Durkheim's overall conceptual system. His epistemology, which is outlined below, is of interest both because he made telling points against other theorists and also because his 'scientific rationalism' anticipates aspects of 'realism' (see Bhaskar, 1978; Keat and Urry, 1975). His epistemology and sociological theorizing, it is true, were flawed by positivistic, Comtean and essentialist elements, but this does not invalidate them as a whole. Since the different levels of concepts within discourses have a certain relative autonomy from each other it is possible to be reasonably selective about what to retain and what to reject and, as will be shown, the coherence of their substantive concepts is often more important than the status of their 'epistemological protocols' (Hindess, 1977a, pp. 223–7). In the latter part of the chapter, particularly when analysing the phenomenon of charisma, we will see just how much can be gained by using and developing some of the more valid aspects of Durkheim's conceptual schema.

Durkheim believed that all human societies have depended for their continuing existence upon the unscientific ideas that men developed about themselves, the world and nature.[1] These function to explain their experience, to regulate their behaviour and to mediate their relationship with the environment (1938, pp. 14–15). But such ideas were only pragmatically useful since only science produced real knowledge. Because mankind is reflective, calculative and capable of making contracts, political theorists tend to explain social order as a conscious creation of individual human beings. These are assumed to be rational prior to and independently of organized social life.

> It follows that veritable miracles are believed to be possible . . . for example, that a legislator can create an institution out of nothing by a mere injunction of its will, or transform one social system into another . . .
>
> (1976, p. 27)

Will–artefact theorists are as superstitious as primitive man and their ill-considered Utopianism has generated unrealizeable aspirations, social disorder and despair.

A quite opposite error is theoreticism – the substitution of theoretical ideas for valid attested experience. Some theories, like those of Spencer, are often developed abstractly and, instead of being used to *explore* the *complexity* of social phenomena, turn to reality merely to illustrate their concepts, thereby assuming that the entities and forms of organization and relationships that they posit determine the real (1938, pp. 17–21). Two other erroneous modes of analysis are variants of empiricism. On the one hand are historians who conceive of societies as 'just so many heterogeneous individualities not comparable among themselves' and on the other philosophers (and anthropologists like Frazer) for whom 'only humanity is real' and who believe that 'it is from the general attributes of human nature that all social evolution flows' (1938, p. 76). The crucial point is that *the status of facts is context-dependent and must be assessed theoretically*.

Durkheim's criticism of these approaches was accurate and is still relevant but his own brand of 'scientific rationalism', whilst relatively coherent and insightful, is less satisfactory and somewhat confused. Science, he believed, should base its concepts *upon* information accurately derived from the senses.

Science, then, has to create new concepts, it must dismiss all lay notions and the terms expressing them, and return to sense perception, the primary and necessary substance underlying all concepts. From sensation all general ideas flow, whether they are true or false, scientific or impressionistic.

(Durkheim, 1938, pp. 43–4)

Here he advocated a systematic empiricism grounded in a positivist epistemology – an ontology of phenomenalism, a stress on the centrality of observation and a combination of inductive and hypothetico-deductive forms of theorization. However, whilst he developed an operational definition of social facts as observable, external, etc., he conceded that their effectivity was mediated by 'representation', which individuals recognized subjectively and dealt with internally. Despite this often-cited quotation, such positivism was in practice a relatively marginal aspect of his thought.

Durkheim's naturalism was not inherently positivistic or reductionist. He believed that 'societies are subject to natural laws and form a kingdom of nature' (1976, p. 27) not because nature is uniform but rather because social facts are 'capable of being explained naturally . . . We reject the term if it is given a doctrinal meaning concerning the essence of social objects' (1938, p. 141). One must 'recognize the natural heterogeneity of things' since social facts 'have their own laws, specific in nature and comparable to physical or biological laws, without being directly reducible to the latter' (1982, p. 178). Natural laws are based upon the accurate specification of *necessary* causal relations between phenomena: 'a given effect can maintain this relationship with only one cause, for it can express only one single nature' (1938, p. 127). Once causal relationships have been established for 'decisive or crucial facts' (1938, p. 79) through 'experiments with method' (1933, p. 220), it is possible to explore other relationships more systematically and make generalizations more confidently (1976, p. 361).

Each science, Durkheim argued, has its own order of reality; the interconnectedness of the elements of this realm constitute its *determining principle* and its province proper. Thus sociology is distinct from biology and psychology in that it has its own realm of facts, social facts that are supra-individual and like all forms of reality coerce human beings by imposing severe limits on what they can do (1938, p. 10). The great merits of this argument are its resolute opposition to methodological individualism, and its recognition of the power that the social order has over individuals and of the importance of the role of 'representations' in social life.

All of reality may not be equally accessible to perception, so 'science chooses . . . only the most objective and most easily measurable' (1933, pp. 66–7). Such observable social phenomena are aspects of a greater, *interconnected* realm partially 'beyond our purview' (1961, p. 86). 'Social solidarity', for example, is a social fact *realized* and known through law, which is both a form and index of this solidarity. Causal relationships can be identified even if inaccessible to 'sense perception' if the mind is not 'enslaved to visible appearances' but connects 'what the senses separated' (1976, p. 237). The object of sociology is a complex of social facts with its own separate level of existence and which is partially inaccessible to perception.

In arguing that there exist phenomena only partially accessible to the senses between which there were *necessary* and at times unobservable relationships Durkheim broke decisively with both common sense and positivism. In arguing that the scientist must play an active role in determining the *criteria* for what constitutes relevant facts and indeed that ideally they should be experimentally *produced* he subverted inductivism and empiricism. But, whilst he correctly attacked nominalism, his alternative view was compromised by an unsatisfactory essentialism, although his view of causation and scientific explanation has more in common with Kuhn, Bachelard and Bhaskar than with positivism (Kuhn, 1962; Lecourt, 1975; Bhaskar, 1978). Nevertheless, the Comtean 'view of nature as a hierarchy of orders of reality . . . possessing an internal homogeneity . . . is close to what Durkheim himself characterises as metaphysics' (Benton, 1977, p. 85). To reject the idea that the social realm is epiphenomenal and to demonstrate that social factors have a coercive facticity does not mean that they are all identical phenomena, merely that they share the characteristics of *facts* as such. To demonstrate that certain social phenomena cannot be explained by psychological, economic or climactic factors *alone* without introducing social factors does not mean that the *only* factors with causal efficacy are social – they are certainly a *necessary* but by no means a *sufficient* component of the relevant causal chains (Benton, 1977, p. 90). Certain aspects of Durkheim's work may then be criticized as tautological and metaphysical.[2] But whilst it is indeed problematic to represent society as a *single* coherent continuous entity, there still may be relational and organizational continuities that may or may not figure in a society's collective representations.

Let us illustrate these criticisms by examining his analysis of the relationship between religion and society. First the tautology. For Durkheim the 'social', the 'stuff' of society, is a primary substance which he identified with the 'horde', the simplest form of social life (1933, p. 174; 1938, p. 82; Hirst, 1975, pp. 122–35). The organizing principle and source of the social realm is the *conscience collective*, which expresses itself through both social institutions and social currents. The *conscience collective*, becomes, in his later work, virtually identical with religion. On the one hand he argued that all phenomena that are sacred (as opposed to profane) are religious and that since religion is caused by society and consists of its worship all religious phenomena are unitary and have a single cause, society (Keat and Urry, 1975, p. 85). On the other hand, he argued that religion is

the most primitive of all social phenomena. It is from it that have emerged, through successive transformations, all the other manifestations of collective activity – law, morality, art, science, political forms etc. In principle everything is religious. (Durkheim, 1982, p. 173; see also, Durkheim, 1976, pp. 423–4)

But this is merely tautological; it explains neither religion nor society.[3]

Furthermore, Durkheim's mode of investigation and explanation is unlikely to *produce empirical knowledge*. He claimed that the 'interior characteristics' of phenomena are betrayed by 'external and immediately sensible manifestations' (Durkheim, 1974, p. 19) and that phenomena with the same external characteristics should be classed together since they are all produced by a single cause, but here the concept of cause functions to refer givens to their essence.

Since, however, the essence is both the condition of existence of the facticity and it exists without conditions in itself, the essence can only exist in the mode of expression. It can only be *referred to* as the order of the facticity behind the facticity. The given facticity is thus the sole '*clue*' to the existence of the essence. . . . Thus the riddle is solved, the essence to which we refer tells us nothing but what we already know.

(Hirst, 1975, p. 101)

For example, *conscience collective* or religion is metaphysically conceived of as the organizing principle and source of energy within society but there is no concrete specification of the nature of its internal order or any analysis of the form of its relationship to its conditions of existence (Hirst, 1975, pp. 90–103).

Durkheim argued that scientists must 'repudiate resolutely the use of concepts originating outside of science for totally unscientific needs' (Durkheim, 1938, p. 32). Yet his own attempts at such scientificity were flawed. This can be seen in his argument that, whilst sociologists should be objective,

> Science tells us simply what is necessary to life. But obviously, *the supposition, man wishes to live,* a very simple speculation, immediately transforms the laws science establishes into imperative rules of conduct.
>
> (Durkheim, 1933, pp. 34–5)

He conceived of society as an organism that can develop only within sharply defined limits of a kind that maintains its essential continuity and develops in a unilinear manner which can be determined by the sociologist. He concluded that revolution is therefore either wrong because it is destructive and 'pathological' or irrelevant because it only affects surface phenomena. But to define 'the desirable' as equivalent to 'health and normality' where 'health is inherent in things' (1938, p. 74) involved a misunderstanding of the nature of medical pathology.[4] His conception of 'normal society' as a non-contradictory unity derives from conservative ideology and is therefore, to be ironic, only too clearly 'what we already know'. Similarly, in using the form of law as an index of the kind of solidarity that exists in a society, he *assumed* that all institutions including the law express such an entity's essence.

It is because Durkheim's mode of reasoning was inherently tautological and he worked with ideological preconceptions that, Hirst argues, his empirical work had little validity:

> each 'positive investigation' is really nothing but the '*Rules*' in a different form, each is an argument for a scientific sociology and in each the 'empirical material' is deployed as a means of illustration and persuasion.
>
> (Hirst, 1975, p. 170)

Durkheim was guilty of the same error as Spencer! Hirst's general point is well made but overstated. All of Durkheim's 'positive investigations' have both some empirical validity and significant potential for development.

Whilst Durkheim's epistemology was locked within a combination of Comtean, positivist and essentialist problematics, it still functioned as a critique of certain forms of social science and made partial breakthroughs to an alternative, more adequate 'realist' approach. His work provides a useful critique of empiricism – both ethnograpic and abstract; of theoreticism – merely referring to reality when one wishes to illustrate one's concepts; of methodological individualism and reductionism; and of positivism and of certain metaphysical concepts of the social realm. Elements of his mode of explanation and concepts of causation are compatible with a more adequate, 'realist epistemology' and it is these that will implicitly and explicitly be retained. At this point it is necessary to explore his conceptual system as a whole.

Durkheim's sociological concepts

A purely psychological explanation of social facts cannot fail, therefore, to allow all that is characteristic (i.e. social) in them to escape . . . sociologists, taking effect for cause . . . have very often designated as determining the conditions of social phenomena certain psychological states . . . which, are, after all, *only the consequence of these social phenomena.*

(Durkheim, 1938, p. 107; emphasis added)

Durkheim's brilliance lay above all in his commitment to social explanations of social phenomena, in his feel for the *power of the social*. He was clear that the social order cannot be conceived of as the sum total of the attributes of its members, nor is it an expression of their individual goals, nor is it exhausted by the interpersonal relations that obtain between them, indeed human subjectivity is *constituted* by the social realm. Society is an extremely complex entity the nature of which, including its capacity to reproduce itself, will only be revealed through rigorous theorizing and empirical research. Although all societies share certain characteristics there are also different kinds of societies. Thus the *significance* of any social fact or any social incident can be determined only when a society's nature and its level of development have been determined.

This section considers how Durkheim conceived of society and explores some of his achievements and the way in which their

potential was fundamentally limited by his misunderstanding of
the relationship between biology and sociology, his conception of
society as an expressive totality and his angelic transcendentalism
– a form of historicist idealism where a society or group is simply
viewed as equivalent to a person (Benoit-Smullyan 1969: 216–21).
Nevertheless this is by no means the only discourse in his texts
and later it will be shown how the fragments of other discourses
in his work can be used to explore charisma as a *social relation* and
to develop a concept of the social realm that anticipates and indeed
in some ways improves upon some aspects of 'post-structuralism'.

For Durkheim, the existence of a realm of social facts justifies
the creation of sociology – 'the science of societies considered
concurrently in their organization, functioning and development'
(1938, p. 194). A society is a territorially located entity with an
external environment, including other societies, and with an
internal environment, the social milieu (1938, p. 113). Its nature is
determined by the extension and concentration of the social group
and the frequency, duration and intensity of the interaction
between individuals who obey the same social rules. The rate of
social interaction determines the energy level of the society and
the *conscience collective* its unity. The *conscience collective* is the
source of 'social facts'. It expresses itself, in a congealed form, as
institutions – 'all beliefs and all modes of activity instituted by the
collectivity' (1938, p. lvi) – and as 'currents of opinion', which,
for example, 'impel certain groups either to more marriages or to
more suicides, or to a higher or lower birth rate' (1938, p. 8).
'Morphological social facts govern the social substratum' (1938,
pp. 12–13) and are important in deciding societies' species and for
determining their normal mode of existence and development
(1938, p. 86). The simplest society, the horde, consists of a group
of individuals in a socially undifferentiated state, unified in
mechanical solidarity. More complex 'societies are only combinations of one and the same original society' (1938, p. 86) which
develop emergent properties. Durkheim's implicit analogy with
the emergent properties of chemical compounds is untenable since
chemical compounds are produced by the combination of *different*
elements, not one and the same element. (He unsuccessfully tried
to defend himself against such criticisms in 1898 – Durkheim,
1982, pp. 251–2.) Nevertheless in attempting to classify societies
Durkheim was pursuing a worthwhile goal, since the social
significance of any social event or fact can only be determined if
there is some specification of the nature of the society and socio-
structural context within which it is produced. It is therefore

worth following through the rest of his argument in which he attempted to develop criteria for distinguishing between normal and abnormal developments.

As societies develop, social differentiation usually produces a division of labour, which 'naturally' creates social solidarity, but not all differentiation is positive – that 'which disintegrates (cancerous, microbic, criminal) is very different from that which brings vital forces together (division of labor)' (1933, p. 353). Differentiation is a more general process than the division of labour since only a functional organ 'joins with others in maintaining general life' (1933, p. 354). Nevertheless a situation can be normal without being useful – if a phenomenon 'is bound up with the conditions of existence of the species under consideration, either as a mechanically necessary effect of these conditions or as a means of permitting the organisms to adapt themselves' (1938, p. 60).

Durkheim believed that, whilst similar processes occur in the biological and social realms, they also differ. On the one hand,

> France has passed through very different forms of civilisation; it began by being agricultural, passed to craft industry and to small commerce, then to manufacturing, and finally to large scale industry. Now it is impossible to admit that the same collective individuality can change its species three or four times. A species must define itself by more constant character-istics.
>
> (1938, p. 88)

This presupposes that France is an entity with an essence unfolding over time thereby implying a narrative history rather than a genealogy.[5] On the other hand, a 'second generation' of societies 'is a different species from the parent-societies because the latter in combining give birth to an entirely new organization' (1938, p. 87). But there is no reason why the internal milieu of a society could not be modified to allow it to cope with changes in its external environment. Since societies are not totally discontin-uous or reproduced *in toto*, neither position is adequate. This emphasis on reproduction is nevertheless important and useful. Social factors will reproduce some institutional forms and sets of meanings, modify others and let yet others fall into desuetude.

For Durkheim, 'the gravest practical problems . . . consist precisely in determining anew the moral health, functionally, in relation to the changes which have occurred in the environment'

(1933, p. 34). Social facts are *moral* facts and there are few phenomena as intimately connected with morality as crime. Durkheim's discussion of crime shows how to begin to distinguish between subjective feelings about, and more objective evaluations of, the nature and significance of social phenomena and particularly how important it is to specify the level of analysis in order to understand the different ways in which the 'social' produces its effects.

Crime and punishment

> A social fact is normal, in relation to a given social type at a given phase of its development, when it is present in the average society of that species at the corresponding phase of its evolution.
>
> (Durkheim, 1938, p. 64)

Let us illustrate Durkheim's arguments about the relationship between the normal and the pathological by exploring his analysis of crime. Crime, he argued, is a a 'normal' phenomenon since it is found universally and a society exempt from crime is impossible. Variations in the content of law and morality show that there are no 'natural laws' and hence the source of the law and of law-abiding behaviour must be found in society, in the collective conscience, not in the asocial individual. Crime's 'only common characteristic' is that it 'shocks sentiments, which, for a given social system, are found in all healthy consciences' and thus 'invokes against its author the characteristic reaction which we call punishment' (1933, pp. 70–3). The societal reaction to crime is spontaneous not calculative – 'what we avenge, what the criminal expiates is the outrage to morality', sometimes expressed as a 'need to destroy' which is 'the instinct of conservation exacerbated by peril' (1933, pp. 87–9). Adults who do not know society's 'fundamental rules or do not recognize their authority' show 'an undeniable sign of pathological perversion' (1933, p. 74). Punishment both controls the delinquent and helps to reaffirm the collective sentiments in the upright thereby increasing the effectiveness of the *conscience collective* (1933, pp. 108–9). In this context the widespread commitment of individuals to the society's values is the 'normal phenomenon'.

The collective conscience necessarily discriminates between minor transgressions of its code and crimes proper but if a society's members become more law-abiding, higher and higher standards of conduct will be enforced. Whilst standards may rise in general, there will be variations in the uniformity of individual consciences due to the different physical and 'social space they occupy, the social influences to which they are exposed and their hereditary antecedents' (1938, p. 69). A certain slackness in the *collective conscience* may have positive and negative consequences since for 'the originality of the idealist' to find expression. 'the originality of the criminal' must be possible. The criminal may thus play 'a definite role in social life' and crime itself may even produce positive effects – did not Socrates' crime help prepare 'a new morality and faith which the Athenians needed' and establish liberal philosophy (1938, pp. 71–2)?

A focus on the crime of suicide makes these arguments clearer. Suicides occur in all societies, but there is a particular rate of suicide that is normal for a particular species of society at a particular level of development which is thus an effect of social processes that are intrinsic to it (egoism, altruism, anomie, etc). An excessive suicide rate indicates that society is not functioning appropriately and that therefore the social organism is suffering from some pathology (1938, p. 75). *Social facts that involve deviation from social norms and are considered to be social problems may, from the scientific viewpoint, be normal phenomena.* Nevertheless the relationship between normality and pathology, and normality and deviance, is unclear.

> To make of crime a form of social morbidity would be to admit that morbidity is *not something accidental*, but on the contrary, that in certain cases it grows out of *the fundamental constitution of the living organism*, it would result in wiping out all distinctions between the physiological and the pathological.
>
> (1938, p. 66; emphasis added)

Here Durkheim is claiming that morbid effects must be produced by pathological causes, *accidental* in that they are *extrinsic* to the essential elments of the organism. In biology, however, morbidity is often simply the effect of a specific mode of functioning of the *same* elements of the organism that produce 'normal' effects (see Hirst, 1975, p. 121).

Durkheim moreover remains ambivalent about the nature of the criminal himself since, although crime is a normal phenomenon, 'it does not follow that the criminal is an individual normally constituted from the biological and psychological points of view'

(1938, p. 66). This ambivalence is related to a confusion of definition and levels in his arguments, which can be traced back to two of his criteria for what constitutes a normal social fact:

> the normal type merges with the average type, and every deviation from the standard of health is a morbid phenomenon.
>
> (1938, pp. 55–6)

> a social fact . . . is every way of acting which is general throughout a given society, while at the same time existing in its own right independent of its individual manifestations.
>
> (1938, p. 13)

At the same time as social facts are *generally* found *in* particular kinds of societies, they are also *general within* a society. Thus it is a social fact that social actors are subordinate to the *conscience collective*, but in Durkheim's schema this means both that social actors *need* to act in concert for a society to survive and that individual social actors *usually* do so because they have 'healthy consciences'; if they do not then they are pathological. This is a misinterpretation of sound biological and evolutionary theory since 'adaption' refers to the survival of individual members of species, and 'evolution' to the fate of whole populations over time. What may benefit one level of phenomenal existence may undermine the other (Frazzetta, 1975, ch. 3). But for Durkheim the general social *need* is seen as simply refracted through the individual consciousness. The macrocosmic social totality is reflected microscopically in the individual – a view of the ordering of the world based upon 'similitude' (see Foucault, 1970, pp. 17–25).

Durkheim, angelicism and vitalism

In *The Evolution of Educational Thought*, Durkheim illuminated the differences between the degree of social organization in pre- and post-Carolingian Europe with a biological analogy. The former was like those animals that 'lack a central nervous system' and are therefore 'only aware in a confused kind of way of what is going on in the furthest reaches of' their bodies. The latter, which had 'a central institution in which the whole of its life both internal and external culminates', was like those 'higher animals' that, 'thanks to their nervous system, are at every instant alerted to any goings-on of importance taking place within them' (1977, p. 40). But whilst here he used the organic analogy creatively and with an awareness that it is always based upon *differences* as well as similarities, nevertheless he underplayed the latter. Elsewhere his faulty reasoning was more blatantly inadequate. He claimed that the individual and society are equivalents, albeit distinct – that 'Collective psychology is sociology' (1974, p. 34), and since 'a moral fact must serve some living and sentient being . . . endowed with consciousness . . . above and beyond those sentient beings who are other individual human beings, there is nothing else but that sentient being that is society' (1961, p. 59). Here Durkheim collapses into 'angelic transcendentalism'.

It has been shown that for Durkheim the social is an irreduceable essence, a phenomenal level, a distinctive and continuous realm, which constitutes the subject matter of sociology. In one version of the organic analogy Durkheim conceives of social currents as if they are the organism's blood, as the 'vital' principle of the social realm. Whilst he explicitly attacked Bergsonian mysticism (1951, p. 320),[6] he inadvertently replicated, albeit in a different mode, significant elements of Bergson's 'vitalism'. He argued, for example, that social life consists

> of free currents perpetually in the process of transformation and incapable of being mentally fixed by the observer, and the scholar cannot approach the study of social reality from this angle. But we know that it possesses the power of crystallization without ceasing to be itself. Thus apart from the individual acts to which they give rise, collective habits find expression in definite forms: legal rules, moral regulations, popular proverbs, social conventions etc. . . . Since, on the other hand, these practices are merely social life consolidated it is legitimate, except where otherwise stated, to study the latter through the former.
>
> (1938, p. 45)

Durkheim has transposed Bergson's account of how the animation of matter develops species to an account of the social realm! The source of Durkheim's error is his belief that there is *a* separable social essence and that societies are 'unities of complex wholes' (Hirst, 1975, p. 131).

Durkheim's aim was to stress and conceptualize the autonomy and constitutive role of social relations and their irreduceability to interpersonal relationships and individual consciousnesses. The major problem was that he did this by conceiving of society as an entity 'animated' by social currents. But a sense of the 'social' can be achieved when society is no longer conceptualized as such an expressive totality but instead is understood as an emergent but mobile set of systems, as an articulation of instances, a complex of discursive practices, and, in part, a series of collective representations. The organic analogy can then be abandoned and the concept of social currents liberated from its function of plugging explanatory gaps.

Durkheim and post-structuralism

Durkheim conceptualized systems of collective representations in different ways. Sometimes, as when he conceived of society as a system organized in and through the *conscience collective*, he was guilty of misusing the organic analogy. His image of both individual and society was often logocentric, prioritizing the word and the speaking subject. Language, social relationships and the social structure are conceived as expressions of individual or collective – bounded, autonomous, feeling – subjects. Derrida (1976) has argued for the displacement of such logocentrism by a more graphocentric conceptualization in order to show that none of these phenomena can be adequately understood as expressions of subjectivity. Whilst Gane (1983a) has already drawn attention to Durkheim's complex analysis of 'sacred language', there is a very striking passage in *Suicide* where Durkheim is quite explicitly graphocentric and where, somewhat ironically given Foucault's often dismissive comments about Durkheim, he anticipates Foucault's spatial and architectural concept of the social realm:[7]

> it is not true that society is made up only of individuals; it also includes material things . . . The social fact is sometimes so far materialized as to become an element of the external world. For instance, a definite type of architecture is a social phenomenon; but it is partially embodied in houses and buildings of all sorts which, once constructed, become autonomous realities, independent of individuals. It is the same with the avenues of communication and transportation, with instruments and machines used in industry or private life which express the state of technology at any moment in history, of written language, etc. . . . A child's taste is formed as he comes into contact with

the monuments of national taste bequeathed by previous generations. At times such monuments even disappear and are forgotten for centuries, then, one day when the nations which reared them are long since extinct, reappear and begin a new existence in the midst of new societies. . . .

The same remark applies to the definite formulae into which the dogmas of faith are precipitated, or legal precepts when they become fixed externally in a consecrated form. . . . The material forms [legislation] assumes are thus not merely ineffective verbal combinations but active realities, since they produce effects which would not occur without their existence.

(Durkheim, 1951, pp. 313–15)

This focus on synchronic processes is a significant advance over his more usual conceptualization of social order and social change in terms of 'evolutionary narratives'.

Further, he often evokes a sense of an extremely dynamic social life. This is in part constituted by continuously 'mutating' systems of signification, discursive practices, social forms and institutions that traverse and are traversed by the different social groups within a society. If there is conflict it is on an (at least partially) shared terrain of intelligibility and there are undoubtedly social processes that must be understood in relationship to the overall society and not just to parts of it (see the discussion of Durkheim's analysis of power/authority in Lacroix, 1979). *Sub*-collectivities, even oppositional ones, draw upon the society's collective representations and, whilst selecting, interpreting and reworking them, are in part constituted by them.

There is a large collective life which is at liberty: all sorts of currents come, go, circulate everywhere, cross and mingle in a thousand different ways, and just because they are constantly mobile are never crystallized in an objective form . . . And all these eddies, all these fluxes and refluxes occur without a single modification of the main legal and moral precepts, immobilised in their sacrosanct forms. Besides, these very precepts merely express a whole subjacent life of which they partake; they spring from it but do not supplant it. Beneath all these maxims are actual, living sentiments, summed up by these formulae but only as in a superficial envelope. The formulae would awake no echo if they did not correspond to definite emotions and impressions scattered through society. If, then, we ascribe a kind of reality to them, we do not dream of supposing them to

be the whole of moral reality. That would be to take the sign
for the thing signified.

(Durkheim, 1951, p. 315)

The fruitfulness of this quotation can be seen by reflecting upon
Cohen's book, *The Symbolic Construction of Community*
(1985), which explicitly draws upon Durkheim's work. Cohen
argues that social scientists should use the term 'community' not
as if it actually refers to a stable, bounded, organized, social entity
but rather to describe how some individuals identify with certain
other individuals and institutions and define themselves in
opposition to yet others. Those individuals who share this
identification will agree on the importance of certain symbols, and
in that sense these will be shared, *but* this does not indicate a
consensus on their meaning since they can be interpreted in quite
different ways (Cohen, 1985). Whilst this argument is clearly
compatible with some of Durkheim's, it fails to recognize that
symbols are produced and *reproduced* throughout society. This is
only possible in so far as such symbols are part of a wider order,
involving a range of other relations, including class relations,
which themselves must be reproduced. Reproduction is only
possible if there is significant continuity in at least some social
relations.

In parts of his book Cohen virtually reduces society to an
expression of the subjective consciousness of individuals. Yet in
some ways there is a strong overlap between some of his
arguments and those of such militant anti-subjectivists as Laclau
and Mouffe. They argue that:

'Society' is not a valid object of discourse. There is no single
underlying principle fixing – and hence constituting – the whole
field of differences. The irresoluble interiority/exteriority tension
is the condition of any social practice; necessity only exists as a
partial limitation of the field of exteriority.

(Laclau and Mouffe, 1985, p. 111)

For them, a hegemonic discourse is one in which many different
positions and social groups are (actively) articulated together and
are rendered partially equivalent in and through a collective
mutual identification. Society only exists momentarily in and
through a hegemonic discourse. They claim, further, that since
they have made 'a break with the discursive/extra-discursive
dichotomy' they are able to successfully abandon 'the thought/

reality opposition' (Laclau and Mouffe, 1985, p. 110). Whereas for Cohen the individual consciousness is the source of social reality, for Laclau and Mouffe discourse becomes both its source and defines its limits.

This is indeed to take 'the sign for the thing signified'. Although at times Durkheim treats collective representations and social relations as both expressive of the same essence, in all of his work he conceptualizes them as separate and often – as in early works such as *The Division of Labour in Society* and late works like *The Evolution of Educational Thought* – he gives priority to the latter. After all to argue that social relations are *affected* by collective representations and that human action must in part be *explained* by the sets of significations to which individuals are subject does not logically mean that either of these adequately or accurately represents the full complexity of social relations.[8]

An implication of the long quotation from Durkheim cited above is that individuals and sub-collectivities do not simply act out pre-given positions but can also transform the signifying systems to which they are subject. The differential distribution of individuals and groups within social relations determines (albeit in a mediated way) their experience and understanding and their capacity to develop their own complex and possibly alternative interpretations of discourses (Foster, 1985, pp. 38–41). These specific issues are taken up again later, in the section on 'Politics and charisma'.

Durkheim and the concept of charisma

The utility of this somewhat different conceptualization of Durkheim's system can be illustrated by using it to analyse charisma. Although he does not seem to have used the actual term, Durkheim certainly discussed the phenomenon to which it is usually applied. What was innovative about his analysis is that for him the phenomenon is a social relation – the attributes of charismatic leaders *and* their followers and others subject to their authority are real and socially produced. First, Weber's discussion of charisma will be briefly commented upon and ways in which Durkheim's work can be used to go beyond Weber's methodological individualism will be suggested.

Much of Weber's discussion of charisma is connected with his ideal-typical analysis of power and domination and of the three types of Legitimate Domination – Rational–Legal, Traditional and

Charismatic. To say that the validity of the claims of a ruler to legitimacy rested upon charismatic grounds is to say that it rested on

> devotion to the exceptional sanctity, heroism or exemplary character of an individual person, and of the normative patterns or order revealed or ordained by him.
>
> (Weber, 1978, vol. 1, p. 215)

But Weber was equivocal as to the nature of charisma, treating it *either* as a real attribute of an individual *qua* individual 'personality' or as merely a projective fantasy of the leader's followers. Thus he stated that:

> The term 'charisma' will be applied to a certain quality of an individual personality by virtue of which he is considered extraordinary and treated as endowed with supernatural, superhuman, or at least specifically exceptional powers or qualities. These are such as are not accessible to the ordinary person, but are regarded as of divine origin or as exemplary, and on the basis of them the individual concerned is treated as a 'leader'.
>
> (Weber, 1978, vol. 1, p. 241)

He certainly believed that charismatic individuals can be found in religious, economic and political contexts – Jewish prophets, entrepreneurs in the 'heroic age of capitalism' and great national political leaders; Jesus, for example, was a charismatic possessing tremendous self-confidence and a consistent and persuasive commitment to some clear set of values (Weber, 1978, vol. 1, pp. 630–2). Indeed, for Weber historical (charismatic) 'personalities' are defined by the single-minded orientation of their whole existence around specific values (Weber, 1949, p. 55). Nevertheless, Weber realized that in no way could all of those who claimed charismatic legitimation – Kaiser Wilhelm II, for example – be taken at their word. In such cases, it is necessary to focus on the projections of the charismatic leader's followers and the ideologies to which they subscribe. Weber's methodological individualism meant that he felt the choice was between those occasions when charisma is a 'real attribute' possessed by a particular individual and hence 'beyond the frontiers of human reason', and those when it is merely a fantasy of the leader's followers.

Durkheim on the other hand was quite clear that charisma is a real phenomenon *and* a social relation. There are individuals who 'become supermen because they share in the superiority . . . of society *vis-à-vis* its members' (Durkheim, 1961, p. 91). Society 'deifies' a man who personifies its principal aspirations. Collective representations 'empower' him and make others experience themselves as relatively inferior.

The simple deference to men invested with high social functions is not different in nature from religious respect. It is expressed by the same movements: a man keeps at a distance from a high personage; he approaches him only with precautions; in conversing with him, he uses other gestures and language than those used with ordinary mortals. The sentiment felt on these occasions is so closely related to the religious sentiment that many peoples have confounded the two. In order to explain the consideration accorded to princes, nobles and political chiefs, a sacred character has been attributed to them. In Melanesia and Polynesia, for example, it is said that an influential man has *mana*, and that his influence is due to this *mana*. However, it is evident that his situation is due solely to the importance attributed to him by public opinion. Thus the moral power conferred by opinion and that with which sacred beings are invested are at bottom of a single origin and made up of the same elements. This is why a single word is able to designate the two.

(Durkheim, 1976, p. 213; see also Lacroix, 1979)

The leader is not only believed to have certain unique qualities but feels himself to possess them and is actively energized by them. Similarly, social subordinates feel deferential and are subjectified by and subject to his leadership. As a result, they may feel deskilled and passive, less autonomous, or less self-involved, and/or inspired to try and imitate him (perhaps as an ego-ideal) (Turquet, 1975). (This does not mean that situations cannot be so stage-managed that an individual can be effectively projected as a leader without he or she feeling himself or herself to be a leader.) Where such feelings do exist, where there is a charismatic personality, this is *socially constituted*. In line with Strawbridge, who has pointed to the relation between Althusser's theory of ideology and Durkheim's account of religion (Strawbridge, 1982, pp. 125–40), I would argue that for both Durkheim and Marx what the latter calls 'ideology' is *inescapable and constitutive*.

The effectiveness of 'charismatic personalities' is not primarily a function of their intrinsic characteristics. 'Charismatic' qualities are inevitably context-dependent and need to be socially *sustained*. The appeal of such leaders to their followers depends upon a shared background of culture – of style, symbols, myths, etc. (Jewish prophets, for example, were accorded a role and a repertoire of rhetoric by a long tribal tradition.) None of this necessarily implies that all individuals are equally suitable for leadership roles. Now Durkheim argued that

> the prophets, the founders of religions, the great saints, in a word, the men whose religious consciousness is exceptionally sensitive, very frequently give signs of excessive nervousness that is even pathological: these physiological defects predestined them to great religious roles. But if, for this reason, it may be said that religion is not without a certain delirium, it must be added that this delirium, if it has the causes which we have attributed to it, *is well founded*.
>
> (Durkheim, 1976, p. 226)

In some contexts only those with particular statuses or attributes may even be considered for a charismatic role, but even so the effect of group processes on the individual depends upon the other discourses that traverse him or her, upon the individual's 'investment' in different 'discursive positions' (Henriques *et al.*, 1984) and his or her 'emotional economies'. It may indeed be relevant that an individual has the capacity to devote himself or herself to a particular set of values (Weber, 1949, p. 55) but, nevertheless, subjection always occurs 'interdiscursively' (Pecheux, 1982).

In Weber's understanding of the nature of politics in industrial society and in his advocacy of a 'plebiscitary democracy' an elitist understanding of charisma played a key role.

> In a democracy, the people choose a leader whom they trust; the leader who is then chosen says 'Now shut up and do what I say'.
>
> (cited in Giddens, 1972, p. 19)

A Durkheimian understanding of charisma, however, helps to develop a more democratic, if still hard-headed, view of politics. It is democratic, first, in that charismatic individuals are seen as primarily produced in and through the collectivity; second, because his concepts enable us to analyse more adequately the role that charisma plays in contemporary politics. (Durkheim himself, on occasion, made clear the intimate connection between plebiscitary democracy and demagoguery – Durkheim, 1957.)

Politics and charisma

When reviewing *The Rules of Sociological Method* Sorel argued that the socialist understanding of the dynamics of class societies is superior to Durkheim's schematic evolutionism and metaphysical organicism.

> Socialism . . . does not separate out the division of labour and the formation of classes: these latter, organised for struggle, exert an important influence on the division of labour, by introducing forces very different from those discussed by Durkheim.
>
> (Sorel, 1895a, p. 24)

Durkheim recognized that there are differences between individuals and between social groups within societies but conceived of these differences as legitimate when they are due to the *circumstantial modification* of 'collective states' (Durkheim, 1951, p. 364). However, he often focused upon the negative and even dangerous aspects of intense unregulated, collective activity – of 'currents of collective melancholy, depression and disillusionment'; of 'morbid effervescences' (Durkheim, 1951, p. 368); of appetites 'seized by a sort of natural erethism simply by the greater intensity of public life' (Durkheim, 1951, p. 253). He warned against *independent* working-class action and particularly anarcho-syndicalism (Durkheim, 1951, p. 370; Lukes, 1975, pp. 542–6). Yet on occasion he did recognize that certain forms of spontaneous collective action could be positive:

> great social disturbances and great popular wars rouse collective sentiments, stimulate partisan spirit and patriotism, political and national faith, alike, and concentrating activity toward a single end, at least temporarily cause a stronger integration of society. . . . As they force men to close ranks and confront the common danger, the individual thinks less of himself and more of the common cause.
>
> (Durkheim, 1951, p. 208)

Durkheim here also acknowledges that society can be seriously divided as to its values and priorities and that groups may emerge each committed to one or other side of the divide and thus in conflict with one another, i.e. that there may be rival collective representations and rival group membership available for individuals. In other words, there are likely to be competing modes of 'interpellation' (Laclau, 1979).

In his exploration in *The Elementary Forms of the Religious Life* of what happens when a mob is addressed by *its* agitator, he implicitly acknowledged that *more than one system of authority can exist within a society*:

> In the midst of an assembly animated by a common passion, we become susceptible of acts and sentiments of which we are incapable when reduced to our own forces. . . . To strengthen these sentiments which, if left to themselves, would soon weaken, it is sufficient to bring those who hold them together and put them into closer and more active relations with one another. This is the explanation of the attitude of a man speaking to a crowd, at least if he has succeeded in entering into communion with it. His language has a grandiloquence that would be ridiculous in ordinary circumstances, his gestures show a certain domination, his very thought is impatient of all rules, and easily falls into sorts of excesses. It is because he feels within him an abnormal over-supply of force which overflows and tries to burst out from him, sometimes he even has the feeling that he is dominated by a moral force which is greater than he and of which he is only the interpreter. . . . It is no longer a simple individual who speaks; it is a group incarnate and personified.
>
> (Durkheim, 1976, p. 207–8)

'Agitators' and 'political chiefs' differ in that the authority of the former depends primarily upon their capacity to personify group aspirations whereas the latter have a formal institutional role. This allows such 'charismatic figures' to control the organizational structure that produces their charisma and renders people susceptible to it. This is unusually clear in Werner Erhard's organization, EST, the organizational and symbolic features of which have been subjected to a detailed ethnographic analysis by Donald Stone in his article, 'The charismatic authority of Werner Erhard' (Stone, 1983). EST 'trainers' follow a detailed programme constructed by Erhard and reproducing his own practice, they

imitate his comportment and style of dress. The EST training and
the whole organization make constant reference to, and are
formally controlled by, a seemingly omnipresent Erhard. Instead
of recognizing how these organizational features produce a 'sense'
of Erhard's charisma, Stone, with a startling inversion of logic,
views the organization and its ethos as an *expression* (and proof) of
Erhard's charismatic powers! Leaders in any organization who
have institutional power may *de facto* become charismatic, even
erotically charged (Zetterberg, 1968). They are able to determine
many of the 'rules of the game', to mobilize resources to punish
or marginalize opponents and, by their distribution of largess, to
guarantee the loyalty of their supporters. Above all they are able
to use their authority as a screen behind which social relationships
can be manipulated and their superordinate position means that
their understanding of the 'common good' will be uncontested
and virtually uncontestable.

Charisma need refer not only to those who have or are thought
to have 'special powers', but also – as Weber acknowledged – to
those who are thought to have 'special qualities . . . regarded as
exemplary' (Weber, 1978, vol. 1, p. 241). The exemplary
individual is then represented as the purest expression of what a
community's members (allegedly) share in common. An informed
political assessment of the programmes and performance of a
leader is unlikely if the members of a society are interpellated
primarily by the human (and particular national or 'racial')
qualities that they have in common with the 'exemplary' master
subject, i.e. such 'structurally obfuscating' attributes as 'Aryanness',
'Decency', and 'Familialism'. On the occasion of the British
Queen's Silver Jubilee, the Royal Family were represented as the
essence, the purest example, of the British family. Such a
representation was no anomaly.

> The essence of the British Monarchy is that the King, while
> lifted far above the nation, should also be the nation itself in its
> most characteristic form.
>   (John Buchan, *The King's Grace, 1910–1935,* pp. 276–7;
>   cited by Tom Nairn in the *Guardian*, 6 June 1988)

It is not difficult to see why socialists are so distrustful of
populism with its proclivity for charismatic leaders (Mouzelis,
1978, p. 51) or why charisma has always played such a key role in
class societies. Thus the charismatic social relation can be present
in a number of different forms. 'Low-key' charisma is perhaps the

most characteristic of contemporary bourgeois societies and it helps explain the contemporary depoliticization of public life.

We are likely to describe as a 'credible' or 'charismatic' or 'believable' leader someone who can make appeals to groups whose interests are alien to his own beliefs, constituency, or ideology. In modern politics it would be suicide for a leader to insist: Forget about my private life; all you need to know about me is how good a legislator or executive I am and what action I intend to take in office. Instead, we get excited when a conservative French President has dinner with a working class family, even though he has raised taxes on industrial wages a few days before, or believe an American President is more 'genuine' and reliable than his disgraced predecessor because the new man cooks his own breakfast. This political 'credibility' is the superimposition of private upon public imagery . . .

(Sennett, 1978, p. 25)

Reagan is the people. On a trip two years ago to a depressed industrial town in Pennsylvania, at a moment when the pundits were doubting whether Reagan would even run again, I met a group of blue-collar workers for whom times were hard. Traditionally Democratic, they planned even then to vote for Reagan. Why? 'Because he's the sort of guy who could be on the town bowling team.'

(Robert Chesshyre 'Idol of the American Dream',
the *Observer*, 30 June 1985)

The extent to which individuals are potentially responsive to specific forms of charisma depends upon the social conditions in which they live: Are they anomic? Are they suffering from *ressentiment*? Are they marginalized? Are they oppressed?

The Christian must consider himself a stranger on the earth.

(Epistle to the Hebrews, 11: 13)

On the contrary the strangers on earth (arising from extremely natural causes e.g. the colossal concentration of wealth in the whole Roman world etc. etc.) had to consider themselves Christians. It was not their Christianity that made them vagrants, but their vagrancy that made them Christians.

(Marx and Engels, 1976, p. 137)

An important implication of this remark of Marx and Engels is that structural conditions can generate non-rational but historically progressive movements and this implies that certain non-rational components may be required to energize those committed to social change. Charismatic social relations are themselves a site of struggle and, as Lasch has pointed out in a critique of Sennett, the non-rational is an inescapable element of all effective politics (Lasch, 1980, p. 67). That this is a somewhat atypical position to adopt within Marxism is perhaps indicated by Hirst's negative comments on the role that 'charisma' plays in Weber's work (Hirst, 1976, pp. 89–90) and by Wolpe's critique of the uses to which the concept has been put by political sociologists. Whilst accepting that many of Wolpe's criticisms are valid, it is clear that this book rejects his conclusion that 'the concept of charisma is not analytically useful' (Wolpe, 1968, p. 306). When retheorized it has a definite utility.

Durkheim has been used to explore the nature of charisma, and his work, together with aspects of that of Marx and Engels, can even help to retheorize some other aspects of Weber's work, particularly his 'Parliament and government in a reconstructed Germany'. In his texts it becomes clear that under capitalism there is a problem in integrating the working class as a necessary but subordinate group within society. The masses have been torn from communal relations (Weber, 1978, vol. 1, p. 337) and, further atomized by their subjection to bureaucracies (Beetham, 1974, p. 206), they are in an anomic condition. The authorities' goal of controlling and integrating them into the 'ideological community' (Therborn, 1980, pp. 219–315) is facilitated, but by no means solely, through the coercive power of the law (Weber, 1978, vol. 1, p. 312). 'Responsible' trade unionism and reformist social democratic politics (ibid., vol. 1, p. 1460) must also play a crucial role since they aid workers in winning 'reasonable' demands and incidentally thereby guarantee the reproduction of a healthy and loyal workforce. Participation in unions and political parties limits the dangers of 'egoism' and 'revolutionary syndicalism' by instilling 'altruistic' feelings, which can be mobilized by the state – the camaraderie of the unions can easily become the camaraderie of the regiment (ibid., vol. 1, p. 1391). This can also be developed through charismatic social relations. A charismatic leader controls the masses through a direct but authoritarian relationship (ibid., vol. 1, p. 1391). However, this leader will be in partnership with or subject to the control of the professional patrician politicians (ibid., vol. 1, p. 1427) and they will rule through or exceptionally without Parliament (ibid., vol. 1, p. 1383). Thus charisma can take various forms and it may or may not be stage-managed, but what is important is that through it individuals should *experience* themselves as part of a national collectivity where differences between social ranks are believed to be a matter of degree rather than signifying irreconcilable antagonistic interests (Laclau, 1979). Charisma is a social relation. In Althusserian terms it is an aspect of ideology.

Conclusion

In this chapter Durkheim's sociological concepts and their relationship to his epistemological position have been examined critically. They have also been looked to for their positive contribution to social scientific knowledge and to its potential development when it is liberated from the shackles imposed upon it by Durkheim's own somewhat limited vision. Here the radical implications of Durkheim's epistemological and sociological analyses will also be reiterated.

His work criticizes empiricism, theoreticism, positivism and reductionism, and elements of it anticipate a 'realist epistemology'. In his conceptual system as a whole he was a resolute opponent of methodological individualism, with a strong sense of the social and how it produces human attributes. He was aware of the complexity of society and of the different kinds of societies and therefore the difficulties in determining the significance of social facts.

Durkheim's anticipation of some of the more recent developments in post-structuralism has also been demonstrated. Indeed, his work can be used to develop a far more dynamic portrayal of signifying systems and social relations than is found in the post-structuralists' work. Undoubtedly one real strength of Durkheim's corpus of work lies in its potential use for the exploration of the relationships between social structures, collective representations and group formation. This potential has been concretely demonstrated in a discussion of the relationship between Durkheim's work and that of Weber. When these two are related to each other it is usually to contrast their methodologies and epistemologies and to suggest that they share a common conservatism. Here, something radically different has been achieved. It has been shown that Durkheim's writings can be used to rethink Weber's concept of charisma and even to reformulate some of his substantive analyses.

Notes

1 This follows the order of argument in Hirst (1975) and Benton (1977).
2 Indeed Durkheim's theory is like a variant on the Kabalistic theory concerning the tree of life (Scholem, 1961; James, 1971). The primary substance – found in the horde – could almost be seen as the breath of the Holy Spirit animating not individuals but societies. *Ab initio* the social is created and then it diversifies and complexifies. In this process the various branches (of this tree of life?) grow at different rates with different degrees of exuberance but also of contamination and sluggishness. In so far as the movement of history is of the initial diversification of societies and their eventual unity under the universal norms of reason we can only assume that history is a process of discovery and rediscovery, wherein the accidents of specificity and ignorance are sloughed off to find the pristine essence now understood – via science – for what it really is. Not the breath of the universal spirit, but the presence of the stuff of society, the social essence.
3 On occasion, however, for example in his discussion of Fustel de Coulanges, Durkheim demonstrated a more complex understanding of the nature of and relationship between religious phenomena and social relationships. He criticized Fustel de Coulanges for explaining social change in terms of the development of religious ideas. Thus whilst Fustel de Coulanges had discovered that primitive societies were familially organized and that

> the primitive family was constituted on a religious base . . . he has mistaken the cause for the effect. After setting up the religious idea, without bothering to establish its derivations he has deduced from it social arrangements, when on the contrary, it is the latter that explain the power and nature of the religious idea.
>
> (Durkheim, 1933, p. 179)

4 And this despite the fact that he was aware of the danger of using analogies incorrectly. Biological sociologists, for example, had not tried 'to control their studies of society by their knowledge of biology' but rather 'tried to infer the laws of the first from the laws of the second' (Durkheim, 1974, p. 1). He claimed in *The Elementary Forms of The Religious Life*:

> The life thus brought into being even enjoys so great an independence that it sometimes indulges in manifestations which have no pleasure or utility of any sort, but the mere pleasure of affirming itself.
>
> (Durkheim, 1976, p. 424)

See above p. 23 and also Durkheim (1933, p. 66).

5 It is precisely this conception of history as a 'narrative' that has dominated much Anglo-Saxon writing. Arthur C. Danto (1968) schematically represents this concept of narrative as follows:

> The form of an explanation in history may be represented as follows:
>
> E: x is F at t-1 and x is G at t-3
>
> F and G are predicate variables to be replaced, respectively, with contrary predicates; and x is an individual variable to be replaced with a singular referring expression which destinates the subject of change. Thus we get E: The Duke of Buckingham favours the marriage at t-1 and the Duke of Buckingham opposes the marriage at t-3.
>
> The shift F-G is the change in x which requires explanation. But to explain the shift requires reference to something happening to x at t-2, an event (of whatever degree of complexity) which caused the change in x. I therefore offer the following model as representing the structure of narrative explanation:
>
> (1) x is F at t-1
> (2) H happens to x a t-2
> (3) x is G at t-3
>
> (1) and (3) together constitute the explanandum, (2) is the explanans. To furnish (2) is to explain (1) and (3) . . . it ought now to be perfectly clear in what sense an historical explanation takes the form of a narrative. It is so in the sense that (1), (2) and (3) simply has already the structure of a story. It has a beginning (1), a middle (2) and an end (3).

Furthermore Danto argues that 'to speak of a change is implicitly to suppose some continuous identity in the subject of change. . . . It is this implicit reference to a continuous subject which gives a measure of unity to a historical narrative' (Danto, 1968).

Althusser amongst others has, of course, criticized this view and it is perhaps in recent film criticism that the questioning of assumptions of identity is most developed (Althusser and Balibar, 1970; McCabe, 1974, 1976).

6 Bergson outlined his metaphysical view of nature in the following manner:

> A great current of creative energy gushes forth through matter, to obtain from it what it can. At most points it is stopped; these stops are transmuted, in our eyes, into the appearance of so many living species, i.e. of organisms in which our perception, being essentially analytic and synthetic, distinguishes a multitude of elements combining to fulfill a multitude of functions; but the process of

organisation is only the stop itself, a simple act analogous to the impress of the foot which instantaneously causes thousands of grains of sand to contrive to form a pattern.

> (Bergson 1958, p. 221; cited in Levi-Strauss, 1963b, p. 98)

7 For Foucault's comments on Durkheim see Foucault (1979a), pp. 27–8 Morris and Patton 1979 p. 66 and for Rose's acerbic assessment of these, see Rose (1984), pp. 175–8. For his spatial and architectural concept of the social realm see Gordon (1980), p. 63 and *passim*.
8 Thus Geras (1987) has rightly criticized Laclau and Mouffe for prioritizing discursive representations over class relations. Mouzelis (1978) had already pointed out that in the earlier text, *Politics and Ideology in Marxist Theory* (1976), by overemphasizing the ideological, Laclau failed to address the issue of the kinds of effects produced by different forms of political organization. Foster (1985) combined both such criticisms of 'discourse theorists' when he attacked Jones (1983) for his prioritization of the discourse of Chartism over Chartism as a movement and organization which was a site of struggle. In that case the dispute was about the meaning and future development of Chartism between groups imbricated within, and thus partially constituted by, class relations external to this particular discourse. Woodiwiss (1987a) provides a trenchant criticism of Laclau and Mouffe's development of discourse theory and of their epistemology. It should be noted that their reply to (selected) critics involves an (unacknowledged) radical change in their position on the latter (Laclau and Mouffe, 1987).

3 Durkheim and politics

Introduction

Although Durkheim believed that his work provided an objective account of social reality, it contained assumptions from a number of different schools of political theory. It has been construed as ideological – as conservative (Nisbet 1965, 1967; Coser, 1960), as liberal idealist (Richter, 1960), as socialist (Taylor *et al.*, 1973), differing evaluations that reflect different aspects of his thought. It is not surprising that a sophisticated thinker opposed to individualistic explanations of the nature and genesis of social institutions and social conduct should be linked with a diversity of political traditions.[1]

> He was in many ways both a moralistic conservative and a radical socialist reformer, who would qualify, in most definitions, as a socialist of sorts.
>
> His conservatism was sociologically based but rested ultimately on a view of human nature as being in need of limits and moral discipline. His socialism likewise rested on a fear of anarchy both within society and within the life of the individual, based on maximum freedom of thought and distributive justice in social relations – these were his ultimate guiding preoccupations.
>
> (Lukes, 1975; see Hunt, 1978, p. 64)

Whilst these different conceptual systems might complement each other, their contradictory logics are more likely to displace or suppress elements of each other. Some of the liberal and conservative elements certainly truncated the development of the socialistic aspects of Durkheim's thought.

In this chapter an account is provided of Durkheim's understanding of the nature and likely development of contemporary complex societies and the role that political action could and should play in this development. This is followed with an excursus into the history of the Third Republic, which Durkheim

42

misread because of the conservative and liberal elements in his thought. Then his interpretation of the nature of socialism and communism is discussed and criticized. Finally, when the implications of some of his arguments are drawn out and related to some other aspects of his work, then it will be seen that they can be developed to provide a sophisticated non-Utopian image of a future socialist society.

Durkheim's social evolutionism

For Durkheim, the history of western societies is one of a dynamic, internally generated increase in social differentiation and interdependence. New types of institutions have been produced. These have either taken over functions formerly fulfilled by other (now) anachronistic institutions or they fulfil new functions. Thus large-scale industrial organizations have emerged and the state has grown in size and importance. This new social order is increasingly meritocratic and solicitous of individual freedom (Durkheim, 1933, p. 379). The general growth of this individualism is due to the increased respect paid to the individual *qua* individual. This phenomenon is associated with secularization (Durkheim, 1973, p. 304), the individuating effects of the division of labour, the location of the individual within a complex nexus of rights and obligations *vis-a-vis* other individuals *and* secondary associations (family, community, employers) which are legally enforced by a state itself subject to the Rule of Law (Durkheim, 1933, p. 24). Social institutions should be compatible with each other and with the fundamental principles of the society – the legal system should correspond 'to the existing state of society' (ibid., p. 66). Nevertheless certain social problems are endemic to social life (crime, for example), others are the unintended consequences of the normal functioning of the complex of social institutions of a particular society, and yet others indicate some kind of social malfunctioning. Whatever the cause, an appropriate social response is called for.

> If today we have a large number of social vagrants, people from all ranks of society, it is because there is something in our European societies promoting such a condition. . . . Such obviously social evils require social treatment. . . . The only effective remedy lies in the collective organization of welfare.
>
> (Durkheim, 1961, p. 84)

In the long run, modifications in the mode of organization of economic life may mean that particular problems disappear.

In the economic sphere, differentiation means that there is and will be an increase in the mutual interdependence of economic activity and in the scale of the economic units. The state is needed to provide an adequate legal and administrative framework and infrastructual basis for the economy and to coordinate it through a form of planning that leaves corporations and professional associations with a significant degree of autonomy (Lukes, 1975, pp. 539–46). This would be facilitated by the development of an 'industrial parliament' of the productive members of society (Durkheim, 1933, p. 25) although corporations and professional associations ought to have a significant degree of autonomy (Lukes, 1975, pp. 539–46). Social integration depends upon the development of a rational morality imposed by the professional associations as well as the state, since the state is often 'too remote an authority' (Durkheim, 1961, p. 246), and a rational legal system. These are rational because their effectiveness depends upon an appeal to reason rather than to authority (ibid., p. 21). A major goal of public morality is to make society as a whole and each group within it limit their aspirations. 'Social integration' and 'system integration', to use Lockwood's (1964) terms, could then be realized.

Social groups, like all other social phenomena, are the product of complex social forces, which may or may not equip them to posit and effectively pursue rational goals. Political action can be effective only if political goals are realistic for that kind of society at that particular stage of development. For example, those active in the French Revolution were successful because they were 'the natural product of everything that went before' (Durkheim, 1961, p. 37).

No one today thinks that we can get together and alter the laws of physical nature. Yet there are few among us who realize that the citizens of a country, even if they are unanimously agreed in promoting an economic or political revolution, can only fail miserably in this enterprise if the revolution is not implied in the nature, in the conditions of existence, of that society. Few people understand that to give France a social organization – one which is only possible centuries hence – is just as unthinkable as to reestablish the social system of the Middle Ages.

(Durkheim, 1961, p. 258)

A total break with the extant institutions is not possible and whilst revolution may act as a catalyst to long-term trends it is usually disruptive and may simply destroy society (ibid., p. 233; Lukes, 1975, p. 543). The search for unrealizable goals is dangerous.

Presented abstractly most of these arguments are sound and most social theorists would concur with them, including many Marxists, who, indeed, have often condemned adventurist political action. The problem remains, however, of determining the underlying social trends and social forces and what groups using what methods are likely to be effective in achieving them. This is a particularly significant problem if there is more than one set of possible outcomes, i.e. if societies can 'evolve' in more than one direction. Durkheim himself was committed to constitutional political activity and to the Third Republic, rejecting the view of those who saw society as 'a Bourgeois administration with the Gendarmerie to protect it' (Durkheim, 1974, p. 74). Rather, the consolidation of republicanism, the role that the Dreyfus affair had played in separating church and state and the secularization of education were all progressive achievements (Lukes, 1975, pp. 354–60). To summarize, if state and society are organized according to the 'nature of things' then Reason can prevail and society's potential can be realized (Durkheim, 1961, p. 21).

Since 'the ideal society is not outside of the real society, it is part of it' (Durkheim, 1976, p. 427), for Durkheim revolutionaries are irrational – effects of and contributors to a 'spirit of anarchy' (Durkheim, 1961, p. 54). They are not really impassioned by social concern:

> The anarchist, the aesthete, the mystic, the socialist revolutionary, even if they do not despair of the future, have in common with the pessimist a single sentiment of hatred and disgust for the existing social order, a single craving to destroy or escape from reality.
>
> (Durkheim, 1951, p. 370)

Although for both individuals and society as a whole there will always be some gap between the ideal and the real, gradual progress can be achieved by moral and prudent activity. All citizens, but particularly workers, should have moderate expectations and accept that many of their desires will be unfulfilled:

> each in his sphere vaguely realizes the extreme limit set to his ambitions and aspires to nothing beyond. At least if he respects

regulations and is docile to collective authority, that is has a wholesome moral constitution, he feels that it is well not to ask more.

(Durkheim, 1951, p. 250)

Moreover there will always be some injustice and we should make children aware that they cannot 'rely for happiness' upon 'power and wealth' but 'that the important thing is to find a goal compatible with one's abilities' (Durkheim, 1961, p. 50).

It is with some reason that Zeitlin writes of Durkheim that:

> He despised and feared restlessness, conflict and 'anarchy', the insatiable appetites of modern man were a sign of his morbidity. . . . Durkheim believed that the decline of religious forces had left a moral vacuum. A morality of contentment was required because social peace could never be achieved as long as men were not content with their lot.
>
> (Zeitlin, 1981, p. 255)

These fears led him to overemphasize one aspect of morality – that concerned with self-denial – and to conflate the general need to develop self-control with the obligation to accept all the restrictions on desire imposed by the dominant public morality. Nevertheless, as will be argued at some length in Chapters 5 and 6, there is nothing inherently reactionary about much of this, and revolutionary syndicalists like Sorel were equally conscious of the need for an effective social morality, one that could stimulate through social change a less rigidly ordered society than Durkheim's ideal.

Without doubt Durkheim too readily dismissed contemporary socialist and working-class movements without concretely exploring the details of their programmes. His faith in 'Reason' and 'evolution', in the impartiality of the state and in the capacity and willingness of the privileged social groups to act disinterestedly and accept 'progressive' social change seems to have been based on a mixture of wishful thinking and an arrogant confidence that his theoretical system was adequate to reality. It was not based upon a detailed 'empirical' analysis of what was taking place in the Third Republic.

Durkheim, authoritarian liberalism and conservativism

Durkheim's characterization of the nature and history of the Third Republic is problematic. If the disestablishment of the church undermined Catholicism it did not produce the kinds of schismatic reforms that Durkheim hoped would have made it less of a 'sociological monstrosity' (Lukes, 1975, p. 534). The moral education found in the secularized educational system did not deny the precepts of Catholicism but rather changed their rationale. Indeed, here there was a contradiction in Durkheim's thought. His search for a religion without God and his belief that 'The duties of a man to himself are always those of his duties to society' were only too compatible with an unthinking moral conformism and with the conservative assumption that society was unified, bound together by a shared culture, that this and the needs of the less able were best interpreted by its elites.[2] On the other hand, he accepted the liberal view that there was a unitary transhistorical and non-contextual form of Reason (Richter, 1960, p. 203). His understanding of both Reason and morality was too often monolithic and hence ultimately undemocratic. Indeed, Nizan argues that Durkheimian sociology itself functioned as a form of ideological control (Nizan, 1971, pp. 109–10). Durkheim's desire to differentiate sociology from and assert its superiority over political theory meant that he parodied it and thus was not able to benefit from its insights (Richter, 1960, p. 185). He often *assumed*, for example, that the state acted in the collective interest, accepting at face value its claim to embody Reason. In practice such Reason was abstract and a counterpart of the Rights of Man that would supposedly be secured by the organization of rational conduct according to the Rule of Law. The emptiness of both this 'Reason' and the 'Rights of Man' for those in material conditions where both were mere abstractions and indeed ideological legitimations for repression meant that Durkheim colluded in maintaining the *status quo* rather than transforming it. Although he also claimed that positive social change required a morality that could be reflected upon, criticized and modified (Durkheim, 1961, p. 52), he did not analyse the conditions under which adequate moralities could be *collectively* produced, how people could articulate their desires and have them taken seriously by those in authority. *Equality of power is a precondition for true dialogue.*

He should, after all, have been disturbed by the career of 'Solidarism', the 'official ideology' of the Third Republic.[3] This claimed that through mutual cooperation all classes could contribute to progress, achieve justice and end social conflict. In practice it meant authoritarian political control and did not limit the power or wealth of the bourgeoisie, who merely made empty gestures towards humanizing and reorganizing capitalism. Although Durkheim was himself disappointed by Solidarism (Lukes, 1975, pp. 350–4), he would have done well to reflect upon Renouvier's angry deathbed judgement: 'The bourgeoisie has not kept its promises: it has worked only for itself' (Zeldin, 1979, p. 295). The implication is clear – the bourgeoisie will only give up their privileges if forced to do so.

Durkheim's image of a future society was underdeveloped and his understanding of the motivating force for social change was woefully inadequate. Many socialists have argued that *class struggle*, including the use of extra-constitutional methods, is necessary because the ruling class and its allies are unlikely to surrender their privileges willingly – an organized force is required to make them do so. Moreover, it is by *their* involvement in struggle that the oppressed classes can develop unity, articulate their own goals and make sure that the new social order is organized in their interests. But Durkheim was unable to recognize the need for such an agency of change. It is not surprising that he was concerned with the attitude and actions of the working class, since by their industrial struggles they were questioning the idea that the distribution of wealth and power was an *expression* of some consensus, the effect of some *conscience collective*, and by implication demonstrating that value systems often *legitimate* rather than *determine* the social structure.

In Durkheim, then, there is a reformist politics based upon evolutionism, elements of liberalism, specifically an abstract belief in Reason, and also a conservative commitment to order-for-its-own-sake. Although Richter is right in rejecting a simple reduction of the complexity of Durkheim's texts to a conservative position, the central role assigned to religion and a consensual morality vindicates Nisbet's view that

> Such concepts as status, cohesion, adjustment, function, norm, ritual and symbol *are* essentially conservative and do form *one of* the coherent systems in his thought.
>
> (Nisbet, 1963)

It was above all his conservatism – in the broad rather than the narrow sense – that led Durkheim to conflate conformity with normality and 'that signficantly limited his perceptions of society'

(Coser, 1960, p. 211). But this conservatism was only one of the discourses that traversed his thought; he was also affected by both technocratic and more radical forms of socialism.

Durkheim and socialism

Durkheim, Zeitlin has argued, was engaged in a debate with the 'ghost of Marx' (Zeitlin, 1981, p. v). Hunt disagrees, claiming rather that Durkheim's debate was with French socialism (Hunt, 1978, p. 66). For Pels (1984), Durkheim's work was, if anything, overly influenced by socialism. In fact, there is little doubt that Durkheim's work had a significant relationship with a wide range of socialist theory. He was clearly sympathetic to Saint-Simon, the German 'socialists of the Chair' and, to some extent, Proudhon.[4] He was familiar with but critical of Marxism in its original, derivative, crude and elaborated forms. He explicitly opposed revolutionary syndicalism but surprisingly shared many concepts with its self-styled spokesman Georges Sorel. In 1893 he published an influential 'Note on the Definition of Socialism' and in 1895 he began a three-year course on its history, of which only the first part was ever delivered.

Socialism, he argued, is a practical doctrine – a 'cry of anguish' – rather than a scientific theory. It is an ideology produced by social forces that its advocates do not understand (Durkheim, 1962, pp. 40–1). Socialism encompasses

> every doctrine which demands the connection of all economic functions, or of certain among them, which are at the present time diffuse, to the directing and conscious centers of society.
> (Durkheim, 1962, p. 54)

Such doctrines are held by diverse social groups who share a commitment to a planned industrial social order, based upon large-scale industry and a developed secular state. It is not necessarily a working-class ideology since the

> amelioration of the worker's fate is only one goal that socialism desires from the economic organization it demands, just as class war is only one of the means by which this reorganization could result, one aspect of the historical development producing it.
> (Durkheim, 1962, p. 58)

It is opposed to both classical economics and to 'communism'. The latter is a sporadically recurring utopian doctrine that believes – 'that economic interests are anti-social and that industrial life should be reduced to strict necessities' (ibid., 237) and that seeks a form of justice and egalitarianism only even remotely conceivable in small-scale homogeneous societies. Durkheim was also critical of socialism – he did not agree that moral transformation depends upon a prior economic transformation (Lukes, 1975, p. 246) or with its 'fundamental axiom . . . that there are no social interests outside economic interests' (Durkheim, 1962, p. 237).

The French socialist tradition was complex and shaded into both republicanism and radicalism. The Saint-Simonians, Guesdists, Blanquists, the followers of Proudhon and Fourier, those organized in the First International and the syndicalists, all took different stands on virtually every issue. True, in line with Durkheim's definition, they were united in their distaste for an economy organized according to *laissez-faire* principles but disagreed whether they wanted to humanize and regulate it, 'restore' petty-commodity production, replace it with workers' cooperatives or nationalize it. Equally there was no unanimity on how wealth and power should be distributed or what should be the role of the state in the regulation of the economy or whether the system would be authoritarian, democratic or libertarian. They advocated different strategies to effect change and for consolidating a new social order. It is impossible to capture the complexity of these positions within Durkheim's simple dichotomy between socialism and communism. But this does sensitize us to recurring thematic issues. He has abstracted from the writings of socialist and communist writers elements that can be articulated together to produce two sets of internally consistent but mutually incompatible discourses. It will be shown in a later chapter that they do usefully describe Marx's quite contrastive portrayals of socialism and communism.

Durkheim and technocratic socialism

Lukes argues that Durkheim's 'study of the technocratic strand in socialist thought . . . is of both historical and contemporary interest' (Lukes, 1975, p. 248). It certainly helps to reveal just how much he was influenced by Saint-Simonian socialism. Saint-Simon argued that 'where economic relations form the basis of common life, social unity is above all the result of the solidarity of interests'. Thus the whole of society ought to be organized on an industrial basis and controlled by the productive members of society, namely, intellectuals and 'immediate producers' (including entreprenuerial capitalists) (Durkheim, 1962, p. 176). Society should organise industry to achieve maximum production and distribute the products so that everyone 'has enough, or better still, as much as possible' (ibid., p. 239). To curb egoistic utilitarianism, Saint-Simon advocated a pantheistic religion since, 'without charity, mutual obligation and philanthropy, the social order – and still more the human order – was impossible' (ibid., p. 227). Even so, such an industrial system could not work if restricted to one society, and thus, for example, a European economic and political system might well be needed (ibid., p. 217). Durkheim was obviously sympathetic to Saint-Simon and there was a significant and often theoretically constructive overlap between their conceptual systems – for example, the *sui generis* concept of society and a vision of organic solidarity, of the need for an 'industrial parliament', and perhaps less fortunately the dismissal of class conflict (Zeitlin, 1981, p. 251). But he believed that Saint-Simon had overemphasized the independence and importance of industry and had failed to understand the need to control and limit human needs and desires; and that the religion he advocated would not be capable of creating solidarity or of enforcing moral discipline.

Durkheim, Marxism and communists

In the late nineteenth century, Marxism was relatively unimportant in France and orthodox Marxists like Jules Guesde and Paul Lafargue were rather crude and overly polemical (Lichtheim, 1975; Zeldin, 1979, pp. 381–93; see Lafargue, 1969). The socialist politician Jaurès (a friend of Durkheim's) was a Marxist of sorts, but of an extremely revisionist kind (see his 'Idealism in History' (1895, in Fried and Sanders, 1964, pp. 403-15). Durkheim had certainly read some Marx (Lukes, 1975, p. 246), and, whilst his explicit and implicit references to it were sometimes inaccurate and his criticism far from adequate to their object (Llobera, 1981a), his review of Labriola's *Essays on the Materialist Conception of History* (Durkheim, 1982) provides a clear and supportable statement of the differences between his mature conceptual schema and nineteenth-century Marxism.

Marxism, he argued, stresses the causal priority of the development of the productive forces and particularly the level of

technology both as the determinant of the existing social structure
and also as the major dynamic in social change (Durkheim, 1982,
pp. 168–9); this aspect of Marxism is socialist rather than
communist. Labriola's Marxism does indeed treat the social
relationships between classes as secondary to technological
development, portrays the politico-legal form of the state in an
instrumentalist manner and sees morality, religion, art, etc., as
secondary phenomena. In opposition to this view, Durkheim
articulated his own:

> In principle everything is religious. Yet we know of no means
> of reducing religion to economics nor of any attempt at really
> effecting this reduction.
>
> (Durkheim, 1982, p. 173)

Now, although Labriola's work is somewhat 'technologically
determinist', he posits the existence of a number of relatively
autonomous but dialectically related levels. His object of analysis
is the 'social complexus', 'the totality of the unity of social life'
(Labriola, 1908, p. 85), and the articulated relationship between
these different elements. A characterization of any society will
involve an analysis of the stage of technological development, the
mode of organization of the productive forces, the relationship of
both production and distribution to the class structure, its *potential*
for satisfying social needs and its performance, and the development
of coercive legal–political and ideological strategies for containing
tensions (Labriola, 1908, pp. 103–4). In class systems a (temporary)
social peace is possible and a society's members may actively
identify with the social order; religion, for example, can play an
integrative role (ibid., p. 181). Within his 'complexus of factors'
the the forces and relations of production are not clearly
distinguished and in no sense function as the 'essence' or 'ultimate
cause' of all social phenomena (ibid., p. 111).[5] In positing religion
as the cause and essence of social life Durkheim mirrored what he
assumed was Labriola's system of concepts. In reality, Labriola
was able to produce a much more mediated and complex
portrayal of the historical dynamic than was Durkheim.

If Durkheim's interpretation of Marxism was inadequate, what
of his concept of 'communism'? Part of Durkheim's understanding
of communism and communists was probably based upon the
theory and practice of Georges Sorel, whose writings had been
known to Durkheim's circle from 1893 (Durkheim, 1962, p. 33).[6]
Sorel had a personal disdain for material comforts (Portis, 1980, p.

8) and was concerned with the general problem of 'determining if there exists a mechanism capable of guaranteeing the development of morality' (Sorel, 1898, p. 189). For Sorel (*contra* Durkheim's socialists), 'economic transformation cannot be realised if the workers have not acquired a superior level of moral culture' (ibid., p. 90). Since classes not societies were the subjects of history, the working class needed to organize and act independently of the state. The corrupt Third Republic had nothing to offer. The same was true of the 'professional associations in which the administrative tends necessarily to dominate' (ibid., p. 91). They should reject both Durkheim's grand plans for 'professional associations' and also Solidarism. Rather it was through the struggle of the syndicates that a working class would be produced with a developed *esprit de corps*, intellectual energy and collective power. The proletariat's 'acts of violence' were ennobling since they were 'acts of war . . . carried on without hatred and without the spirit of revenge' (Sorel, 1908, p. 115). For Sorel, class relations are not only a crucial *determinant* of the contradictions that might lead to the emergence of antagonistic social groups within society but directly *constitute* them: class subjects *express* class relationships. This whole quasi-left Hegelian notion is problematic and, indeed, has worked against the sophisticated exploration of social formations (Poulantzas, 1978).[7]

Sorel often referred to Durkheim's work, writing a long review of *The Rules of Sociological Method* (Sorel, 1895a), and shared his view that in order for society to be coherent it needed a unifying morality. In his Marxist phase he believed that this would only be possible if class relations were eliminated and a proletarian hegemony was established. 'Myths' like that of 'the general strike' were mechanisms for stimulating a continuous moral regeneration, a 'permanent revolution'. He later rejected Marxism and lost interest in the proletariat. It would seem that his involvement with their struggles had derived not primarily from a concern with social justice or proletarian self-emancipation but rather from a belief that they might produce the superior individuals and morality that could regenerate society. Later, when they no longer seemed likely to be history's moral vanguard, he played down the importance of class divisions[8] and looked instead to neo-fascism and the charismatic promise of monarchism.[9] Durkheim never adopted such views. Indeed, in his wartime writings on Germany he recognized that legalism was only too compatible with oppression and external aggression and in his 'Two laws of penal evolution' that even in a developed society the state could be tyrannical and partisan (Durkheim, 1973, pp. 66–7).

Durkheim criticized communists for having a conception of the social order that could only even begin to make sense in a small-scale and homogeneous community. Yet the same can be said of the importance he gave in his later work to the *conscience collective* when he no longer drew such a contrast between mechanical and organic solidarity. Furthermore, Durkheim's ideal citizen, a deservingly privileged individual willing to make sacrifices in the name of charity, bears some affinity to a moralistic communist. As is so often the case, each of these critics seems to have been subtly ensnared by a variant of what each of them criticized in the other.

Yet the issue of the relationship between morality and socialism remains an important one. Once a simple-minded economic determinism is abandoned, then any society associated with any mode of production, no matter how democratic and egalitarian, will face a problem of developing a hegemonic integrative ideology (including significant moral components). It is one mechanism by which individuals develop self-control. It provides a framework for defining the appropriate ways to pursue self-interest. It makes individuals aware of the interests of others and of the collective as a whole and could make the relatively powerful act charitably, i.e. abandon narrow self-interest for love of the society as a whole. If one has a crude Rousseauian view of man, the elimination of class inequalities will lead individuals to act spontaneously and naturally in an altruistic way. One would not need moral pressures and moral inspiration actively to recognize 'charity, mutual obligation and philanthropy' (Durkheim, 1962, p. 227). Durkheim showed that one cannot deduce a normative order from the ontological characteristics of human beings. Society helps constitute human subjects as moral subjects. Both the normative order and human subjectivity have to be socially produced and *reproduced*.

There is little doubt that a strong motivating force for socialists is a sense of disgust that under capitalism resources are squandered – a minority have been wealthy beyond their needs whilst the majority have been poor. A more equal society could also be an affluent society, but how affluent? Durkheim argued that the needs of human beings, above a basic minimum, are not givens but are socially determined, but 'how fix the quantity of well-being, comfort, luxury, that a human being ought to possess?' Socialists like Saint-Simon have imagined that social peace would occur if 'economic appetites' were both freed 'of all restraint' and also satisfied. This Durkheim argued is an impossibility (ibid., pp. 241–2). Individuals must moderate their appetites and will only do so if they subordinate themselves to the authority of a collective morality, which therefore is as essential to a socialist as to any other society. One does not need to agree with every element of Durkheim's arguments to recognize that *acceptable* standards of life and therefore of the legitimate level of desires would have to be set in a socialist society – productive capacity, ecological constraints, the degree to which individuals wish to dwell in 'the realm of necessity', all provide parameters within which decisions are to be made but also pose the problem how to make them acceptable and how to enforce them.

Durkheim's radical socialist vision

The purpose of society, it is held, is the individual and for the sole reason that he is all that there is that is real in society. Since it is only an aggregate of individuals, it can have no other aim than the development of individuals. Indeed, by the very fact of the association, society makes human activity more productive in the realm of science, the arts and industry. Thanks to this greater yield, the individual finds more abundant nourishment, material and moral as well as for the intellect and so he thrives and develops. But the State is not itself a producer. It adds nothing and can add nothing to this wealth of all kinds that the society stores up and that the individual benefits from. What then is the part it should play? The answer is to ward off certain ill effects of association . . . the State should be limited to administering a wholly negative justice.

(Durkheim, 1957, pp. 51–3)

There is no such thing as Society. There are individual men and women and there are families.
(Margaret Thatcher, quoted in the *Observer*, 1 November 1988)

In earlier parts of this chapter I spelt out some aspects of Durkheim's arguments with which sociologists of virtually any political persuasion might agree: that social movements are produced by social processes; that their goals may or may not be realizable; and that their actions may produce chaos instead of constructive social change. Many would also agree with his representation (see above), and his critique (below), of *laissez-faire* ideology. How this draws upon socialist discourses (both technocratic and the German 'Socialists of the Chair') and communist discourses can be seen in his discussion of the social functions of the state. For a complex society to function effectively more is required than an increase 'in the exchanges of goods and services'. These transactions must be done

> by rules that are more just; it is not simply that everyone should have access to rich supplies of food and drink . . . each one should be treated as he deserves, each freed from an unjust and humiliating tutelage, and that in holding to his fellows and his group, a man should not sacrifice his individuality. And the Agency on which this special responsibility lies is the State. So the state does not inevitably become either simply a spectator of social life (as the economists would have it), in which it intervenes only in a negative way, or (as the socialists would have it), simply a cog in an economic machine. It is, above all, supremely the organ of moral discipline.
>
> (Durkheim, 1957, p. 72)

The state then is socially productive. It can enhance economic activity, facilitate the establishment of a just social order, protect groups and individuals and thereby help to generate constructive social activity. As Fenton (1984, p. 42) points out, Durkheim's corporatist view of the state and the role that he gives to professional associations makes his work near to the British guild socialists and it is no coincidence that a commentator on Durkheim's work, Paul Hirst, should similarly advocate corporatist political forms (1986, 1988).

Now the evaluation of historical possibilities is not simply an objective exercise but one structured by one's general theoretical position, and particularly by one's understanding of the nature of existing societies, the societies that could possibly exist and the society that *could* emerge from this one. Durkheim's understanding of the nature of and mechanisms for political change was often limited by his overly sanguine concept of the state. On occasion, as we have seen, in his wartime writings and in the 'Two laws of penal evolution', he was less confident that the state acts in the general interest. If oppression and external aggression are compatible with legalism, then to bind political action by constitutional restraints would not be morally or politically correct, and non-conformists and revolutionaries would not necessarily be irrational.

Moreover Durkheim by no means believed that social evolution was over with bourgeois society. There is also a radical conception of a future society to be found in his work. First of all let us notice that he was aware that many social problems are due not to individual inadequacies but to the extant socio-economic organization; welfare, for example, becomes a social responsibility. Secondly, he argued that some level of planning is essential in the economy and, instead of the economy determining social relations, the economy should be subordinated to social goals (Durkheim, 1951, p. 253). Thirdly, Durkheim's concern for some level of decentralization is by no means inherently reactionary and there is an interesting ambiguity about the composition of his industrial parliaments – namely who counts as 'productive' citizens as economic organization is modified. Fourth, since 'morality must not be internalized in such a way as to be beyond criticism' (Durkheim, 1961, p. 8), and since the idea of 'equality and fraternity' leaves 'too large a place for unjust social inequalities' (Durkheim, 1976, p. 427), the search for *justice* and *solidarity* should be continued (Durkheim, 1961, p. 102). This entails an equality of condition and the abolition of inherited wealth (Durkheim, 1957, pp. 210-11). Inherited wealth is at odds with another crucial social principle, and one that would also play a role in a socialist society – efficiency and justice require that social positions be distributed according to merit (Durkheim, 1933, p. 377). 'The characteristic of injustice is that it is not founded in the nature of things' (Durkheim, 1961, p. 21). In Chapter 4 these issues will be taken up in more detail and it will be shown that his thought, although underdeveloped, was complex with far more radical potential than Nisbet, for example, has ever adequately comprehended.[10]

Conclusion

In this chapter Durkheim's political positions have been outlined and assessed. These include elements of conservative, liberal, and socialist discourses. The latter has both technocratic and more radical elements. Although the radical potential of his work has been somewhat vitiated by the effects of these other discourses, it can nevertheless be identified. My argument is that these aspects of Durkheim's work are worth studying both for their positive contribution to social scientific knowledge and for their potential development. In the next chapter I shall look somewhat critically

at Durkheim's causal explanation of social development and its
likely trajectory. I shall critique this and develop further the more
radical aspects of his vision.

Notes

1 Hartz (1964) has argued, for example, that socialist thought
  synthesized elements of both democratic liberalism and conservatism
  and these in turn had been reactions to, and developments of, the
  Whiggish liberalism of the eighteenth century. Marx's own view was
  that his work extracted the rational kernel from and synthesized
  elements of German idealism, French socialism and English political
  economy (Marx 1859, reprinted in Tucker, 1978, p. 2).
2 There is far more overlap between conservative and liberal thought
  than is often recognized. Burkean conservatism, for example, accepted
  the market economy and did not aspire to an ultra-conservative *status
  quo ante* (Macpherson, 1980).
3 The solidarists placed their main hope on the development of
  voluntary mutual benefit societies. They hoped that these would
  provide the whole range of social services – employment exchanges, loans, medical attention, pharmacies, pensions and insur-
  ance – all without much cost to the state. 'The French Republic',
  said Paul Deschanel, 'must become a vast mutual benefit society'.
      The solidarists gave this movement an enormous boost. A law of
  1898 gave the societies the same freedom as the law of 1884 had
  given trade unions, but adding financial privileges and the promise
  of state subsidies on an elaborately calculated scale, proportionate to
  their achievements. By 1902 over a million more people had joined,
  to which should be added half a million school children enrolled in
  a junior branch. In 1910 it was claimed that there were 15,832 societies
  with 3,170,000 active members and 400,000 honorary members.

                                          (Zeldin, 1979, pp. 296–7).

  Durkheim was strongly influenced in this by Renouvier and Hamelin
  (Lukes, 1975, pp. 54–7).
4 Durkheim prepared lectures on Fourier and Proudhon which he was
  never to give (Lukes, 1975, p. 248). Proudhon believed that all wealth
  is socially produced and condemned the way in which property right
  makes it possible to exclude individuals from access to the means of
  production and thus from making the contribution they otherwise
  could to their own and the collective welfare. This is not so different
  from Durkheim's critique of the effect on society of inherited wealth.
  Both also believed that limits should be placed on the role of the state
  (Fried and Sanders, 1964, pp. 199–229).
5 The extent to which he somewhat simplistically anticipates Althusser
  is also evident when he writes:

It is not a question of separating the accident from the substance, the appearance from the reality, the phenomenon from the intrinsic kernel . . . but of explaining the connection and the complexus precisely in so far as it is a connection and a complexus.

(Labriola, 1908, p. 228)

6 Sorel made frequent reference to Durkheim's works. In 1895 his article 'Les Théories de M. Durkheim' was a review of *The Rules of Sociological Method*. The same year he wrote an article on 'Théories pénales de M. Durkheim et Tarde' for *Archivio di Psychiatria, Scienze Penali ed Antropologia* and he refers to Durkheim's work in 'The socialist future of the syndicates' (1896). Sorel wrote the introduction for the French edition of *The Materialist Conception of History* (1897), reviewed by Durkheim. This introduction was translated in part and transposed to the American edition of another of Labriola's books, *Essays in Socialism and Philosophy* (1906). In this later book Labriola made clear that he and the now anti-Marxist Sorel had parted company.

7 Hegel synthesized elements from many liberal and conservative theorists and others have made similar syntheses, albeit less adequately. Thus what often seem to be neo-Hegelian arguments do not necessarily have their source in Hegel himself. In Durkheim (1957 and 1983) Durkheim briefly refers to Hegel's work. For a discussion of the similarities and differences between Durkheim and Hegel and of the importance of (indirect) Hegelian influences on Durkheim's work see Knapp (1985).

8 Recently Laclau and Mouffe (1985) have cited Sorel's critique of Marxism approvingly and have also moved from a position where they prioritize the position of the working class as a vanguard to one where they look to a radical democratic revolution based upon a new unity constructed from the 'new social movements – urban, ecological, anti- authoritarian, anti-institutional, feminist, racist, ethnic, regional or sexual minorities' (1985, p. 159). It would seem that for them, too, socialism is not primarily about justice and does not require a massive working-class participation. Marxism has always involved a concern with justice and Marxists have rightly made working-class activity central – without a fundamental change in class relations capital's logic will always eventually reassert itself.

9 Portis is quite disingenuous in his account of the relationship between Sorel and fascism (Portis, 1980, p. 16) as indeed are Laclau and Mouffe (1985, pp. 41–2), though perhaps to a lesser degree.

10 Here I am arguing that there were explicit elements in Durkheim's work that were socialist, in that sense agreeing with Taylor, Walton and Young (1973, pp. 87–8) rather than Hunt (Hunt, 1978, p. 162), but I also believe that other socialist elements were underdeveloped. At the same time I would argue that socialists have a great deal to learn, much of it uncomfortable, from Durkheim's system as a whole.

4 Durkheim and the division of labour

Introduction

In this chapter I examine the discussion in *The Division of Labour in Society* of the different forms of solidarity, how law can be used as their index and and how one kind of society can develop from the other. In the next chapter the issue of the nature of the 'juridical relation' will be dealt with in some depth. Here I first attend to the dominant discourse in the text in order to demonstrate its incoherence. I shall then show that there is another more coherent, although somewhat underdeveloped, discourse also present, particularly in the section on 'the forced division of labour'. Traces of this are also to be found in other of Durkheim's texts but in an attenuated form and, indeed, sometimes more as a source of aporias than as a positive discourse. This discourse will be elaborated and then used along with other of Durkheim's concepts to develop new readings of his texts.

Solidarity and social order

In *The Division of Labour in Society* Durkheim argued that there are two different kinds of society grounded in different kinds of social solidarity, i.e. forms of social regulation that lead individuals to engage in activities that create feelings of identification with other members of society and with society as a whole. The first of these, mechanical solidarity, is a form of social unity based upon the similarity of individuals who share a uniform way of life and have an identical belief system. The second, organic solidarity, is present when there is extensive social differentiation and the exchange of services leads individuals to recognize that they are mutually interdependent and have shared interests.

60

Whereas the previous type implies that individuals resemble each other, this type presumes their difference. The first is possible only in so far as the individual personality is absorbed into the collective personality, the second is possible only if each has a sphere of action which is peculiar to him; that is, a personality.

(Durkheim, 1933, p. 131)

The totality of these phenomena is not directly available to experience but is partially manifested in law, which *produces* (and is an index of) solidarity (ibid., p. 65).[1]

Law is created when a collectively sanctioned tribunal passes judgement on and coercively regulates social conduct (ibid., p. 96). It protects the fundamental conditions of social life for each 'social type'. There are two different kinds of legal regulation – repressive and restitutive law. The former is associated with mechanical, the latter with organic, solidarity although in empirical analyses it is necessary to to recategorize legal codes, to separate

juridical rules into two great classes, accordingly as they have organized repressive sanctions or only restitutive sanctions. The first comprise all penal laws, the second, civil law, commercial law, procedural law, administrative and constitutional law, after abstraction of the penal rules which may be found there.

(Durkheim, 1933, p. 69)

Overall, then, 'social life comes from a double source, the likeness of consciences and the division of social labor' (ibid., p. 226). Similitude gives rise to repressive law, the division of labour to restitutive law. Repressive law, which is a direct expression of the *conscience collective* (ibid., p. 109), enforces conformity and eliminates diversity by an often vengeful punishment of acts that offend the shared sentiments of the members of a society (ibid., p. 73) – 'what we avenge, what the criminal expiates is the outrage to morality' (ibid., p. 89). The destruction of a dangerous menace protects society (ibid., pp. 87–8) and increases the commitment of the righteous to the *conscience collective* (ibid., p. 109).

If the normal pattern of social interaction between social organs – be they individuals, collectives or institutions – is disturbed and the law intervenes and asks the guilty party to make some reparation, thus restoring the *status quo ante*, this is restitutive law, which helps create/express organic solidarity.

The members of a society based upon organic solidarity form recurring cooperative relations with others who are involved in different but complementary activities. These relations are then institutionalized and regulative codes develop that eventually take a legal form (ibid., p. 216). Since these do not usually express general social values, the *conscience collective* has little role in the formulation and imposition of restitutive sanctions (ibid., p. 129). But there is an ambiguity here since even relationships originally initiated by individuals will be stable only if they are predictable and legally legitimated, for

> if the contract has the power to bind, it is society which gives this power to it . . . Moreover it lends this obligatory force only to contracts which have in themselves a social value, . . . those which conform to the rules of law.
>
> (Durkheim, 1933, p. 114)

These must also be based upon the principles of social justice (ibid., p. 216) and may be extremely radical (see below). Therefore the *conscience collective* needs to play some role even in these 'private' arrangements: 'Members are united by ties which extend deeper and far beyond the short moments during which the exchange is made' (ibid., p. 227). Although Durkheim believed that organic solidarity is the normal outcome of differentiation and interdependence, his remarks on social justice make better sense if we assume that it also has to be struggled for – organic solidarity does not evolve as automatically as Durkheim sometimes implied.

The genesis of the division of labour

Durkheim acknowledged that all known societies have at least a rudimentary division of labour and thus are based upon a combination of mechanical and organic solidarity. Whilst some of his work focuses on the ways in which both function together in the same society (Cohen, 1985), here we are interested in his exploration of 'limit cases', where societies are exclusively characterized by *either* organic *or* mechanical solidarity. The pure form of 'mechanical solidarity' is one where cohesion is 'exclusively the result of resemblances' and the society is an 'absolutely homogeneous mass' (Durkheim, 1933, p. 174). The minimal basic unit of social life, the horde, is a social aggregate which does not include, and has never included, within itself any more elementary aggregate, but is directly composed of individuals . . . they are in atomic juxtaposition. Plainly a simpler society is impossible, the horde is thus the protoplasm of the social realm . . .

(Durkheim, 1938, pp. 82–3)[2]

Durkheim accepts that there is some differentiation in simple societies. But in this early text, as opposed to some of his later work (Durkheim and Mauss, 1963; Gane, 1983b), Durkheim argued that it is not men and women who are differentiated – since even sexual differences are modified by the demands of the collective order – but rather adults and children are distinctive groups, organized into cohorts. For any *individual* childhood is, of course, only a temporary status (Durkheim, 1933, p. 175). True, some individuals may adopt the mantle of leadership, but this implies neither differentiaion nor hierarchy since the leader's followers only comply with his wishes if they are of a mind to do so (ibid., pp. 177–8). Whilst in matters of social control 'the assembly of the people in their entirety functioned as the tribunal' (ibid., p. 104), they might sometimes delegate power to a chief, who might use this for for his own ends rather than those of the collective. But since no *exchange* of services would then occur this rudimentary division of labour would not generate any further differentiation. There would be a unilateral relationship between the ruler and his 'property', the people.

The horde's static social system could last indefinitely but changes in its external environment and its internal state could undermine the viability of the whole eco-system of which it was a part. If this were to happen, the society would have to adapt in order to survive, for example by developing a division of labour within its boundaries. Now Durkheim's discussion of the process of transformation from a homogeneous to an undifferentiated form of society is replete with ambiguity and incorporates many different forms of explanation. He suggested, for example, that there might be a transformation of the society's internal environment – in that there was a greater frequency of interaction between its individual members.

The division of labor varies in direct ratio with the volume and density of societies, and, if it progresses in a continuous manner in the course of social development, it is because societies become regularly denser and generally voluminous.

(Durkheim, 1933, p. 262)

This is simply a way of conceptualizing and describing change, not a way of explaining it.

A horde, however, would rarely remain completely isolated. It would usually border on to other similar societies and form alliances with some of them, thereby developing a segmental form of organization, but the more contiguity with other societies, 'the more are our relations enclosed within the limits of the cells to which we belong' (ibid., p. 211). Implicit in Durkheim's work is a concept of differentiation based upon an analogy with the gaseous systems subject to Boyle's Law (and explained by statistical thermodynamics), and undoubtedly the encroaching presence of other societies could be seen as increasing the pressure on the horde thereby constraining the atomized individuals enveloped by it. But in the case of gases there are no processes that would produce the equivalent to a division of labour and as becomes abundantly clear in Durkheim's later work, the analogy is inherently misleading (Stone and Farberman, 1967).

Durkheim's second kind of explanation also focused on the interactions between individuals in segmental societies. If cellular isolation is somehow breached, giving 'rise to a relationship between individuals who were separated' (he adds the confusing rider 'or, at least, a more intimate relationship than there was' – Durkheim, 1933, p. 256), then

> Social life, instead of being concentrated in a multitude of little centers, distinctive and alike, is generalized. Social relations – more exactly, intra-social – consequently, become more numerous, since they extend on all sides, beyond their original limits.
>
> (Durkheim, 1933, p. 257)

Here he introduces a distinctly human element, since now when social interaction takes place at the outer limits of previously separated cells it is the 'moral gap' between the cells and the pressure from inside the cells that generate a division of labour – 'there are more individuals sufficiently in contact to be able to react and react upon one another' (ibid., p. 257). But this is not an explanation, since once again there is no logical reason why increased contact itself should generate a division of labour. Furthermore, although Durkheim asserts that 'gaps are filled in as the system is levelled out', it is clear that here there is a sphere of interaction unconstrained by any *collective conscience*, therefore that a potentially disruptive area of *anomie* would be always present from the beginning of the division of labour.

Durkheim's third explanation invokes extra-social factors to explain differentiation. Whilst he stated categorically that differences between individuals that derive from their exposure to variations in their physical milieux would 'make possible the division of labour, they do not necessitate it' (ibid., p. 265). Quite inconsistently he turned to differences in the individual's internal and external environments to explain differences in their consciousnesses.

the *immediate physical milieu* in which each one of us is placed, *the hereditary antecedents*, and the social influences vary from one individual to the next, and consequently diversify consciousness. It is impossible for all to be alike, if only because each one has his own organism and that these organisms occupy *different areas in space*. That is why, even among the lower peoples, where individual originality is very little developed, it never the less exists.

(Durkheim, 1938, p. 69; emphasis added)[3]

We know from his discussion of criminality that innovative as well as destructive deviance occurs and therefore such individual differences can be the source of new values and activities and hence of social differentiation: 'in order that the originality of the idealist may find expression, it is necessary that the originality of the criminal shall be possible'. On occasion the criminal may even be an idealist – for example, Socrates' claim to have the right to think independently was 'an anticipation of future morality' (ibid., p. 71). Here Durkheim explains such differences between individuals as the effect of extra-social factors – the physical milieu and genetic inheritance – or as an effect of varying social influences. This latter explanation would only makes sense if Durkheim had abandoned his view that the horde was completely uniform and homogeneous. It might then be like a force field with a power that weakens as one moves from its centre to its periphery – but this would be a metaphor, not an explanation. Alternatively, differentiation might already have occurred. If sociology is the science of social institutions (ibid., p. lvi) and institutions are aspects of the divison of labour, then, since they are part of the subject matter of sociology, simple societies must contain institutions. They must therefore be already differentiated also.

There is a similar flaw in another of Durkheim's attempts to explain the genesis of the division of labour. This was the neo-Darwinian argument that, because the identical self-contained segments in a segmental society are forced to compete with each other for survival,

> Each segment has its own organs, protected and kept apart from like organs by divisions separating the different segments. But as these are swept away inevitably like organs are put into contact, battling and trying to supplant one another. But no matter how this substitution is made, it cannot fail to produce advances in the course of specialization. For on the one hand, the triumphant segmental organ, as it were, can take care of the vaster task devolving upon it only by a greater division of labor, and, on the other hand, the vanquished can maintain themselves only by concentrating their efforts upon a part of the total function they fulfilled up to then.
>
> (Durkheim, 1933, p. 269).

Here we again find a division of labour already installed within each segment and Durkheim has again failed to find its originary cause.[4]

To explain difference and differentiation, then, Durkheim is forced either to invoke extra-social factors or to recognize that society is already differentiated and structured. His assumption that primitive societies are initially homogeneous is not viable, and is not even useful as a limit case. It is not a coherent conceptualization of any social form, nor was it based upon empirical observation but rather it was required by Durkheim's faulty epistemology, namely his belief that the scientificity of sociology requires it to have its own distinctive realm of phenomena.

The genesis of primitive social orders

Is it possible to develop an explanation of the genesis of a primitive social order? Durkheim recognized that 'specialization' is not the 'only solution to the struggle for existence'. Various strategies could be developed to rid a society of its surplus population. Marginal individuals might be sloughed off – forced to emigrate or to attack other societies, or simply expelled or abandoned. Is it possible to conceive of a way in which a society could be generated from the situation where individuals have left their societies to confront a 'precarious disputed existence'.

Durkheim's answer would be no. The horde is the irreduceable 'protoplasm of social life' and, to use an argument with some affinity to Hobbes,

> If the relationships becoming established during the period of grouping were not subject to any rule, if no power moderated the conflict of individual interests, there would be chaos from which no new order could emerge. It is thought, it is true, that everything takes place through private conventions freely disputed. Thus, it seems that all social action is absent . . . contracts are possible only where a juridical regulation, and, consequently a society, already exists.
>
> (Durkheim, 1933, p. 277)

Whilst he is surely right that under such conditions it would be impossible to secure a viable social contract, he is probably incorrect that social order could not be generated.

Rene Girard has developed neo-Durkheimian concepts that explain how this might occur. Those individuals who have drifted away from segmental societies would already have the human capacities produced by a social existence. Whilst these capacities might aid survival, they of themselves would be insufficient to generate a stable social order. Girard agrees with Hobbes (1960, p. 80) that in the 'state of nature' murder would be commonplace and the potential fate of anyone however strong. But he adds that equality of condition itself is also conducive to strife. With no social restrictions on what people could desire, each would be in potential competition with all others for every object of desire. Each would equally be an obstacle to the others. All desires would increase mimetically by the individual's knowledge that his or her object of desire was shared by others. There would be a situation of ever-spiralling frustration and anger. But if all but one were to join together and commit a murder, if the 'pack' turned on some particular individual, then

(a) Collective action would be instituted and
(b) Collective murder would discharge the violent impulses that men experience and cannot control. It would produce calm allowing rational collective thought.

> (Girard, 1977, p. 16)

For Girard it is the memory and fear of this violence that leads men to invent the distinction between the sacred and the profane.

The murder of this victim becomes defined retrospectively as the ritual sacrifice of a being with special qualities.

> But anybody can play the part of a surrogate victim . . . the choice of victim is arbitrary . . . religious interpretations . . . are at fault precisely because they attribute the beneficial results of the sacrifice to the superhuman nature of the victim or of the other participants, insofar as any of these appears to incarnate the supreme violence.
>
> (Girard, 1977, p. 257; see also Durkheim, 1976, p. 257)

Because human beings must necessarily mis-remember the origins of their social order, 'they need to reflect upon the miracle, to rethink it. Myths, rituals and kinship systems are the first fruits of this endeavor' (Girard, 1977, p. 235).

Whilst Girard and Durkheim agree that human society begins with religion (Girard, 1977, p. 307; Durkheim, 1982, p. 173), Girard claims also to explain the genesis of religion itself.

> All religious rituals spring from the surrogate victim, and all the great institutions of mankind, both secular and religious, spring from ritual. Such is the case, as we have seen, with political power, legal institutions, medicine, the theater, philosophy and anthropology itself.
>
> (Girard, 1977, p. 306).[5]

Durkheim observed that although some primitive societies might have chiefs, there would be no dynamic division of labour:

> The solidarity that they express remains mechanical. The whole difference is that it links the individual not more directly to the group, but to the image of the group.
>
> (Durkheim, 1933, p. 180)

This could be interpreted to mean that unity of a static social order need depend not upon the uniformity of the *social position* of its members but rather upon a *shared image* of the social order and a *shared evaluation* of the worth of its various differentiated elements. Girard develops this view of a static but differentiated social order by reflecting upon these lines

> . . . O when degree is shaked.
> Which is the ladder to all high designs,
> The enterprise is sick! . . .
> (Shakespeare, *A Midsummer Night's Dream*, 1.iii.101–3)

The word *degree* from the Latin *gradus* (step, degree, measure of disorder), means exactly what is meant here by difference. Culture is conceived not as a mere collection of unrelated objects, but as a totality, or, if we prefer, a structure, a system of people and institutions always related to one another in such a way that a single differentiating principle is at work. This social transcendence does not exist as an object, of course. This is why, as soon as an individual member, overcome by hubris, tries to usurp Degree, he finds imitators; more and more people are affected by the contagion of mimetic rivalry, and Degree collapses, being nothing more than the mysterious absence of such rivalry in a functional society.

(Girard, 1979, p. 207; and see Girard, 1977, pp. 207, 242)

'Difference' of a structural hierarchical kind, he argues, is a precondition for any stable social order. Tendencies towards homogeneity and social levelling would create dissatisfaction and rivalry which, if unchecked, would destroy the precarious social fabric.

Girard's arguments are interesting not least because they also involve a reworking of Durkheim's concepts. Although there is no space here adequately to assess these arguments – for this see White (1978) – it is worth noting that Girard confuses differentiation and hierarchy and assumes that throughout societies there is some uniform consistent set of standards. This is unlikely to be true for even the simplest of them. In the next section when discussing relationships between simple societies it will be assumed that each of them is differentiated to some degree and that unifying ideologies play an important role in their stability.[6]

Societal rivalry and the division of labour

Durkheim recognized that, even if societies had begun to differentiate, the process as a whole might be aborted (Durkheim, 1933, p. 284). One way in which its dynamism could be sustained would be through the fusion of two already partially differentiated societies. This could occur in a number of different ways. Societies could enter into symbiotic relations, one with another, albeit with a dominant organism.

> But it must be recalled that a group can, while keeping its individuality, be enveloped by another, vaster and containing several of the same kind. It can be affirmed that an economic or any other function can be divided between two societies only if they participate from certain points of view in the same common life, and, consequently, belong to the same society.
>
> (Durkheim, 1933, pp. 280–1)

In *Suicide*, Durkheim wrote of the Jewish people that 'each community became a small compact and coherent society with a strong feeling of self-consciousness and unity' (Durkheim, 1951, p. 160). But this is an ambiguous statement since it is unclear how much they had become a part of the wider society and what they might have surrendered in order to do so. If Christianity is conceived of as a development of Judaism, then within Durkheim's idealist schema the interaction between the two communities would have been unproblematic.

> For social units to be able to be differentiated they must first be attracted or grouped by virtue of the resemblances they present . . . higher societies result from the union of lower societies of the same type. It is necessary first that these latter be mingled in the midst of the same identical collective conscience for the process to begin or recommence.
>
> (Durkheim, 1933, p. 278)

Since, for Durkheim, 'type' is synonymous with 'species' and these retain 'the same collective individuality', their nature is determined by their origins.[7]

> Japan may in the future borrow our arts, our industry, even our political organization; it will not cease to be a different social species from France or Germany.
>
> (Durkheim, 1938, p. 188)

The fusion of societies will only be possible if they are of the same species. But here we are in the realm of myth. Two societies of the same species must be of the same social stuff – either they share the same *ancestor* which is itself autochthonous or each is independently autochthonous and yet still of the same species, in which case the same social 'stuff' must have simply materialized at different places and times. We are with Adam's rib or Cadmus's dragon teeth (Lévi-Strauss, 1963a, pp. 206–31).

An alternative interpretation of the situation of Jewish people is that, whatever their affinity with Christianity, they, as involuntary émigrés, had no choice but to live in often hostile societies. Some protection had been provided by retaining their culture and identity. After all, Durkheim had also acknowledged that the 'unity' of their communities was an effect of 'their need of resisting a general hostility, the very impossibility of all communication with the rest of the population' (Durkheim, 1933, p. 160). In the Middle Ages, Jews carried out 'deviant' activities, such as usury, precisely because they were marginal pariahs. They were easy targets of hysteria and envy and often persecuted and robbed of any possessions that they might have accumulated (see also Lukes, 1975, p. 53). If, during the Dreyfus affair, Durkheim emphasized that the universalistic principles of the Revolution of 1789 protected French Jews against the 'chronic and traditional' anti-Semitism found in Germany or Russia, nevertheless he acknowledged that (at that time) they still remained vulnerable to scapegoating.

> When society undergoes suffering, it feels the need to find someone whom it can hold responsible for its sickness, on whom it can avenge its misfortunes: and those against whom public opinion already discriminates are naturally designated for this role.
> (Durkheim cited in Lukes, 1975, p. 345; see also Fenton, 1984, pp. 118–20)

Colonialism, class and conflict

Durkheim's conception of the continuity of specific kinds of society and the separateness of species was an element of the more metaphysical aspect of his sociology. In so far as society is conceived of as a non-contradictory unity, then difference does not engender antagonism. If, however, two societies of different species were to fuse then antagonism would be endemic. Now, whilst Durkheim may have failed to provide an adequate explanation for the genesis of the division of labour, he was aware that it did not automatically occur and was not the only solution to changes in a society's eco-system:

specialization is not the only possible solution to the struggle
for existence. There are also emigration, colonization, resignation
to a precarious disputed existence, and, finally the total
elimination of the weakest by suicide or some other means.

                                        (Durkheim, 1933, p. 286)

Emigration has already been discussed, 'compulsory altruistic
suicide' is dealt with in Chapter 7; of more immediate interest is
the question of colonialism. Durkheim does not explore this issue
systematically, but in an aside in *Moral Education* he makes a
revealing comment.

> Whenever two populations, two groups of people having an
> unequal culture, come into continuous contact with one
> another, certain feelings develop that prompt the more cultured
> group or that which deems itelf such – to do violence to the
> other. This is currently the case in colonies and countries of all
> kinds where representatives of European civilizations find
> themselves involved with underdeveloped peoples. Although it
> is useless and involves great dangers for those who abandon
> themselves to it, exposing them to formidable reprisals, this
> violence almost inevitably breaks out. Hence that kind of
> bloody foolhardiness that seizes the explorer in connection with
> races he deems inferior. The superiority that he arrogates
> produces a veritable intoxication of self, a sort of megalomania,
> which goes to the worst extremes, and the source of which is
> not difficult to fathom. We have seen, in fact, that the
> individual controls himself, only if he feels himself controlled,
> only if he confronts moral forces which he respects and on
> which he dare not encroach . . . because of the inferiority he
> imputes to them, he sees in them no authority requiring his
> deference.

                                        (Durkheim, 1961, p. 193)

Durkheim's liberal internationalism rendered him incapable of
recognizing any problems in the *establishment* of these relations.
Despite his explicit opposition to reductionist 'race theory', he still
tended to equate modern western civilization with civilization
itself and hence, by implication, to endorse the view that such
underdeveloped peoples were not suited to self-government
(Fenton, 1984, p. 132). Thus, although he was appalled by and
sought to explain 'excess', he did not problematize the nature of
the social relations between colonial powers and their colonies.

Rather, he focused upon the subjective attitudes of the colonialists and their relationship to their fatherland.

> Thus it is that the abuses into which the civilized so easily fall in their dealing with inferior societies are beginning to be checked, since a better-informed public opinion is in a better position to keep a watch on, and to judge what is going on in distant countries.
>
> (Durkheim, 1961, p. 196)

These abuses, then, could be controlled by the power of the fatherland's *conscience collective*. Whilst Durkheim's comments on the cruel excesses of colonialists are not without interest, he failed to recognize the role that force has played in the establishment of such social relations and that, in so far as there are social contradictions, it will continue to do.

If we continue to follow Durkheim's reasoning, a likely feature of a colonial or any other society where there has been a fusion of different species – and this is true of virtually every modern state – will be an ever-present anomie. At each stage of the division of labour when similar organs, informed by different collective consciences, come into contact there will be a struggle for dominance. Then, either the dominant collective conscience will try to repress the other, which will nevertheless remain a constant source of anomie in relationship to the 'regulative rules that emerge', or, if neither of the original societies consistently wins the struggle for dominance, a uniform combined *conscience collective* cannot emerge. In colonial and most other societies Durkheim's reasoning must be held suspect when he characterized the growing importance of state intervention as follows:

> since their functions become more numerous and complex, it is necessary for the organ which serves as their foundation (the State) to develop, just as the body of juridical rules which determine them.
>
> (Durkheim, 1933, p. 224)

For, after all, there is no good reason to assume that in most societies there is a *conscience collective* that acts in the general interest.

On occasion Durkheim acknowledged the existence of *struggles* between different forms of collective consciousness within the same society where it would be difficult to conceive of them as deriving from different societies. For example, he contrasted the cooperative relations between masters and workers in the medieval guilds with the antagonism between employers and workers in industrial societies. Since both employers and their organizations and workers and their organizations have the same historical roots it would be difficult to use an ever-present anomie to explain this antagonism.[8] If society is no longer conceived of as a historically continuous unity there is no need to do so. A conception of society in terms of class relations, structural contradiction and differentiation of interests provides a far better theoretical starting point. Durkheim provided no adequate analysis of changes within societies or the nature of the interactions between them. If one abandons his social metaphysic, it becomes possible to explain some changes in social conditions as a necessary although unspecified effect of changes in a society's ecology – modifications in fertility, changes in climate, flooding, land exhaustion, etc., etc. These changes might also be due to a restriction of movement produced by imperialistic territorial expansion by neighbouring societies or by its simple desire to dominate other people.

Using somewhat modified Durkheimian categories we can see that the possible sets of relations between societies are extremely complex. One society may simply dominate another. Two or more societies might be involved in a continuous but inconclusive warfare, producing the static, barbarous *modus vivendi (et moriendi)* of the Yanomamo and the Maring (Harris, 1974, pp. 61–107). Or, again, two might unite against a third – producing in this one case a genuinely new *conscience collective*. (None of this, needless to say, means that there would *necessarily* be a continuing increase in the division of labour.) It is in this particular situation that one finds an appropriate context for one of Durkheim's much-maligned metaphors.

> a combination of elements produces new properties that do not characterize any of the elements in isolation. The combination is then something new through the linking of the parts that compose it. In combining tin and copper, basic elements that are soft and malleable, we get a new substance with an altogether different property. It is bronze which is hard.
>
> (Durkheim, 1961, p. 61)

Yet even when different societies fuse willingly it is not at all clear whether this new structure will be dynamic or static. One possibility is the development of a neo-feudal order. Since we are assuming that it would be born out of conflict, much production would be for war and warriors would be the dominant group. But if new needs were to develop and production was expanded to satisfy them, then a dynamic division of labour might develop, but this process itself might well be accompanied by further internal conflict. I have deliberately shifted here towards the view argued in *The German Ideology* (1845, in Marx and Engels, 1976, pp. 33–5), since at a certain conceptual level a great deal of useful compatibility can be developed. It is useful because Marx and Engels have no *one* explanation of the division of labour and would indeed question such an aspiration and because there is a great deal of overlap between their concepts and those of a reconstituted Durkheimism.

Durkheim and the pathological forms of the division of labour

If Durkheim's discussion of the genesis of the division of labour is incoherent and yet illuminating, the same may also be said of his analysis of the nature of societies based upon organic solidarity. In these societies individuals are committed to each other and to the society as a whole because, through the exchange of variegated services, they contribute to their own, each other's and the society's well-being. The division of labour is stimulated by individuals developing capacities and skills that enable them to work in, and indeed create, occupations that they find satisfying and that are socially useful. The 'spontaneous' division of labour itself calls forth forms of localized regulatory mechanisms, which regulate cooperative activities and which are supported by the citizenry because they facilitate the achievement of individual and collective goals. Organic solidarity is a form of social organization wherein complementarity allows differences to coexist with equivalence.

The system, however, may not function properly. The interactions between individuals may be inadequately regulated – because appropriate institutions are lacking or because appropriate norms have not been developed; because some of the interacting agents are not committed to the regulative rules or because they do not feel involved in the collective enterprise. These problems can be coped with by developing an industrial parliament and by various *ad hoc* strategies. Durkheim tends to imply that the major problems are the maintenance of order and the engineering of consent without asking if the order is a just one or the consent rational (Zeitlin, 1981, pp. 279ff).

His discussion of the 'forced division of labour' is not subject to these strictures because he specifies the nature of the rational order that could emerge from the division of labour and also what stops this happening. In such a social order the potential of both individuals and the collective would be realized and conformity would only be elicited by a successful appeal to reason (Durkheim, 1933, pp. 20, 52). Thus it would no longer be the case that individuals would be committed to 'the group under *any* circumstances' (ibid., p. 380; emphasis added). In any social order an effective morality regulates the system in accord with the reality of its organization; therefore the widespread valorization of and pursuit of social equality in complex societies must express 'some aspect of reality'. When there is a simple exchange of goods or services between individuals who are in a position of substantive equality – as, for example, in petty-commodity production – this is not too problematic. Durkheim shared with Proudhon this concern with substantive equality and a distrust of those forms of property that allowed one set of individuals to exercise power over others (Fried and Sanders, 1964, pp. 199–299). Durkheim differed from Proudhon, however, in recognizing that the division of labour necessarily produces large hierarchical organizations. There will be therefore

> an ever growing inequality, the equality which public conscience affirms can only be . . . equality in the external conditions of conflict.
>
> (Durkheim, 1938, p. 379)

Society as a whole will only be solidaristic if any hierarchically stratified positions are, in both principle and practice, filled by meritocratic recruitment. This is the only way that the energy of individuals is likely to be used constructively, since only then will they fulfil their occupational role enthusiastically.

In this text Durkheim often used physicalist metaphors – talking of energy levels, degrees of excitation, etc. These are legitimately taken as evidence of his somewhat positivistic naturalism (Stone and Farberman, 1967). They can also be seen as a part of his attempt to assess under what conditions individuals will work at their jobs with the energy, commitment and imagination that guarantees social continuity, stimulates innovation and thus creates further advances in the division of labour:

if they bend all their efforts, and must so bend them, to doing away with external inequalities, as far as possible, that is not only because [the] enterprise is good, but because their very existence is involved in the problem.

(Durkheim, 1933, p. 380)

The rewards allocated to different functionaries within a society will depend upon how that society determines their relative value.

In societies with an advanced division of labour, equity can be achieved in day-to-day contracts only if in a formal and substantive sense 'the contracting parties are placed in conditions externally equal' (ibid., p. 383). A contract is only fully 'consented to if the services exchanged have an equivalent social value' and the value of services 'is represented by the quantity of useful labor which it contains' (ibid., pp. 382–3). Useful labour is that which produces 'useful social effects' and its magnitude varies according to

the sum of efforts necessary to produce the object, the intensity of the needs which it satisfies, and finally the extent of the satisfaction it brings.

(Durkheim, 1933, pp. 383)[9]

Durkheim argued that just social order could be undermined by 'a forced division of labour'. This is produced by a form of social organization that prevents individuals 'from occupying the place in the social framework which is compatible with their faculties' (ibid., p. 377) and from receiving the rewards appropriate to their social contribution.

. . . all constraint is not normal. Only that constraint which corresponds to some social superiority, intellectual or moral, merits that designation. But that which one individual exercises over another because he is stronger or richer, above all if this wealth does not express his social worth, is abnormal and can only be maintained by violence.

(Durkheim, 1938, p. 123)

Now, when individuals are negotiating contracts, 'the individuals who are exchanging must have no other force than that which comes from their social worth' (Durkheim, 1933, p. 384). Here Durkheim was not only referring to overt coercion but also to situations where people are differentially subject to necessity.

If one class of society is obliged, in order to live, to take any price for its services, while another can abstain from such action thanks to resources at its disposal, which, however, are not necessarily due to any social superiority, the second has an unjust advantage over the first at law. In other words there cannot be rich and poor at birth without there being unjust contracts.

(Durkheim, 1933, p. 384)

The major source of such inequality is the hereditary transmission of wealth. This is

enough to make the external conditions under which the conflict takes place very unequal, for it gives advantages to some which are not necessarily in keeping with their personal worth. Even today among the most cultivated peoples, there are careers which are either totally closed or very difficult to be entered into by those who are bereft of fortune.

(Durkheim, 1933, p. 378)

The institutions of inherited wealth create a gap between the needs of the social order, its legitimations and the actual experience of its subjects, subverting the possibility that they could make a *rational* commitment to the social order.

Durkheim reiterated these arguments in the lectures that he delivered from 1890 until near his death on 'The nature of morals and of rights' (posthumously published as *Professional Ethics and Civic Morals*, 1957). If individuals or groups are to be in genuinely equivalent circumstances when negotiating contracts and if a genuine equality of opportunity is to be achieved, individuals should not be able to inherit wealth. Any already accumulated wealth should be shared out or auctioned off, but by the professional groups rather than by the 'blundering and wasteful' state (Durkheim, 1957, p. 217). Even these principles of equity, which mean that individuals are still rewarded unequally because of the unequal contributions that they make to society, will be superseded by ones based on charity – as 'the depth of feeling of human fraternity will go on increasing . . . the best amongst men' will be 'capable of working without getting an exact recompense for their pains and services' (Durkheim, 1957, p. 221; Lukes and Scull, 1983, p. 237). In Chapter 8 I shall explore further Durkheim's arguments and relate them to those of Marx in his *Critique of the Gotha Programme*.

Nevertheless, Durkheim's analysis of the nature of historical development and the conditions under which the individuals and society might be in harmony is ambiguous, relatively under-developed and overly individualistic. The major social problem that he seems to identify explicitly is that talented lower-class individuals might be excluded from positions of high social status for which they are eminently qualified by the less talented and even mediocre children of the privileged. In any kind of society – and certainly in a socialist one – this might seem unjust. He draws an historical analogy:

> When the plebians aimed to dispute the right to religious and administrative functions with the patricians, it was not only in imitation of the latter, but it was also because they had become more intelligent, richer, more numerous, and their tastes and ambitions had in consequence been modified.
>
> (Durkheim, 1933, p. 376)

But this passage deals not just with individual mobility but with a situation where a *whole class* became capable of participating in the exercise of social and political power. We know that elsewhere Durkheim stressed that the differences between individuals that were due to hereditary characteristics were of little real significance because, in social life,

> inherited general aptitudes must be submitted to active elaboration, they must acquire a whole world of ideas, movements, habits, they must co-ordinate them, systematize them, recast their nature, give a new form and new face to it.
>
> (Durkheim, 1933, p. 320)

The capacities of individuals can be developed to the point where the majority of them can participate as equals in social life. Indeed, in *Professional Ethics and Civic Morals*, he questions the belief that a meritocracy is an adequate solution to the problem of justice.

> To us it does not seem equitable that a man should be better treated as a social being because he was born of parentage that is rich or of high rank. But is it any more equitable that he should be better treated because he was born of a father of higher intelligence or in a more favourable moral milieu. It is here that the domain of charity begins. Charity is the feeling of human sympathy that we see becoming clear even of those last

remaining traces of inequality. It ignores and denies any special merit in gifts of mental capacity acquired by heredity. This, then, is the very acme of justice.

(Durkheim, 1957, p. 221)

Further, any unequal distribution of rewards is likely to lead individuals to buy *relative* privilege for their families, if they can, and thus undermine the equal access to the necessities of life – from food and shelter to education, etc. – and therefore equal access to these would have to be guaranteed.

This is not merely an abstract ethical position. Durkheim argued (in some of his most conservative texts) that through a collectively generated self-discipline virtually all social actors were *capable* of developing themselves and particularly of extending their reasoning capacities.[10] He was concerned to articulate some of the sets of practices that make it possible for individuals to be *active, rational, human beings*. All human beings are subject to a plurality of desires and needs – some inherited, some recast – which require some degree of satisfaction, but the search finally and fully to satisfy one or other of them is doomed to failure and indeed such a search would itself preclude articulating them together in an *organized form*.

All life is thus a complex equilibrium where various elements limit one another; this balance cannot be disrupted without producing unhappiness or illness. . . . A need, a desire, freed of all restraints, and all rules, no longer geared to some determinate objective, and through this some connection, limited and contained, can be nothing but a source of constant anguish, for the person experiencing it. What gratification indeed can such a desire yield, since by definition it is incapable of being satisfied.

(Durkheim, 1961, p. 39–40)

He elaborates on what would now be recognized as a Lacanian theme:[11]

Discipline even contributes in large measure to the development of that which is of fundamental importance to each of us: our personality. The capacity for containing our inclinations, for restraining ourselves – the ability that we acquire in the school of moral discipline – is the indispensable condition for the emergence of reflective, individual will. The rule, because it teaches us to restrain and master ourselves, is a means of emancipation and freedom.

(Durkheim, 1961, p. 48)

Even the rational non-conformist must secure the conditions that make his or her rationality possible.

Conceptually there is no necessary connection between psychic health and social conformity. In contemporary societies,

Individuals, while conforming, must take account of what they are doing; and their conformity must not be pushed to the point where it completely captures intelligence.

(Durkheim, 1961, p. 52)

What is required is on the one hand the development of a morality based on the nature of things, and on the other hand social arrangements that realize society's true potential. Only when they are in accord will the rational social actor be a conformist.

Durkheim tended to appropriate for sociologists the position of philosopher kings, but the obvious logic of this analysis is that all social actors should have a role in determining their society's morality and its social arrangements. This could be realized through an 'industrial parliament'. Now a careful reading of the passage in which this argument is expounded in the 1902 preface to the second edition of *The Division of Labour in Society* demonstrates that this concept is still potentially compatible with the most radical implications of his work. Durkheim believed that industrial crises, whether due to the anarchic relations between industries or those between employers and employees, can best be regulated through a 'corporative regime'. Whilst the general principles of regulation would be laid down by governmental assemblies, the generalized application

could be made only with the aid of elected assemblies charged to represent the Corporation. *In the present state* of industry, these assemblies, in the same way as tribunals charged with applying the occupational regulations, should evidently be comprised of representatives of employers, as is already the case in the tribunals of skilled trades, and that in *proportion corresponding to the* respective importance attributed by opinion to these two *factors to production*. But, if it is necessary that both meet in the directing councils of the corporations, it is no less important that at the base of the comparative organization, they form distinct and independent groups, for their interests are too often rival and antagonistic. To be able to go about their ways freely, they must go about their ways separately. The two groups thus constituted would then be able to appoint their representatives to the common assemblies.

(Durkheim, 1933, p. 25; emphasis added)

Clearly this can be interpreted as an integrationist and corporatist statement, as did Gouldner in his introduction to Durkheim's essays on *Socialism* (1962). It can also be put to work in another manner. Durkheim acknowledged the depth of conflict between employers and employees. Whilst a few lines earlier he treated trade unions as merely aspects of those organizations that include both employees and employers, here they are only roped together as antagonists. In order to achieve true organic solidarity a new social order will need to replace the 'present state' of industrial organization, which leaves 'too large a place for unjust inequalities' (Durkheim, 1976, p. 427).

Durkheim's work shows us that such a society will be one wherein there is a spontaneous division of labour. At any time each individual will fulfil a useful task fitted to his or her relative capacities as they have been developed. It will not be a static society since many of each new generation will develop different attributes from those of their parents. There will be a progressive rise in the numbers, intelligence and collective wealth of the people and some *forms of collective assemblies* will be required to develop a non-repressive form of social regulation.[12] Furthermore, since inherited wealth will have been abolished, production will be organized through collective forms of ownership. Thus those employing others will no longer be private owners of capital but rather functionaries, representatives of the (democratically controlled) enterprises.

In an excellent recent article, Mike Gane (1984) has shown how Durkheim believed that such a system would be similar to that of the guilds, in that it could produce an equivalent *degree* if not *type* of solidarity. Its creation would be a slow process – it would occur in phases and only when the times were propitious. But these would be periods of 'creative effervescence' (Durkheim, 1976, p. 476) when men would be revolutionaries, primarily in a constructive rather than a destructive sense. However, Gane has also shown that it was often in Mauss's writings that we find Durkheim's arguments taken furthest. He argues that Mauss's article 'A sociological assessment of Bolshevism' (1984) 'is a consistent development of Durkheim's critique of revolutionary communism', since although 'the Bolsheviks aimed to liberate the newly emerging corporate institutions, the soviets (seen by Mauss as the new form predicted of occupational groups by Durkheim) . . . they did not know how to allow them to develop' (Gane, 1984, p. 323).

Durkheim's (and Mauss's) image of a future society remains somewhat speculative. But it is not simple-minded and it certainly is not an example of a crude Rousseauism. It may lack the precision of Marx's *Critique of the Gotha Programme*, but in some ways it shows a far greater awareness of the complex conditions of existence of an active (realizable) socialism where mature individuals can be rational, energetic and socially conforming with some protection from the collective tyranny of their immediate communities and from that distant and 'relatively autonomous' 'higher organ', the state.

Conclusion

In this chapter the dominant discourse within *The Division of Labour in Society* has been shown to be incoherent and incapable of fulfilling the task set for it by Durkheim, i.e. the development of a purely social explanation for the genesis of the division of labour. The very concept of 'mechanical solidarity' is problematic and Durkheim's account of 'organic solidarity' is distorted by untheorized conservative assumptions. On the other hand, the concept of organic solidarity is more useful particularly when elaborated along the lines of his discussion of the 'forced division of labour'. These issues are explored further in the next chapter on 'Durkheim and the juridical relation'.

Notes

1 Clearly the question that must then be addressed is what determines the level and movement of the division of labour. At this point it is worth noting in Durkheim a certain ambiguity as to whether the phenomenon of the division of labour is exhausted by those examples cited by him and accessible to observation or, whether, like the *conscience collective*, it is only partially manifest. In terms of his overall

conceptual scheme there seems little doubt that the latter is the case. For him science, art and economic activity are only aspects of a superficial phenomenon, civilization. 'If science, art and economic activity develop, it is in accordance with a necessity that is imposed upon men. It is because there is, for them, no other way of living in the new conditions in which they have been placed' (Durkheim, 1933, p. 336). Civilization 'can explain neither the existence nor the progress of the division of labor, since it has, of itself, no intrinsic or absolute value, but, on the contrary has a reason for existing only in so far as the division of labor itself is found necessary' (Durkheim, 1933, p. 337; cf. also p. 282).

Civilization is seen as an aspect of the division of labour – but this itself, in the case of England, is also seen as *superficial* (Durkheim, 1933, pp. 339–40).

2 This is more precise than (but compatible with) the definition found in the *Division of Labour in Society*. Durkheim illustrates his argument and thinks it through by using empirical evidence gathered from simple societies and then incorporates these rather specific factual observations into his argument as general propositions.

3 Indeed, when Durkheim elsewhere explains social change in terms of innovative deviance we find him again either explaining a social phenomenon by extra-social factors or leaving unspecified the social mechanisms that might produce difference. Thus a relatively 'slack' *conscience collective* may produce positive effects whilst allowing negative ones (Durkheim, 1938, p. 71). Was Socrates born with such a capacity or was it instilled? If so, how?

4 Much as Hindess and Hirst argue that Balibar's conception of a 'transitional mode of production' is an impossibility, we must say that undifferentiated segmental societies could not be the source of a modern complex one (see Hindess and Hirst, 1975).

5 He goes on to justify his argument with a very Durkheimian conception of scientific proof.

> Even if no example taken above offers conclusive proof of my theory, their cumulative effect is overwhelming; all the more so because they coincide with archetypal myths that tell, in apparently naive fashion, how all man's religious, economic and social institutions grew out of the victim. The surrogate victim as founder of the rite, appears as the ideal educator of mankind.
>
> (Girard, 1977, p. 306)

6 Girard himself makes further claims for his analysis. I have already mentioned but not explicated his concept of mimetic desire. It was initially developed as a critique of those individualistic explanations of human conduct, whether romantic or existentialist, which located the source of human desire within the consciousness of the actor and which saw social relationships and social products – such as literary

texts – as expressions of the individual. He argued that it is through the process of identification with others that we learn what is *worth* doing and how to do it. We also learn *who* (and with what attributes) is worth desiring. In situations therefore where we desire someone who is already desired by our *living* model we have set the agenda for some kind of conflict. This may be the angry reaction of the model to his 'disciples'' actions as in the *initial* violence of Laius to the child Oedipus. If they are in a more equal situation this may lead both or either of the rivals to engage in a continuous guerrilla warfare with ever-increasing violence. The model's own desire may be fuelled by that of the disciple, and so on, and so on. Girard analyses texts as diverse as those of Dostoievski and Proust (Girard, 1965), Seneca and Shakespeare, and questions the methods and conclusions of structuralist luminaries like Freud and Lévi-Strauss.

Much of this analysis is sound and thought provoking. However, on occasions he makes excessive claims for his analysis.

> The origin of symbolic thought lies in the mechanism of the surrogate victim. . . . To refer to the origin of symbolic thought is to speak as well of the origin of language.
>
> (Girard, 1977, p. 235)

He argues further that mimetic desire is a process to be found also in animals – and can thus exist prior to the explanation of the different effects of this process in animals and humans is to invoke the 'black box' of an enlarged brain.

> One must realize that mimetic desire is not even specifically human. There must be a mimetic element in the intra-species fighting of many animals since the absence of an object – the flight of the disputed female, for instance – does not always put an immediate end to the fighting. Eventually, however, the fighting comes to an end with a kind of submission of the vanquished to the victor. The dominated animal always yields to the dominant animal who, from now on, turns into a model and guide of all behavior, except appropriation.
>
> Unlike animals, men engaged in rivalry may go on fighting *to the finish*. To account for this a *violent* instinct, in contradistinction to an *instinctual* inhibition of intra-species murder in animals, results in an impasse. It is more productive, I believe, to assume that an increased mimetic drive corresponding to the enlarged human brain must escalate mimetic rivalry beyond the point of no return.
>
> (Girard, 1978, pp. 32–3)

Thus he wishes to argue that mimetic rivalry is a universal phenomenon in the animal kingdom. But the human potentiality of its development, as well as for other development, is greater than for any other animal. This in turn leads to an unending cycle of violence, which will only end if it happens that the group turns on one individual, murders him, then has a period of peace. At this moment symbolic thought is born. Yet no logical/scientific *connection* is demonstrated between the size of the human brain and spiralling mimesis, or indeed between a past blood-letting peace and the development of symbolic thought. We must treat this as pure speculation.

7 See Chapter 2.

8 Durkheim believed that the major example of a disruptive disturbance was the speed that 'a strike becomes general today in a body of workers' (Durkheim, 1933, p. 224).

9 On this point, here and elsewhere (see 1957, pp. 121–6), Durkheim's work is somewhat ambiguous and confused. Is social worth determined by negotiation between those engaged in exchange or is it determined authoritatively (Sirianni, 1984, pp. 454–5)? Or, again, is it the relative 'intensity of the needs' that requires more satisfaction for some than for others that necessitates higher rewards for the former? In Marxist terms this ambiguous formulation conflates use value and exchange value and Durkheim fails to develop the implications that the different relative costs in producing various forms of labour power have for their unequal valuation (see Filloux, 1977, p. 194–8; Lacroix, 1978, p. 339).

10 Zeitlin is partially correct in arguing that 'social constraint is transformed by Durkheim into an unqualifiedly *positive* phenomenon for it keeps "our vital forces within appropriate limits"' (Zeitlin, 1981, p. 41). On the other hand, he fails to think through the implications of Durkheim's own qualifying comments. It is a form of conceptual empiricism to believe that the conservative slant of Durkheim's work necessarily invalidates his more general discussion of 'discipline'. Durkheim continuously truncated the potential development of his concepts by the intrusion of his metaphysical assumptions and socio-political values.

In his later works he presupposed a social consensus on the relative value of different activities and he assumed that conformity is a positive good. Thus in *Suicide* and in *Moral Education* he did argue that, if workmen and children demand more rewards or opportunities greater than those in authority believe to be appropriate for them, it is because there has been a breakdown in order. Their appetites have not been appropriately regulated. It is because Durkheim assumed that there is an active consensus on the relative value of different occupations and on the criteria to determine capacity and merit that disruptions must derive from an irrational asocial source. As soon as these assumptions are questioned – and they are elsewhere in that text – then the argument fails. Both workers and students may *rationally* question their situations because there is a gap between certain of the social values and certain of the social arrangements.

11 To a large extent the discussions of desire by Lacan and Durkheim complement each other:

> . . . man's desire finds its meaning in the desire of the other, not so much because the other holds the key to the object desired, as because the first object of desire is to be recognized by the other.
> (Lacan, 1968, p. 31)

> Need is directed towards a specific object and is satisfied by it. Demands are formulated and addressed to others; where they are still aimed at an object, this is not essential to them, since the articulated demand is essentially a demand for love.
> Desire appears in the rift which separates need and demand; it cannot be reduced to need since, by definition, it is not a relation to a real object independent of the subject but a relation to phantasy; nor can it be reduced to demand, in that it seeks to impose itself without taking the language of the unconscious of the other into account, and insists upon absolute recognition from him.
> (Laplanche and Pontalis, 1973, p. 483)

Sheridan further explicates the meaning of this by relating desire and language:

> All speech is demand; it presupposes the Other to whom it is addressed, whose very signifiers it takes over in its formulation. By the same token, that which comes from the other is not treated so much as a particular satisfaction of a need, but rather as a response to an appeal, a gift, a token of love. There is no adequation between the need and the demand that conveys it; indeed, it is the gap between them that constitutes desire, at once particular like the first and absolute like the second. Desire (fundamentally in the singular) is a perpetual effect of symbolic articulation. It is not an appetite: it is essentialy extrinsic and insatiable.
> (Translator's introduction to Lacan, 1977, p. viii)

For Lacan, then, desire can never be satisfied, but in so far as it is recognized in speech it can in some sense be controlled (Lacan, 1968, p. 190). For Durkheim of course not only must it be recognized but there must also be some organized active 'authority' – not too dissimilar from Lacan's 'the Name of the Father' – which imposes itself on the individual.

12 There is a strong similarity between this reformulation of Durkheim's concepts and that by Habermas of Weber's (Habermas, 1971, pp. 118–19).

5 Durkheim and the juridical relation

Introduction

This chapter returns to Durkheim's discussion of the nature and role of law. After a brief summary of his theory, I use recent work in anthropology to assess the viability of the distinction he drew between the role of law in primitive and differentiated societies. This leads to a consideration of the differences between legal and juridical relations and then to the exploration of the concept of the juridical subject. In the second part of the chapter I shall explore in some detail Durkheim's early article 'La Science positive de la morale en Allemagne', which differs in important ways from his mature theory. A consideration of these differences will raise conceptual issues the resolution of which can help the development of a more adequate theory of the juridical relation and of law.

Durkheim's systematic theory of law

A stable social order, Durkheim argued, depends upon a coherent and effective moral order. Law is the element of the moral order the precepts of which are made explicit by a specially designated tribunal or individual and which 'produces those rules which are essential' for a society (Durkheim, 1957, p. 66).

> Every precept of law can be defined as a rule of sanctioned conduct.
>
> (Durkheim, 1933, pp. 68–9)

The other non-legal sanctions at work within society are more diffuse, imprecise and relatively unimportant and can be modified by law, as when, for example, it clarifies ambiguities in custom that generate disruptive interpersonal disputes. As society develops and law's conditions of existence are modified, law is also transformed. There are two main kinds of law characteristic of two different kinds of societies. The first, repressive law, punishes the offender, often vindictively, thus enforcing conformity. The second, restitutive law, demands satisfaction for an offence only in order to restore the *status quo ante* (ibid., pp. 74–5). The first is an index and source of 'mechanical solidarity', a social order based on the similarity of its members; the second of 'organic solidarity', an order based upon the complementary differentiation of its members. Historically there has been a general evolutionary movement from mechanical to organic solidarity, from collectivism to individualism, from repressive to restitutive law.

Durkheim and contemporary anthropology

In examining the empirical foundations of his arguments, we should emphasize that although Durkheim does not document his sources when he writes on law, except in key passages in *The Division of Labour in Society*, this does not mean that he lacked a detailed knowledge of the area. Throughout his career he read and reviewed a large selection of sociological, anthropological and historical books on various aspects of the role of law in a wide range of societies (Besnard, 1983; Nandan, 1980). In this section, amongst others, the writings of Roberts, Mauss, Lévi-Strauss, Diamond and Moore are used to assess the accuracy of his account of the role of law in 'primitive societies' and to understand where, how and why he erred. These considerations will help in the task of developing a more adequate theory of law, of specifying and explaining the various roles it can play in different social orders and distinguishing between juridical and legal relations. A quite different aspect of Durkheim's work – his discussion of the 'soul' in *The Elementary Forms of the Religious Life* – will be used to help develop an understanding of the fundamental importance of the concept of 'responsibility' in all social formations.

Durkheim's simple dichotomy between modern differentiated societies and *sociétés inférieures*, and indeed the way that he uses evidence to sustain this, whilst by no means lacking in interest, partially obscures a more complex picture. The societies that Durkheim grouped together as *sociétés inférieures* include nomadic hunters and gatherers, settled segmentary acephalous societies and rudimentary class societies. In *Order and Dispute: An Introduction to*

Legal Anthropology (1979), Simon Roberts provides a useful summary of much of the evidence on the control of disruptive actions in many of these societies. Hunters and gatherers display many of the characteristics described by Durkheim. They are usually made up of relatively small groups of undifferentiated kinsmen and kinswomen. They tend to make decisions collectively and if there are individual leaders this does not mean that there is any continuity of office. Repressive means of dealing with disputes and/or non-conformity sometimes are and sometimes are not a feature of these societies. It is true that if communities are actively worried about the intervention of supernatural agencies then, in line with Durkheim's view of the typical *société inférieure*, there is sometimes a stress on the active production of conformity. Perhaps more important is that when groups cannot easily disband and regroup then those individuals defined as persistently disruptive may be dealt with repressively. But such repressive measures are certainly not the norm. First, supernatural entities are often seen as akin to the deists' watchmakers, in that having created the world they leave its inhabitants to their own devices. Second, more often than not, such societies can easily disband and regroup. Durkheim himself acknowledges in *Professional Ethics and Civic Morals* that such simple societies are not 'subject to authority of any kind' (1957, p. 46).

In the bulk of both the nomadic and the settled segmentary, acephalous societies we find that the conduct of individuals usually becomes a problem when somebody defines himself or herself as an offended party and initiates action against the offender. In such cases both parties usually make the issue of more general concern by involving their kin, who may then negotiate for them, or who may bring in some third party. The authority of any such third party is conditional and any solution proffered by them has no binding power but depends upon the mutual acquiescence of the opposing parties. A compromise of some kind is usually sought, but if this cannot be achieved the main sanction used by the aggrieved party is the withdrawal of the services it used to provide to the other group. This can have serious consequences since social solidarity is as much dependent upon the mutual economic interdependence of different sub-collectivities and their bonds of shared ancestry and mutual descendants as it is upon absolute uniformity of values and of conduct. Thus a restitutive rather than repressive approach to socially contentious behaviour is normal in such societies and their members are less emotive, more rational and variegated than Durkheim believed.

In fact, some elements of Durkheim's portrayal of modern complex societies can be usefully transposed to the primitive realm. Organic solidarity is allegedly based upon the exchange of equivalents by differentiated members of collectivities: cooperation and unity do not depend upon the conformity of values, perspectives and goals intrinsic to societies based upon mechanical solidarity. But, as Mauss (1970) and Lévi-Strauss (1969) have shown, primitive communities have their own complex systems of exchange relations and are not dull and conformist. Mauss argues that in all societies there are institutions and practices that organize the obligation to give, receive and repay gifts. These gifts may be useful, or useless, accumulated or destroyed, one-sided or reciprocal. This system is not inspired by any simple utilitarian calculus but it does help produce alliances and sets of obligations between groups thereby contributing to the 'morphological' foundations of social life:

> Everything that happens in the course of gatherings, fairs and markets or in the feasts that replace them, presupposes groups whose duration exceeds the season of social concentration, like the winter potlatch of the Kwakiutl or the few weeks of the Melanesian maritime exhibitions. Moreover, in order that these meetings may be carried out, in peace, there must be roads or water for transport and tribal, intertribal or international alliances – *commercium* and *conubium*.
>
> We are dealing, then, with something more than a set of themes, more than institutional elements, more than institutions, more even than systems of institutions divisible into legal, economic, religious, and other parts. We are concerned with wholes, systems in their entirety.
>
> (Mauss, 1970, p. 77)

Here we have a 'total social phenomenon'. This phrase, with which Mauss displaced Durkheim's concept of 'social fact', indicates how his understanding of the 'stuff' of social life is rather different from Durkheim's. He believes that the behaviour of individuals is both produced by, and produces, social bonds, that the exchange and circulation of gifts produces reciprocal obligations and alliances between individuals, groups and whole societies. This bonding is intimately connected with the sacredness of all the elements in an exchange – and these are sacred because they are elements of the same social totality. However, the boundaries of this totality are flexible – groups remain a part of it in so far as reciprocal relations are maintained between them and the rest of the complexus.[1]

Lévi-Strauss has explored the nature of these totalities in some detail. He argues that it is possible, by circulating women between individuals and groups, to produce alliances even when there are differences in values and in interests. Consider, for example, the different groups of the nomadic and warlike Nambikwara of Western Brazil.

> There is a continuity between hostile relations and the provision of reciprocal prestations. Exchanges are peacefully resolved wars, and wars are the result of unsuccessful transactions. This feature is clearly witnessed to by the fact that the transition from war to peace, or at least from hostility to cordiality, is accomplished by the intermediary of ritual gestures, a veritable 'reconciliation inspection' . . .
>
> And from being arrayed against each other they pass immediately to gifts; gifts are received, gifts are given, but silently, without bargaining, without any expression of satisfaction or complaint, and without any apparent connection between what is offered and what is obtained. Thus it is a question of reciprocal gifts, and not of commercial transactions. But a supplementary stage may be reached. Two bands which have thus come to establish lasting commercial relations can decide in a deliberate manner to join by instituting between the male members of the two respective bands the artificial kinship relationship of brothers-in-law. Given the marriage system of the Nambikwara, the immediate consequence of this innovation is that all the children of one group become the potential spouses of the other group and vice versa. Thus a continuous transition exists from war to exchange, and from exchange to intermarriage, and the exchange of brides is merely the conclusion to an uninterrupted process of reciprocal gifts, which effects the transition from hostility to alliance, from anxiety to confidence, and from fear to friendship.
>
> (Lévi-Strauss, 1969, pp. 67–8)

The circulation of women, then, produces shared interests between rivalrous and potentially conflictual groups – a pool of future marriage partners and the existence of mutual grandchildren make for strong bonds.[2]

We have here a concept of order that acknowledges the dynamic (and volatile) nature of individual and group interests. It recognizes that there are many mediations between individuals and any social totality of which they are a part. It posits the *conscience collective* not as the source or essence of the totality, but rather as a potential element of it with its own specifiable (and unguaranteed) conditions of existence. Durkheim's belief that there is some separate social essence was the consequence of a laudable desire to develop social rather than individualistic explanations of human conduct and to differentiate sociology from psychology, but this foundered on his mistaken belief that each science dealt with a distinctive separate kind of phenomenon. In so far as we are dealing with human beings in society the issue is rather the level of analysis. Everything from the forms of consciousness that individuals develop (including the unconscious) to the reproduction of the mode of production can be explained by using social categories, but this is not to conceive of the social as a self-subsistent realm, or, indeed, to believe that these categories exhaust empirical phenomena.

Repressive law and class societies

In his discussions of the nature and role of repressive law in primitive societies Durkheim claimed that offences against religion are particularly severely punished. These arguments were in part based upon the work of Maine. More recently, after a systematic examination of the evidence, Diamond (1935) has concluded that collective punitive action is most likely if there are successful accusations of witchcraft, incest, illicit sodomy or bestiality. It is only in class societies, when there is an alliance between the aristocracy and the organized priesthood, that the sacrilegious aspects of conduct become important – when offences against the powerful are defined as *lèse-majesté* (Diamond, 1935, pp. 277–300).[3]

In Alpert's view, Durkheim's discussion of repressive law does not refer to simple, acephalous societies, and therefore anthropological data are irrelevant.

> Although throughout his study Durkheim speaks of law in 'primitive societies' (*dans les sociétés inférieures*) he is really dealing not with *primitive* law as anthropologists understand the term today, but rather with what more closely corresponds to *ancient* and *feudal* law.
>
> (Alpert, 1939, p. 196)

In fact, much of Durkheim's general discussion of primitive societies is grounded in data derived from acephalous societies, but nevertheless Alpert is correct about the source of Durkheim's materials on law. When he systematizes Durkheim's evidence in tabular form it clearly indicates that repressive law predominated in early (although not the simplest) societies.[4] Nevertheless there are problems about Alpert's interpretation of these data. Alpert and Durkheim both assume that *law* is the source of order and, therefore, that if there is a centralized political structure it will be the locus of law *and* order. Yet in the Greek and Roman systems, for example, day-to-day issues of 'order and dispute' were dealt with in and through the extended household. The centre of gravity of these systems, like that in acephalous societies, lay in the *patria potestas*, the extended household.[5] This is not a simple inversion of Durkheim's position, indicating the primacy of restitutive *law* over repressive *law*; rather it shows the limited role of law, properly so called. That Greece and Rome can be considered as (unstable?) hybrid cases is connected with the degree of differentiation, stratification and bureaucratization of these societies, however rudimentary this might have been.

The contemporary American anthropologist, Stanley Diamond, has argued that there is a radical disjuncture between social orders based upon the rule of law and those based upon the rule of custom.

> Custom – spontaneous, traditional, personal, commonly known, corporate, relatively unchanging – is the modality of primitive society; law is the instrument of civilization, of political society, sanctioned by organized force, presumably above society at large, and buttressing a new set of social interests.
>
> (Diamond, 1971, p. 120)

Law is produced as a new principle of social order as a way of securing and buttressing privilege. Its seeming impersonality and impartiality and the concept of a public offence facilitate the control of social life by a class living off the economic surplus as well as allowing them to generate personal wealth from the operation of law itself (law was also an important source of ruling-class revenue in Anglo-Saxon England – Weisser, 1982). These inequalities generate social problems – vagrancy, poverty – which may themselves be criminalized and which may also lead to criminal actions such as robbery, larceny, etc.

The laws of intermediate societies are unprecedented:

They rise in opposition to the customary order of the antecedent kin or kin-equivalent groups;they represent a new set of social goals pursued by a new and unanticipated power in society. These goals can be reduced to a simple complex imperative; the imposition of the interrelated census, tax–conscription system. The territorial thrust of the early state, along with its vertical social entrenchment, demanded conscription of labor, the mustering of an army, the levying of taxes and tribute, the maintenance of a bureaucracy, and the assessment of the extent, location, and numbers of the population being subjected. *These were the major or indirect occasions for the development of civil law*.

(Diamond, 1971, p. 126)

As the integrity of local groups declined, a process which in the autochthonous state must have taken generations or even centuries, conditions doubtless developed which served as an *ex post facto* rationalization for edicts already in effect. In this sense, laws became self-fulfilling prophecies. Crime and the laws which served it were, then, covariants of the evolving state system.

(ibid., p. 132)

Whilst Diamond may be right that law and crime have been generated by social and economic inequalities, and that certain elements of the customary order had undoubtedly been socially beneficial, it seems unlikely that the principles of this primitive order could provide much meaningful guidance for the construction of any industrial (or post-industrial) social order. Even in the most egalitarian of complex societies, the sheer scale of its political units and the degree to which its individuals and institutions are interdependent would indicate the need for predictable and rationally justifiable decisions and judgements. At least some elements of a legal order would be necesary – legal systems, individuation, abstractness and formal procedures provide the individual with some protection against arbitrariness. It is for this reason that, in *Geist des Romischen Recht* (in a passage cited approvingly by Diamond), Ihering argued that 'Form is the sworn enemy of the unlimited discretion (of the sovereign power) and the twin sister of freedom' (cited in Diamond, 1971, p. 139).

Sally Moore (1972, 1978) has explored some areas of *continuity* between customary and legal orders and explains certain aspects of the legal systems of contemporary societies as a function of their size, rather than of the internal development of the law. In line with my earlier comments, she points out that whilst in simple societies most disputes are negotiable and settled between the protagonists themselves, nevertheless there are circumstances when the conduct of some individuals may become of collective concern. Anybody who is unable or unwilling to conform to the general patterns of social life without being continually threatened with sanctions and who disrupts the normal flow of social interaction may undermine the society's very conditions of existence.

> Again and again in the literature, where expulsion is mentioned, or execution by one's own group, it is the gross violator or recidivist who is mentioned. This has a bearing on Durkheim's argument about the presence of criminal penalties in technologically simple societies, and the punishment of the criminal for assailing the basis of group cohesion, part of which is surely conformity without physical force. From the way Durkheim writes, it was not in terms of recidivism that he conceived of primitive criminal penalties, but rather as falling immediately on anyone who broke the rules. That he erred on this score does not matter. What is significant is that he was right about the larger picture, the existence of ultimate penalties for that source of group disruption, the trouble maker, the individual who will not conform.
>
> (Moore, 1978, p. 124)

There may also be individuals who are so disputatious that they become a burden on their kin. If an individual's personal disputes regularly implicate members of his own extended kin group, they will find themselves a party to conflicts that they have not initiated and from which they suffer rather than benefit.

> Even in a society which stresses that ultimate liability is entirely individual it is possible for social collectivities to be vulnerable to seizures of property or other attacks from outsiders because a member has defaulted on his obligations. In many of the pre-industrial societies in which the principle of expanding dispute is allowed expression in self-help, a group bearing corporate liability may be committed to potential liability by any member, acting on his own, without authorization or sanction of the group for his particular acts. It is my hypothesis that *where every member of a corporate group has the power to commit it in this way to a collective liability, a corollary rule always exists whereby*

the corporation may discipline, expel or yield up to enemies members
who abuse this power or whom the corporation does not choose to
support in the situation in which he has placed them.

(Moore, 1978, p. 121)

Individuals unable or unwilling to contribute to the normal,
generally accommodating, patterns of interaction within a society,
then, may be denied the chance of continuing to participate in
group life. They will be held responsible for the consequences of
their actions. But to whom they are responsible is a complex
question. Moore argues that this issue can be addressed by
conceiving of societies as made up of a series of different rule-
governed orders, of 'corporate groups'. Following Smith (1974),
she defines 'corporate groups' or 'publics' as:

'enduring, presumably perpetual groups with determinable
boundaries and membership, having an internal organization
and a unitary set of external relations, an exclusive body of
common affairs, and autonomy and procedures adequate to
regulate them.' In some societies corporations are all discrete
units, in others they overlap or some contain others. The
corporations within a society may be structural replicas of one
another, or they may have varied rules of internal organization
and external relations . . . 'corporations provide the framework
of law and authoritative regulation for the societies that they
constitute' . . . A corporate definition of 'public' permits one to
consider the distinction between public and private legal matters
in everything from a village in acephalous societies to a
sophisticated state. What is public in the context of one group
may be a private matter in the context of a larger unit which
encompasses it.

(Moore, 1972, p. 100)

This analysis can be applied to national states, to sub-
collectivities that accept their authority and those that do not; to
loose confederations of kinship groups and to kinship groups
themselves. Every collectivity will impose obligations on its
members and impute to them the capacity for responsibility, and
collectivities may hold each other responsible for their members'
actions. The more a corporation needs to regulate the members of
the sub-collectivities it encompasses, and the more they move in
between these sub-collectivities, the more atomized and anonymous
they become, then the more will individual, as well as or instead

of, corporate responsibility become generalized. This, then, may well be an important source of the concept of a general human legal personality, and it complements Durkheim's view that individualism is linked with individuation, itself the effect of increased social differentiation and of a complex matrix of legally sanctioned rights and obligations.

Hirst and Woolley (1982) have argued that in many societies there has been no general belief in 'free will' or any unitary concept of the human personality. In ancient Greece, for example, a man acting under the compulsion of *Ate* would be considered liable but not morally responsible for any anti-social conduct, yet there was still conduct for which he was believed to be responsible. Yet to reject the 'metaphysical fiction' that men and women are 'free agents' does not mean

> rejecting social categories which organize practices, categories like 'contract', 'obligation', 'responsibility', 'fault' and 'guilt'. These categories do not depend on individuals being in some inherent, ontological sense responsible or guilty, but they do require that conduct is attributable to individuals, not as its origin but as its locus.
> (Hirst and Woolley, 1982, p. 132)

Even if one questions Althusser's claim that there is a universal form of interpellation/subjection (Althusser, 1971, p. 149), he is surely right in arguing that the belief in some kind of personal responsibility is a universal phenomenon in, and a necessary support for, human societies.

Socially enforced and personally acknowledged rights and obligations – whether legally codified or not – are for Durkheim the essence of the universally present 'juridical moral bond' –

> a relation conceived by the public consciousness as existing between two subjects, individual or collective, or between these subjects and a thing, and by virtue of which, one of the parties in question has at least a certain right over the other.
> (Lukes and Scull, 1983, p. 193)

The importance of the 'juridical relation' is well illustrated by Malinowski's discussion of the fate of a young man who committed (altruistic?) suicide after being publicly accused of breaking the rules of exogamy. Whilst his offence had been generally known, it was only when an interested party, the girl's discarded lover, took the initiative and mobilized public opinion that the culprit was subjected to a punitive public pressure (Malinowski, 1926, pp. 77–80). A Durkheimian view would be that the spurned lover, whatever his own feelings, would have had to do something if he wished to retain the respect of the community.[6]

In this section there has been an exploration of certain recent analyses of the nature of order in simple societies and particularly what role, if any, law plays in them. We have concluded that Durkheim was clearly wrong that these societies are dependent upon 'mechanical solidarity', rather we find in them many of the features that he associated with 'organic solidarity'. Nevertheless the use of extreme measures against recidivists in some senses vindicates elements of Durkheim's view, not so much that 'repressive law' predominates in such societies but that the 'juridical relation' is endemic to social order itself. However, here this term is being used to refer not so much to formal legal relations but rather to the ways in which individuals are held responsible for their actions. Whilst Hirst and Woolley have provided us with a useful discussion of the different ways in which people are held responsible for their actions, it is to Durkheim that we turn for a brief exploration of how responsible subjects are produced.

The soul, the personality and the responsible subject

What attributes must the members of a society possess for the concept of obligation to make sense? In *The Elementary Forms of the Religious Life*, Durkheim argued that there is no known society without a religion and no religion that does not have a concept of the soul. It is because an individual possesses a soul that he will be treated with respect by his co-religionists. In totemic religions the soul is 'the totemic principle incarnate in each individual' (Durkheim, 1976, p. 248). Each individual is seen as an aspect of, or a manifestation of, *mana*, the sacred force. Since religion is, in reality, the worship of society (and the sacred is associated with collective activities), in the primitive societies that Durkheim was studying the religious and tribal communities were coterminous; however, the same arguments apply in our more secular cultures. The soul is the social aspect of our dualistic human nature; the other part is the body and its appetites and passions.

For society, this unique source of all that is sacred, does not limit itself to moving us from without and affecting us for the moment; it establishes itself within us in a durable manner. It arouses within us a whole world of ideas and sentiments which express it but which, at the same time, form an integral and permanent part of ourselves. When the Australian goes away from a religious ceremony, . . . all these numerous ideals which he has elaborated with the co-operation of his fellows, continue to live in his consciousness and, through the emotions which are attached to them and the ascendancy which they hold over his entire being, they are sharply distinguished from the vulgar impressions arising from his daily relations with external things. Moral ideas have the same character. It is society which forces them upon us, and the respect inspired by it is naturally extended to all that comes from it, its imperative rules of conduct are invested, by reason of their origin, with an authority and a dignity which is shared by none of our internal states: therefore we assign them a place apart in our psychical life. . . . This is the objective foundation of the idea of the soul: those representations whose flow constitutes our interior life are of two different species which are irreduceable one into another. Some concern themselves with the external and material world; others with an ideal world to which we attribute a moral superiority over the first.

(Durkheim, 1976, pp. 262–3)

Members of a tribal community, then, respect each other because they are all sacred and at the same time 'feel' a socially induced compulsion to act morally.

All the beings partaking of the same totemic principle consider that owing to this very fact, they are morally bound to one another; they have definite duties of assistance, vendetta etc., towards each other; and it is these duties which constitute kinship.

(Durkheim, 1976, p. 190)

If they have a soul, human beings will, on occasion, have to repress their instincts and desires (ibid., p. 316). Through such self-control they can develop a relative autonomy from their immediate environment and then act in conformity with reason. This is a Kantian definition of personality – its cornerstone is the 'will' and 'the will is the faculty of acting in conformity with reason' (ibid., p. 271).[7] Differences of social position, and of the body's spatial location, however, will produce different personal (and somatic) experiences and perspectives and thus the nature of rationality is often contextually determined.

> Passion individualises, yet it also enslaves. Our sensations are essentially individual; yet we are more personal the more we are freed from our senses and able to think and act with concepts. So those who insist upon all the social elements of the individual do not mean by that to deny or debase the personality. They merely refuse to confuse it with the fact of individuation.
>
> (Durkheim, 1976, p. 272)

If an individual is believed to have a soul, or a personality, then he or she will be treated with respect and will be expected to use the faculties associated with it – i.e. autonomy, self-control and the ability to follow social rules and fulfil social obligations; failure means culpability. Thus society, social obligations and personal responsibility are mutually interdependent. *The juridical relation is central to social life.* It is only if individuals are, on occasion, considered responsible for their actions that they are recognized as personalities; thus punishment can rejuridicalize subjects. None of this necessarily endorses any Kantian metaphysic of the human subject, or any assumption that the juridical order is a just one or obeyed primarily out of a rational sense of duty. These issues will be returned to in later chapters.

Social life and social obligations

All societies need a a system of relatively defined social obligations. Specific rights and duties provide the family's moral foundations and this nexus structures the lives and emotions of the different members of the family.

> Suppose we are faced with a question of domestic ethics? The case is far from complete when it has been said that children must obey their parents, who must in turn protect their children; that husband and wife must be faithful to each other and co-operate. The *real* relations uniting different members of the family are more numerous and more defined. . . . There are specifically the right of punishment which law and custom

limit; the right of the father over the lives of his minor children; rights and duties to wardship, others concerning heredity; they take different forms, depending upon whether the child is illegitimate, legitimate, or adopted; according to whether the powers are exercised by father or mother, etc.
          (Durkheim, 1933, p. 419; see also Durkheim, 1933, p. 207)

Here law clarifies, codifies, supports or modifies practices that have often developed relatively independently of it. But since domestic law can alter familial organization Durkheim is undoubtedly too sanguine about the necessarily positive consequences of state intervention. Donzolot's (1979) somewhat hysterical position is its equally flawed, libertarian antithesis (Minson, 1985). Detailed evaluations of the effects of specific legal decisions should replace such *a priorism*.

Lukes and Scull admit that in his discussion of the family Durkheim comes closest to an enabling and constitutive concept of the law (Lukes and Scull, 1983, p. 7). They fail to appreciate that in his view it was by duty and responsibility that the family and the human personalities within its ambit are constituted (see also Durkheim, 1951, pp. 171–202, 259–76). The strength of the family is primarily due not to the 'community of sentiments and beliefs' of its members but to its structure of rights and obligations (some legally codified); indeed, if anything, the latter probably generated the former (Durkheim, 1933, pp. 122–3). Thus this consideration of the treatment of the soul in Durkheim's *The Elementary Forms of the Religious Life* and of the family in *The Division of Labour in Society* shows the power of Durkheim's argument that juridical relations are universal but that he was wrong in conflating these with legal relations.

Whilst socially organized forms of exchange provide a basis for solidarity in primitive and complex societies, in the latter this is often mediated through specifically legal forms. In a society characterized by an advanced division of labour, many individuals will exchange their capacity to work for a wage, by means of an employment contract. But this will not produce social solidarity unless it is a just arrangement. The two parties would have to be in conditions of formal and substantive equality and the wage levels would have to be determined with reference to general social evaluation of the kind of work performed (Durkheim, 1933, pp. 383–8). The legal forms and the principles upon which the legal system is based would have to be appropriate to the structure of the society. Society would need to be actually organized in way that let its structure function properly. Law, then, clearly has effects – formal juridical categories can produce negative consequences. To evaluate its social role it is necessary to examine in detail the specific legal system and the overall social context within which it operates. These statements are deduced from the implicit logic of Durkheim's position, and it is of no little interest that they are compatible with Marx's remark that

> Right can never be higher than the economic structure of society and its cultural development conditioned thereby.
>
> (Marx, 1875, reprinted in Tucker, 1978, p. 320)

Durkheim, sovereignty and the law

This part of the chapter explores the nature and function of developed legal systems, properly so called. Although Durkheim often wrote in rather general terms about law and juridical relations and sometimes conflated overlapping but distinctive forms of relationships, in *Professional Ethics and Civic Morals* he discussed formal law in some detail. Since the aspects of these arguments that are of most interest – the principles of justice on which complex societies should operate and the material conditions necessary for just contracts – have already been discussed, the focus here is on one of his earliest articles. His other texts will be referred to only when particularly pertinent.

In 'La Science positive de la morale en Allemagne' (1887/1986), Durkheim produced a detailed (and relatively uncritical) exegesis of the treatment of moral facts in the work of German sociologists, economists, jurists and psychologists. In the article he anticipated many of the themes of his own later work – the poverty of abstract deductivism, the nature of moral and social facts, the definition of 'normal phenomena', the *sui generis* reality of society, and, of most interest to us, the relationship between law and morality. In his later work these concerns are articulated together in a unique conceptual system, to its credit far more sophisticated than the partial insights to be gleaned from the 'objective idealism' of German social science; yet, on the debit side, his more systematic theory disregards important issues that are addressed in this article, particularly in the section on Ihering.

First the 1887 article will be briefly summarized with particular attention to the position that Durkheim develops on the nature of law. Then continuities and discontinuities in his thought will be identified. In his later work there is clear evidence of the influence of the conservative 'historical school' producing a more complex sense of the 'social' but also, unfortunately, a tendency to treat society as a 'single subject'. Durkheim's earlier article was more Hobbesian in its stress on the separateness and indeed coerciveness of the sovereign, and therefore less ideological and more coherent and sophisticated. Moreover Ihering, whose ideas Durkheim generally endorsed, had elsewhere developed a radical liberal position that had certain affinities with Durkheim's arguments on the 'forced division of labour'. Thus an understanding of Durkheim's work is aided by relating it to political theory, and I show its importance by using the sub-discipline of jurisprudence, particularly the works of John Austin and H. A. L. Hart, to clarify and evaluate Durkheim's different positions on law. By the end of the chapter it will have been shown how the elaboration of certain of Durkheim's 'repressed' concepts helps realize some of the radical potential of his work.

The first part of 'La Science positive de la morale en Allemagne' examines the economics of the 'Socialists of the Chair', Wagner and Schmoller,[8] and particularly their criticisms of the 'Manchester School'. Utilitarianism assumes that the pursuit by individuals of egoistic ends in a *laissez-faire* economy will produce, through the hidden hand, a society of material abundance with a positive morality. The German economists argued that economic activity and morality are necessarily related and that the state, above all through the legal system, provides concrete connections between them. State intervention in the economy is therefore quite normal and is not necessarily socialistic. Whilst endorsing much of their argument Durkheim was critical of their overemphasis on legislation as the source of social arrangements. Schaeffle provides a healthy antidote to this rationalist statist view when he argues that both morality and law emerge and evolve so as to fulfil society's changing needs. The last section of the article focuses on the work of the psychologist Wundt, which is notable for recognizing that social phenomena were produced in a way that had little to do with individual calculation and will.

The article's middle section deals with some of the work of R. von Ihering, who, with Stammler and Jellinek, was one of the influential nineteenth-century German jurists whose work was drawn upon by, amongst others, Weber (Weber, 1978). It has been said of Ihering that 'he was at once the fulfillment and end of the historical school' (Friedrich, 1962, p. 154) – which was true in more ways than one. For Durkheim, Ihering's importance lies in his exploration of the nature of, social functions of and interrelations between law, custom and morality. In his *Der Zweck im Recht* (translated as *Law as a Means to an End*, 1924), Ihering argued that if social phenomena are widespread and persistent this is because they are useful to society. Both morality and law help guarantee the social order by specifying and imposing social obligations. Morality is more diffuse and 'internal', whereas law – as the 'minimum of morality absolutely indispensable for society to be able to endure' – is enforced by the armed might of the state. Custom differs from them both in that it is less of a guide to proper conduct than a prophylactic against dangerous situations. It is society, moreover, through the legal system that creates individual rights and institutions, such as private property, and as society evolves the state plays an ever more active role in all spheres of social life. This is because there is a need for the state to guarantee the provision of essential services (education, defence) and to regulate and coordinate the increasingly diverse activities of individuals, and also because even their most private acts inevitably affect the interests of others.

Law's ultimate justification lies in its indispensable contribution to the reproduction of society. The source of a legal system is less important than its social consequences. Any kind of social order depends, in part, upon constraining its members – whether through morality, law or brute force. What is important is not so much the source of order, the kind of coercion used, but whether it is relevant and effective. Thus 'force' can and should nullify ineffectual or counterproductive legal systems.

Critiques of Durkheim's theorization of law

In the introduction to their book *Durkheim and the Law*, Lukes and Scull offer three major conceptual criticisms of Durkheim's work: that he underestimated the importance of conflict within and between legal and moral rules (see also Vogt, 1983); that he neglected to explore the effects of how the law is organized; and, finally, that his

> focus on the negative and constraining aspects of law, on sanctions and obligations, precluded any systematic enquiry into its positive or enabling aspects, as a set of procedural rules, permitting individuals and groups to act in certain ways, and constitutive rules, defining practices and relationships (for

example drawing up a will or forming a company).
(Lukes and Scull, 1983, p. 7)

There is some truth to all of these criticisms. The first two *lacunae* were an effect of the conception of society as an 'expressive totality', which informed much but by no means all of his work.[9] As was shown in Chapter 2, this led him to treat law as both an index and an element of social solidarity. Since all social phenomena express the same essence, no real conflict between them would be possible, and since the significant feature of a social fact is its social function, its organizational features are epiphenomenal (Keat and Urry, 1975, pp. 83–7; Hirst, 1975, p. 101).

Whilst, as Lukes and Scull acknowledge, in his *substantive* work Durkheim by no means ignored the more positive aspects of law, it is certainly accurate to suggest that his arguments are grounded in the tradition that conceives of law as coercive and constraining. Now it seems indisputable that law can play a constitutive role, as an essential (but not the sole) means of constructing socially effective agents, and even organizational forms that are often irreduceable to interpersonal relations (Hirst, 1980, p. 63). Moreover, if law is constitutive it can also be enabling – it can help 'to control, to guide and to plan life out of court' (Hart, 1961, p. 39). But does this mean, as Hart argues, that the coercive theory of law should be abandoned (ibid., p. 27) or rather that the issue then becomes how to develop a theory that can adequately explore the relationship between law's 'coercive', 'enabling' and 'constitutive' aspects? If the latter, it will be necessary to confront the issue of 'sovereignty' in some detail, not least because this is an area where theorists like Hart have stressed the 'constitutive' role of law.

The argument that law necessarily functions, in part, through coercion does not entail a belief that it has only negative effects. In his 1887 article Durkheim explicitly distanced himself from those who subscribe to a totally negative view of law and criticized those who believe that 'law's only function would be the protection of individuals against each other' (Durkheim, 1887, pp. 54–5). He also confronted the relationship betweeen law and force in a way that was at odds with his later system:

In origin, law is nothing but force limiting itself in its own interest. In the material world and in that of primitive man, when two forces are in battle, the conflict only ceases with the annihilation of the weakest. But men were not slow in perceiving that it was often more economic not to go as far as eliminating the adversary; from that developed the institution of slavery, that of contracts and peace treaties, the first forms of law. All treaties are in fact rules which restrain the power of the victor; doubtless, it is the victor who imposes this on himself, but, nevertheless, law benefits the vanquished. Thus in principle force is essential and law is only secondary. Today the relation of the two terms is reversed and force is no more than an ancillary, merely the servant of law. We should not judge the past by the present. Besides even now the previous relation between the law and force might be temporarily re-established; then force, instead of letting itself be regulated by the law, would overturn it to create a new version of it. This is what happens in all coups d'états and revolutions; we shouldn't always condemn this deployment of force in the name of an abstract principle. The law is not something holy, it is a means to an end. It only has value when it fulfils its function well, that is to say when it guarantees the continued vitality of society. If it interferes with this it is natural that force intervenes to take its place. *Primum vivere*.

(Durkheim, 1887, p. 55)

There are some obvious problems and ambiguities in this formulation. On the one hand, society is seen as more 'fundamental' than the state and as a non-contradictory, albeit complex, entity unified by a common interest.[10] On the other, the basis of the law is no longer law itself (or the state) and, since the law does not automatically 'function' in society's interest, here a conceptual space is opened up – one pre-empted in his later schema – to explore whether and how conflict might exist between law, morality, etc. and how organizational forms might affect the law's operation. Durkheim's use of the term 'force' is somewhat similar to Hobbes' use of Leviathan as a coercive sovereign. It is thus possible to conceptualize a separation between the sovereign and society and that they may have different – although not necessarily antagonistic – interests. Overall this Hobbesian element makes it possible to pose such questions as: What determines sovereignty and what are its material foundations? When law is 'enabling', who is being enabled to do what, with what consequences for whom?

This formulation of the relationship between law and force is grounded in Ihering's work, which had incorporated utilitarian

elements and elements derived from the 'Historical School' of
Savigny. But whilst Ihering's early work on Roman law was
firmly within the framework of the Historical School, by 1872 he
had already published a work, *The Struggle for Law*, in which he
criticized his own previous work and that of Savigny and Putche.
(The two volumes of *Der Zweck im Recht* were published in 1877
and 1883.) They had all subscribed to the view that law, like
language, evolved painlessly. However, a more realistic view was
that:

> The life of the law is a struggle, a struggle of nations, of the
> state power, of classes of individuals. . . . This struggle reaches
> its highest degree of intensity when the interests in question
> have assumed the forms of vested rights. Here we find two
> parties opposed each to the other, each of which takes as its
> device the sacredness of law; the one that of the historical law,
> the law of the past; the other that of the law which is ever
> coming into existence, ever renewing its youth, the eternal
> primordial law of mankind. . . . All of the great achievements
> which the law of mankind has to record – the abolition of
> slavery, of serfdom, the freedom of landed property, of
> industry, of conscience, etc., – All have had to be won, in the
> first instance, in this manner, by the most violent struggles,
> which often lasted for centuries.
>
>   (Ihering, 1879, pp. 11–12)

Ihering's association of the growth of individualism with the
progress of 'the law which is ever coming into existence . . . the
eternal primordial law of mankind' has an affinity with the radical
evolutionism to be found in Durkheim's discussion of 'the forced
division of labour' (Durkheim, 1933, pp. 374–88). (It must be said
that there are importance differences. Ihering's liberalism had
something in common with the views of the Weber who collected
duelling scars – he resented the state's interference in the
individual's right to exact personal revenge from those who
offended honour.)
     Perhaps if, in his more systematic theoretical schema, Durkheim
had retained the Hobbesian conceptualization of the relationship
between law and force and enriched it with the more fruitful
aspects of Ihering's treatment of the role of conflict and power in
shaping the direction of social evolution he might have developed
a more adequate theory of law. True, he recognized that some
laws might be anachronistic and others might not totally represent

public sentiment (Durkheim, 1951, p. 426); that at times the state might itself act illegally, as in the Dreyfus affair (Lukes, 1975, p. 334); and even that formal legality might produce a lawful but unjust and aggressive society like Imperial Germany (LaCapra, 1972). Such insights were so marginal to the main thrust of his work that he failed to recognize that progressive ideas usually have to overcome opposition – that, for example, whilst social evolution might be facilitated by the abolition of inherited wealth and whilst organic solidarity might be strengthened if contracts are legally binding only if made by substantially equal partners (Durkheim, 1933, pp. 374–88), those powerful vested interests who would thereby suffer would be unlikely to agree to such developments unless forced to do so by some form of organized political struggle, and certainly something more than 'public opinion'. Ironically, then, whilst in his later work Ihering moved away from the 'painless evolutionism' of the Historical School, in some ways at least Durkheim moved closer to it.

Sovereignty and the command theory of law

Like Ihering, the English legal theorist John Austin made use of Savigny's work and much of his argument was a sophisticated elaboration of Hobbes' utilitarianism. Furthermore, in *Professional Ethics and Civic Morals*, Durkheim defined political society and sovereignty in a manner virtually identical to Austin's but did not really follow through the implcations of these definitions (Durkheim, 1957, pp. 45–7; Lukes, 1975, pp. 268–9). Thus an exploration of Austin's work will help us to develop a more adequate understanding of the nature of sovereignty and of law and provide some indication of how Durkheim's work could be developed.

For Austin, the source of law is the sovereign:

> if a *determinate* human superior, *not* in a habit of obedience to a like superior, receive *habitual* obedience from the *bulk* of a given society, that determinate superior is sovereign in that society, and the society (including the superior) is a society political and independent.
>
> (Austin, 1955, p. 194)

Although such a sovereign might be accused of acting in an unconstitutional way, they could not be accused of acting illegally because – *qua* sovereign – they are not themselves subject to law (Austin, 1955, p. 259). The legal system, then, is only an aspect and expression of the power of the 'sovereign'.

This formulation of the nature of sovereignty is in sharp contrast to Hart's:

> Rules are constitutive of the sovereign, not merely things we should have to maintain in habits of obedience to the sovereign.
> (Hart, 1961, p. 103)

For Hart, *contra* Austin, the law not only facilitates social life in that 'it provides individuals with faculties for realising their wishes by conferring legal powers upon them' (Hart, 1961, p. 27), but it provides the ultimate criteria for assessing the legitimacy of those able to exercise coercive power.

However, this is by no means an advance on Austin's command theory. First, the command theory was much more sophisticated than Hart has acknowledged. For example, Austin was quite explicit that constituent members of a complex, 'mixed or heterogenous sovereign' can themselves be subject to legal rules, that authority can be delegated and that rights are often, in fact, 'legally endowed faculties' (Austin, 1955, pp. 286–7, 124) and thus law can function in an enabling and constitutive manner. Secondly, these aspects of his theory are in no way incompatible with his view that law must have a coercive dimension and that power ultimately determines sovereignty (Austin, 1955, p. 220), that is *which* set of constitutive rules, 'official certificates' (Hart, 1961, p. 93), '*Grundnorm*' (Kelsen, 1945), or what have you, will be treated as the foundation of the legal order and function as the criteria of legitimacy.

Austin's formulation opens up the possibility of exploring issues of power and domination and how groups and institutions make 'claims' to legitimacy. It is therefore more likely to be fruitful than the pre-emptive 'enabling' imagery of Hart – and the *assumption*, central to the theories of Hart and the 'systematic' Durkheim, that effective legal systems are primarily obeyed by individuals because they are useful to the individual and from 'a sense of duty'.[11]

This not to say that such an Austinian position is adequate.

> A true theory of law would . . . question Austin's tendency to conflate official authority and power and would specifically reject the identification of the official sovereign accepted by the

courts ('The Queen in Parliament', say) with the dominant power in the land. An adequate theory would also question Austin's failure to look at legalism as an ideological force reinforcing relations in capitalist society, with its individual 'rights and duties' and its whole ideology of individual responsibility.

(Skillen, 1977, p. 94)

Thus, even if a theory of law is developed that is able to specify how its coercive, enabling and constitutive elements can be articulated together, it will still be necessary to explore how the legal system is related to other forms of social relations and particularly to ideology.

Austin might have begun to confront some of these issues if he had grasped other implications of Hobbes' arguments.

If power is taken as the basis of right, as Hobbes, etc. do, then right, law, etc. are merely the symptom, the expression of other relations upon which State power rests . . . an expression whose content is always determined by the relations of this [ruling] class, as the civil and criminal law demonstrate in the clearest possible way.

(Marx and Engels, 1845, in 1976, p. 329)

These comments of Marx and Engels, divested of their neo-Hegelian and reductionist elements, suggest that a legal system cannot be adequately described without analysing its relationship to the other elements of the social formation. This formulation can be combined with recent work that analyses law as a relatively autonomous ideological instance. Althusser (1971) and Edelman (1979) suggest that the concept of the 'sovereign' as a class or individual subject is problematic. (Indeed, even when Austin writes of a 'mixed or heterogeneous sovereign' this mainly refers to a complex of 'governing' institutions within the state.) The persistence of social formations cannot be adequately explained in terms of interpersonal or even inter-institutional relations. A wider concept of the state and other modes of domination need to be developed in the direction of a neo-Gramscian notion of hegemonic domination.

Rational–legal orders

Nevertheless law, properly so called, inevitably plays an important role in any complex social formation and a developed legal system will be an aspect of its system of hegemonic institutions. Durkheim would have endorsed Weber's view that any complex differentiated society would require a 'rational–legal order', where

> obedience is owed to the legally established impersonal order. It extends to the persons exercising the authority of office under it by virtue of the formal legality of their commands and only within the scope of authority of the office.
>
> (Weber, 1978, pp. 215–16)

But where Durkheim's analysis of codified law focused on its function and its content, Weber's focused more on its formal properties. In his view, 'legal–rational orders' are based upon an independent and self-contained legal system, consisting of an internally coherent, gapless system of abstract rules, which regulate the actions of individuals. Every act is to be visualized as 'either an "application" or "execution" of legal propositions or as an infringement thereof' (ibid., p. 658).

Whilst Weber acknowledged that no such legal–rational system has ever existed, he argued that it is an ideal type – the purified essence of legal systems or that towards which they constantly tend. Hunt rightly argues that it is an unrealizeable legal Utopia (Hunt, 1978, p. 106). Whilst there is *a necessary strain to consistency within any sophisticated legal system*, and whilst such systems have some autonomy, nevertheless law is a secondary phenomenon. Its effectiveness depends upon its relevance and 'if it no longer corresponds to the existing state of society' (Durkheim, 1933, p. 66) it will be modified. To conceive of law in functional terms does not entail a functionalist concept of society. As Ihering argued, there may well be dispute and conflict within societies as to what the role and content of the law, i.e. its function, should be – it will be based upon principles generated by forces that largely originate outside of the legal realm. Therefore, *contra* Weber, substantive concerns inevitably affect legal development.

Yet such concerns are themselves always constructed and expressed within and through ideologies associated with heterogeneous forces and subject to dispute. And Weber is clearly right that there is a 'strain to consistency' in the legal system and a need to achieve some level of coherence within legal discourse. It is the concept of sovereignty that fulfils the necessary 'symbolic function' of supporting the 'juridico political processes of attribution and deduction' (Cousins and Hussain, 1984, p. 237). Nothing could be more in the spirit, if not exactly in accord with the letter, of Durkheimian concepts than a conception of sovereignty as a 'symbolic function'. Moreover, such an 'ideological construct' will to some extent inhibit even the actions of powerful individuals who might wish to manipulate or criminally abuse their own or state power.

Any legal system will be confronted with the need to produce categories that clarify issues deriving from the imperatives of social life. In the arena of criminal law it is the perception of an act as offensive or dangerous (because it may be unprecedented or excessively disruptive or because there are new criteria of acceptability) that provides the stimulus for certain groups or agencies to criminalize it (Durkheim, 1938, pp. 65–75). Neither lawful nor criminal behaviour can be interpreted as the expression of human nature. Laws are examples of norms – to be understood as rules that *should* be followed and that therefore *can* be disobeyed. The content of criminal law will be variable and not necessarily consistent and some criminal behaviour is inevitable. After all, social relationships and the constitution and functioning of the human subject cannot be exhausted by legal categories, and individual human action is by no means always 'conscionable' – it is often the effect of processes that elude consciousness and control. Similarly, civil law develops because of a perceived need to clarify which duties, obligations and rights can be legally enforced on whom (or what) and/or to develop social forms that require the support of legal categories.

Legal systems, then, are always based upon relatively heterogeneous principles that are in an unstable relationship with each other, and that will be internally consistent only at particular moments, if at all. A variety of substantively rational concerns will therefore be in a constant tension with each other and with the formally rational requirements of the legal system *qua* system. Since some of these 'principles' are derived from substantive concerns to be found in more than one kind of social formation, they will also be present in more than one kind of socio-legal order. A complex differentiated socialist society will equally require the 'fiction of sovereignty', a point to which I shall return later in this book.

Conclusion

The early part of this chapter explored the adequacy of Durkheim's understanding of the nature of primitive law and of primitive societies and concluded that to some extent he misconceived both of them. It also became clear that certain of his concepts are useful and others could be relatively easily reconstituted. Obviously fruitful is his exploration of the 'juridical relation', for this has made it possible to develop an understanding of the key role that the concept of 'responsibility' must play in any social order. Not only do Durkheim's categories, albeit reworked, help to make sense of acephalous and modern complex societies but they also enable one to begin to theorize how the subject as a responsible agent is generated within ideology as a desirable goal and as a subjective experience.

Durkheim's 1887 article provides some of the earliest intimations of his overall conceptual system. He found in German thought some themes and concepts that later, in his mature system, he would elaborate, redefine and synthesize with other concepts to produce his mature system. His work would undoubtedly have benefited from a closer and more sustained relationship with the work of the German jurist Ihering. That this did not happen meant that, regrettably, certain potentially fruitful concepts and avenues of exploration were abandoned or suppressed. Otherwise there might have been the development of a theory that took account of the enabling, constitutive and repressive aspects of law and that could theorize the relationship between legal systems and social structures. Nevertheless, it is clear that, whilst Durkheim may have paid insufficient attention to the political foundations of legal systems and to the formal logic of legal discourse, his view that it is an institutional structure the function and content of which is largely determined extrinsically has significant merit.

Notes

1 Whilst accepting much of the argument in *The Gift*, Sahlins (1972) rightly criticizes Mauss for somewhat ethnocentrically imposing a distinction between religious and economic phenomena on cultures where no such differentiation occurs. This does not affect the use that we make of Mauss.

2 Not surprisingly, Lévi-Strauss's discussion of the 'circulation of women' has been subject to some strong criticism. See for example,

Cowie (1978). It has been put to work in a useful way by Gayle Rubin in 'The traffic in women' (1975). Durkheim's understanding(s) of the position of women is analysed in Gane (1983b).

3 The conceptual basis of the importance that Durkheim gave to religion was due to his assumption that religion is, in essence, the worship of the collectivity (and his rather unconvincing attempt to make absolute distinctions between religion and magic) (Durkheim, 1976). These arguments have been adequately criticized elsewhere (Keat and Urry, 1975, p. 85; O'Keefe, 1983, pp. 158–75) and in Chapter 2 above.

4 Alpert provides a detailed table of the relative proportion of repressive and restitutive laws in four societies, based upon *The Division of Labour in Society* (Alpert, 1939, p. 197).

5 Thus, overall, restitutive practices predominated over repressive law. Durkheim's misunderstanding of the role of law in the classical period was probably due in part to his misguided confidence in the factual accuracy of the study of *The Ancient City* (1972) by his former teacher, Fustel de Coulanges.

6 Becker has used this example to illustrate his argument that the public condemnation of deviance requires a moral entrepreneur to mobilize public opinion (Becker, 1963, pp. 10–11). Lemert, however, points out that

> Malinowski's instance of incest, which impressed Becker, actually was between cousins, quite different from incest within the nuclear family, almost invariably punished in primitive societies.
> (Lemert, 1972, p. 21)

The dilemmas that such social pressures might produce receive a beautifully understated fictional representation in Gabriel García Márquez's novella *Chronicle of a Death Foretold* (1984), set in a small town in Latin America. On her wedding night a woman confesses to her husband that she is not a virgin and blames a local man. The distraught husband returns her to her family. Her brothers are obliged to avenge the family's humiliation and restore her honour by killing the culprit. When the brothers realize that they are expected to kill the man, since this is a somewhat complex society with a state and a local police force, they do everything they can to get arrested before they can commit the crime. At least then they would have obeyed the 'letter', if not the 'spirit', of the customary code and would still not have committed murder. They do not manage to get arrested and have to kill the accused man, a rich local Arab. Although this story is set in a relatively 'advanced' society it is a poignant evocation of the power of social obligations and the costs of avoiding them – very Durkheimian! The social enforcement of obligations is universal, but this may or may not involve the law, and the normative and legal systems may or may not be compatible with each other.

7 These arguments are similar to those of Weber in his discussion of the role of personality in the explanation of social events (Weber, 1975, pp. 192–3).

8 Weber's essay 'Objectivity in social science and social policy' (Weber, 1949) was to a large extent a public repudiation of the position taken by Schmoller and his coterie, the previous editors of the *Verein für Sozialpolitik*. Therborn (1980) and Coser (1977) discuss the political and theoretical position of both Wagner and Schmoller.

9 The chapter 'Saint-Simon – critical conclusions' in his *Socialism* (Durkheim, 1962) and his 'Two laws of penal evolution' (Durkheim, 1973) largely escape these strictures.

10 Durkheim often implies that a society, whilst changing, nevertheless sustains its identity over time. For example, he argues that:

> There are certainly differences between present-day France and France of the past, but these are, so as to speak, differences in age. . . . However there is an identity between the France of the Middle Ages and contemporary France that one cannot fail to recognize. While generations of individuals succeed one another, throughout this perpetual flux of particular personalities society persists, with its own mode of thought, its particular temperament.
> (Durkheim, 1961, p. 62; see also Durkheim, 1938, p. 88)

However, societies which at different moments in history are signified by the same name may be radically different social formations, not in an evolutionary relationship with each other but in one more characterized by discontinuity (Hirst, 1975, pp. 122–35). Moreover, his overly sanguine comments here on 'imperialistic' regimes are not radically repudiated in his later work. For example, if he was ever critical of France's colonial ventures, it was not to question the colonial administrations' claims to legitimacy, but rather to condemn the extravagant, megalomaniacal and unlawful behaviour of some colonialists. This, from the social viewpoint, was inherently irrational and counterproductive and due to a lack of discipline (Durkheim, 1961, pp. 193–6).

11 The English jurist Lloyd, albeit reluctantly, has acknowledged the importance of Austinian concepts for any exploration of the foundations of particular legal systems.

> When, for example, the Cromwellian regime succeeded in super-seding the monarchy, or when William was called in to replace James II after the latter's expulsion, the Austinian conception of habitual obedience to A rather than B is clearly relevant to explaining how legal authority can pass from one to the other regardless of the legal regulations hitherto in operation. . . . When however this transitional stage where law and power are

largely merged is passed, it is no longer relevant for the purpose
of determining what is legally valid to explore the sources of
ultimate *de facto* power in the State.

(Lloyd, 1964, p. 1983)

6   *Fatalism*

Introduction

In this chapter aspects of the text of Durkheim's *Suicide* will be worked upon with concepts developed from my earlier consideration of the 'forced division of labour'. First, there are some brief introductory comments about the attitudes of certain social scientists to this text,[1] then Durkheim's concept of 'fatalistic' suicide will be discussed in the light of more recent analyses of 'fatalism'.

Suicide and the critics

Durkheim believed that in *Suicide* he had succeeded in applying the scientific method outlined in *The Rules of Sociological Method* and that he could therefore isolate the causes of suicide, diagnose their structural bases, and propose practical remedies to it as a social problem (Durkheim, 1951, pp. 36–7). That *Suicide* has played an important role in the development of sociology there is little doubt, yet his claims for the overall validity of his methods and findings have been subjected to hostile and ultimately devastating criticism. Some have merely wished to correct his theory and methodology, to systematize it or make it more testable. Selvin (1965) has shown that, whilst Durkheim had developed innovative modes of multivariate and contextual analysis, the validity of his conclusions was undermined by his lapse into the ecological fallacy. Gibbs and Martin (1964) have 'clarified' and 'developed' his arguments to produce testable social integration theories with which to explain differing rates of suicide (and other forms of deviance). Nisbet (1963) rejects Durkheim's claim to have used a sophisticated form of inductivism since, far from having put aside his preconceptions, 'The idea, the plot, and the conclusion of *Suicide* were well in Durkheim's mind before he examined the parish register' (Nisbet, 1963, p. 156).

Whilst for Nisbet this does not constitute a reason to reject the text, his understanding of theoretical activity is inadequate – the text of *Suicide* is seen as the 'objectivation' of the author's intention and no worse for it. Thus for the objectivity of the factual realm Nisbet substitutes a problematic subjective idealism.[2]

Douglas (1967) who also believes that *Suicide* is less an empirical analysis than an abstract theoretical argument, is markedly more hostile to the whole Durkheimian project. He has shown how Durkheim relied uncritically on coroners' reports, and was generally very selective in his use of statistics. He could always find suicide statistics and statistics measuring other forms of social relationships that were covarying – the economy, religious affiliation, etc. – and thus claim to *explain* variations in suicide rates. Durkheim argued that there is a specific kind of suicide associated with each such element, and then assumed this to be the *kind* of suicide registered in the changes in the suicide rate. The same states of the *conscience collective* are known and expressed both through the condition of social institutions and through the effects of suicidogenic currents (Douglas, 1967, pp. 73–6).

For Douglas, Durkheim's work is simply wrong and without value, and so in his own substantive discussion of suicidal acts he dogmatically rejects it, and virtually inverts it by replacing it with an extreme form of subjectivism. He develops sound arguments why the sociologist must attend to the realm of social meanings but errs in reducing social reality to that realm. He constructs a typology of different types of suicide through an untheorized reading of suicide notes (and short stories and newspaper articles) and only introduces socio-structural considerations to provide a context for his 'narratives'. His concept of social structure is abstract and universalistic and again untheorized. He fails to distinguish between the major cause of an event and the contingent occasion for it; for example, Douglas cites the case of Marguerite S., a Frenchwoman who eventually killed herself after being rejected by her lover (Dougas, 1967, pp. 315-19). This he somewhat speculatively explains as an aggressive act designed to make the lover suffer guilt. Even if this is an accurate interpretation of her motives, it does not explain why his rejection of her left her so devastated. What in the Paris of 1943 was the social significance of her status as a widow and of her age (she was 43 when the affair ended)? What opportunities for social involvement were open to her? What was her emotional condition at the time and what determined this? To pose and answer such questions would help explain her vulnerability. It could explain why that event (and perhaps others), *at that time*, could precipitate her suicide. Durkheim's sociology allows us to pose and answer such questions, and he is only exaggerating slightly when he states that if the conditions are appropriate and individuals are vulnerable 'there is nothing that cannot serve as an occasion for suicide' (Durkheim, 1951, p. 300). As will be shown below, there is within the text of *Suicide* the beginnings of a sophisticated sociology of emotion. Whilst some of these criticisms are accurate, the mode of critique here is radically different, as will be illustrated through a discussion of the concept of 'fatalism'.

Fatalism: a suppressed, displaced and condensed concept

Until recently, most discussions of *Suicide* have focused on the three pure types of suicide the analyis of which makes up the bulk of Durkheim's book. There have, as a result, been a number of detailed explorations of the relationship between differences in suicide rates and the levels and forms of social integration, but there has been a corresponding lack of attention to two other elements of Durkheim's conceptual scheme – the role that social currents play in social life and the importance of fatalistic suicide. In *The Rules of Sociological Method* Durkheim argued that, because sociologists have tended to focus on

> established beliefs and practices, one might be led to believe that social facts exist only where there is some social organization. But there are other facts without such crystallized form which have the same objectivity and the same ascendancy over the individual. These are called 'social currents'.
>
> (Durkheim, 1938, pp. 4–5)

Suicide, that most private of acts, is an effect 'of the currents of egoism, altruism and anomy' which are 'the source of all individual inclination rather than their result' (Durkheim, 1951, pp. 299–300). Douglas has accurately pointed out, however, that there is a certain logical and conceptual asymmetry in Durkheim's discussion of suicidogenetic currents, which can be rectified by introducing Durkheim's own concept of fatalism.

> Now just as egoistic and altruistic forces restrain each other, so the anomic force has an opposite force that restrains it –

fatalism. This dimension is one of legitimate discipline or control (fatalism) and the lack of legitimate discipline or control (anomie).

(Douglas, 1967, pp. 56–7)

Durkheim devotes two chapters totalling 75 pages to egoistic suicide, one chapter of 23 pages to altruistic suicide, and a chapter of 25 pages to anomic suicide. This last chapter contains, in a footnote to a discussion of marriage, his only explicit analysis of fatalism. He argues that, contrary to conventional wisdom, men benefit more from the marital state than do women. Reflecting upon the implications of his own argument he suggests that

there is a type of suicide the opposite of anomic suicide, just as egoistic and altruistic suicides are opposites. It is the suicide deriving from excessive regulation, that of persons with futures pitilessly blocked and passions violently choked by oppressive discipline. It is the suicide of very young husbands, of the married woman who is childless. So, for completeness sake, we should set up a fourth suicidal type. But it has so little contemporary importance and examples are so hard to find aside from the cases just mentioned that it seems useless to dwell upon it. However, it might be said to have historical interest. Do not the suicides of slaves, said to be frequent under certain conditions (See Corre, *Le crime en pays créoles* page 48), belong to this type, or all suicides attributable to excessive physical or moral despotism. To bring out the ineluctable and inflexible nature of a rule against which there is no appeal, and in contrast with the expression 'anomy' which has just been used, we might call it *fatalistic suicide*.

(Durkheim, 1951, p. 276)

Now if Douglas's treatment of Durkheim's work is dogmatic, the recent work by Steve Taylor, *Durkheim and the Study of Suicide* (1982), is exemplary. He uses a 'realist' epistemology to critique, reformulate and make use of Durkheim's work, and argues that any sociological explanation must take account of both social meanings and other levels of social reality (Taylor, 1982, p. 163). He identifies four major kinds of suicide – Submission, Thanation, Appeal and Sacrifice. The first of these is related to fatalism.

Submissive suicide . . . is produced by *revelation*: all is now known, the individual's existence has been completely demystified and drained of possibility. The world of the submissive is one of constricting horizons, of closed doors, blind alleys and cul-de-sacs. . . . The apparent prevalence of submissive suicide suggests that Durkheim, possibly because of the implications for his own theory, underestimated the importance of fatalism in the causation of suicide.

(Taylor, 1982, p. 172)

Aside from the intrinsic merit of this reworking of *Suicide*, Taylor's arguments are important in that they suggest that fatalism is not simply of historical interest but very relevant for the explanation of certain contemporary kinds of suicide.

In a different context David Lockwood (1982) has also drawn attention to Durkheim's concept of 'fatalism', which he argues can be used to make sense of somewhat neglected aspects of the relationship between ideology and the social order. He is particularly interested in the implications of Durkheim's comments on the connection between fatalistic suicide and 'excessive physical or moral despotism', thereby calling into question Douglas's glib reduction of 'fatalism' to an effect of 'legitimate discipline'. Lockwood suggests that an examination of 'moral despotism' can help us to specify two different, albeit complementary, ways that people come to accept the extant social arrangements as the only possible ones. The first of these, 'conditional fatalism', is present if individuals experience distressing social conditions

as unavoidable 'facts of life', privations that are due to anonymous forces over which one has no control. [The second] refers to some aspect of the collective conscience which has the capacity to make individuals accept their life situations as unquestionable because any alternative disposition is, by virtue of the beliefs they hold, unthinkable.

(Lockwood, 1982, pp. 103–4)

Fatalism is likely in those societies where the role of religion in social integration is more an effect of its ritualistic elements than of the coherence and consistency of its belief systems.

Although in this article the concept of 'fatalism' is explored creatively, it seems to be abstracted out and borrowed from Durkheim primarily to strengthen certain of Weber's arguments about the soteriology of the world religions, particularly the relationship between Hinduism and caste systems. It is of some significance that in 1908 Durkheim explicitly rejected arguments very similar to Lockwood's when they were put by the moral philosopher Parodi.[3] Neverthless Parodi and Lockwood would seem to have the better case – not least because their more sophisticated formulations are not 'conspiracy theories', whatever Durkheim claimed, and because Durkheim's arguments are flawed by conservatism and functionalism. This leaves unresolved the question of the utility of the concept of fatalism and the effect its elaboration might have on Durkheim's conceptual schema. Moreover, whatever the merits of his arguments Lockwood shares with Durkheim (and Weber) a tendency to separate out and overemphasize the cognitive basis of social order. For example, he endorses Weber's view that the doctrine of *karma* has played the key role in sustaining caste inequalities. True he agrees that Weber is open to criticism for underestimating the role of material sanctions and the exercise of economic and other forms of power in maintaining the system, but he does not integrate these factors into his own analysis.[4]

Fatalism and slavery

Let us explore the complexity of these issues by a brief discussion of slavery, a phenomenon mentioned by Durkheim in his cryptic footnote on fatalism. Although the societies within which slavery has been important have been heterogeneous (as have the forms of slavery), most have used naked coercion as one of their mechanisms for controlling the slaves. In both the Ancient World and in the plantations of the American South there was an abiding danger of rebellion by significant sections of the slave population. It is likely in both cases that this stemmed not so much from some inherent human desire for freedom (Hindess and Hirst, 1975, pp. 113-21) but from contradictions within the legitimating and practical ideologies of the societies. In any concrete analysis it is necessary to theorize the relationship between the forms of physical coercion and the nature of the legitimating ideologies.

In the Ancient World problems were created by the fact that slaves were treated both as the property of their masters and as human beings with souls. Since there were no consistent racial differences between slaves and their masters and and since slaves fulfilled virtually every kind of economic and social role, it was difficult to represent them as inherently different and to represent their status as following naturally from their intrinsic qualities. This contradiction explains why there so often emerged one or other form of ritual degradation ceremony that signified difference between the two groups.

> If a slave is a property with a soul, a non–person and yet indubitably a biological human being, institutional procedures are to be expected that would degrade and undermine his humanity and so distinguish him from human beings who are not property. Corporal punishment and torture constitute one such procedure.
>
> (Finley, 1980, p. 95)[5]

These particular forms of coercion were designed to instil fear in the slave population, but they also humiliated and degraded the immediate victims. In so far as these were emotionally as well as physically wounded, many would, indeed, have *felt* themselves to be shamed and inferior. This exercise of power would have confirmed the ruling classes' own feelings of superiority and made their position of mastery seem self–evident.[6]

The social relationships between Southern Whites and Black American slaves were different but pose equally complex questions. The masters found the marked racial characteristics of their slaves a convenient reason to deny them any shared humanity. The Black field hands often showed that lack of personal initiative and mute resistance so often associated with unskilled, backbreaking labour, particularly when subjected to authoritarian supervision. Such behaviour was used by the masters as *prima facie* evidence of their brutishness. Nevertheless, many slaves did not simply accept these stereotypes or adopt them as their own self-images. They had their own traditions from which they could derive alternative ways of understanding themselves and the world, and they were also exposed to Christianity and its rhetoric about the universal brotherhood of man in Christ (Stuckey, 1971). Their masters may not have been bothered by the contradiction between statements about universal humanity on the one hand and brutalizing treatment on the other – Calvinism, after all, could be easily adapted to the circumstances – but for the slaves it was not so easily rationalized away.

While there is evidence that there were rebellions by the field hands it is also clear that the behaviour of domestic slaves was significantly different. They lived in intimate contact with their owners and developed complex multi-layered relationships with them. Some formed emotional attachments with their immediate masters and mistresses, even identifying with the goals and sympathizing with the distress of such Whites – even if this distress was caused by the behaviour of other slaves. The complexity of the master–slave relation led many Southerners, for example the sociologist Ulrich Phillips, to claim that whilst the relation was at times characterized by 'injustice, oppression, brutality and heartburning' there was also between the paternalistic master and his childlike Blacks 'gentleness, kind-hearted friendship and mutual loyalty to a degree hard for him to believe who regards the system with a theorist's eye and a partisan squint' (1918, p. 514; cited in Elkins, 1968, p. 11). I would contextualize it differently: it is likely that in the period prior to the Civil War the outlook of many slaves was fatalistic – the conditions under which they lived seemed to be 'unavoidable facts of life' and no alternative seemed conceivable.

In line with Phillips' interpretation of the master–slave relationship were the many sentimental Southern tales of Black slaves – particularly household servants – remaining loyal to their masters during the Civil War and in its immediate aftermath. D. W. Griffith's film, *The Birth of a Nation* (1915), based upon Thomas Dixon's novel *The Klansmen*, is a not untypical example. In fact the vast majority of all slaves escaped whenever and wherever this was possible. Once the power of the state was broken, once the everyday threat of violence from the White community receded, once the plantations ceased to be the one viable source of the necessities of life, what slave needed to stay? What slave wanted to stay? Under such conditions domestic servants somehow no longer experienced those feelings of loyalty that were allegedly the *source* of their bonding to their masters or mistresses. They were no less eager to leave than were the field hands. The complex articulations of repressive state apparatuses, of an economic system based upon a race's monopolization of the means of production and subsistence, of the relationships and rhythms of everyday servitude, were all disrupted. These had, in part, structured and been constitutive of the attitudes and the 'emotional economy' of those who had successfully lived as domestic slaves. They were subsequently able to constitute themselves and be constituted in other ways.[7]

The theoretical and empirical question that needs to be explored, then, is that of the complex articulations that produce as an outcome certain forms of social relationships, attitudes and 'emotional economies'. There may be a number of different levels on which to focus – the relationship between different attitudes of an individual, different aspects of an ideology, the different elements of social relationships, the articulation of apparatuses, instances, or discursive practices.[8]

'The forced division of labour' and 'forced solidarity'

Zeitlin has argued convincingly that Durkheim's central and abiding concern was

> how best to adapt the individual to 'society' and how to prepare him to fulfil his specific function in a morally dutiful manner.
> (Zeitlin, 1981, p. 280)

Yet Durkheim recognized that societies can be based upon despotism. Indeed, even in 'caste societies' all might not be well.

> Constraint is not every kind of regulation, since . . . the division of labor cannot do without regulation. Even when functions are divided according to pre-established rules, this apportioning is not necessarily the result of constraint. This is what takes place even under the rule of castes, in so far as that is founded in the nature of society . . . constraint only begins when regulation, no longer corresponding to the true nature of things, and accordingly, no longer having any basis in customs, can only be validated through force.
> (Durkheim, 1933, pp. 376–7)

By treating custom and force as mutually exclusive modes of control Durkheim avoided the question of their articulation. But social orders can exist that legitimate themselves in one way but are organized in another. Private property and inherited wealth, for example, may once have been functional for a social order but if – as in the case of complex differentiated societies allegedly based upon organic solidarity – this is no longer true, and yet they persist, this must, in part, be through force. On the other hand, it is unlikely that this is the only means of achieving stability. Ideology presumably plays some role – a point at which to return to 'fatalism'.

Douglas argues that fatalistic suicide is produced by 'legitimate discipline or control' when this is not counterbalanced by anomic forces. Lockwood focuses upon the ideological effects of 'excessive physical or moral despotism'. Both of these are acceptable but only partial interpretations of Durkheim's concept. They can be used to explore some of his substantive examples but they are not adequate for the task of unpacking, evaluating and reformulating the whole of his condensed and confused discussion. To achieve this it is necessary first to turn to the part of the footnote on fatalism that deals with sexuality.

> It is the suicide deriving . . . from futures pitilessly blocked and passions violently choked by oppressive discipline. It is the suicide of very young husbands, of the married woman who is childless.
>
> (Durkheim, 1951, p. 276)

Young men's 'passions are too vehement' (ibid., p. 275) for them to be tied down before they have achieved some general satisfaction, i.e. before they have 'sown their wild oats'. A married woman who has no children is a failure; she cannot satisfy her desires or fulfil her natural function (or social role). For Durkheim, such men and women are both suffering from a confrontation between nature and culture and are therefore to be coupled together.[9]

There is common conceptual ground between Durkheim, Douglas and Lockwood in that they define 'fatalistic suicide' in relationship to 'the ineluctable and inflexible nature of a rule against which there is no appeal'. Where they differ is in their interpretation of the nature, source and significance of such rules. A woman's inability to have a child indeed be tragic if she desires one or if motherhood is a virtually mandatory element of her social role. It is clear that there is 'no appeal' against certain kinds of infertility. In the hypothetical case concerning the young husband, however, the constraint lies in the forms of social arrangements and his relationship to them. Does he publicly subscribe to monogamy but cheat? Could he and would he simply desert his wife? Is divorce possible? Could they have a free 'rational' marriage? It is the nature of the rule and its viability that will determine its degreee of ineluctability. There may be, as Douglas argues, individuals who believe that the norms governing their activities are legitimate and yet feel unable to live up to them because they are too demanding or obtrusive; by making privacy impossible they may preclude the presence of spontaneity and exhilaration in an individual's life. If the frustrations that individuals experience are treated as 'facts of life', if the institutional arrangements are seen as immutable and natural or if people cannot even imagine any alternatives, then it will certainly *seem to be* 'a rule against which there is no appeal'. They would fit within Lockwood's understanding of 'fatalism', but would not involve questions of legitimacy. But the way that Durkheim relates many of the suicides of slaves to 'excessive physical or moral despotism' raises other issues. True, slaves were often subject to continuous surveillance and brutality but, as the slave revolts demonstrate, many of them resented the rules imposed by an illegitimate social order as much if not more than the unpalatable material conditions under which they lived. They knew that 'their yoke' was not only painful but also unjust. Since most of the time they could still do nothing to alter their circumstances suicide was a reasonable option.

In the latter part of *The Division of Labour* Durkheim argued that in his day many were still the victims of injustice, condemned to lives of low status and, often, frustration. Their work was uninteresting and poorly paid, whilst others, because of the advantages derived from inherited wealth, although less worthy, filled the more prestigious positions. Now there are a number of possible responses to this situation. An individual might fail to recognize the contradiction between the meritocratic legitimating ideology and the extant structural inequalities. The myth that the *privileged* are typically self-made men with honest fortunes and that anybody can make the journey 'from log-cabin to White House' might be accepted uncritically.[10] Some of the displaced might believe, wrongly, that their social position accurately reflected their worth. There are many ways of living within ideology. People might also feel their society to be unjust but misdiagnose the reasons for this, scapegoating certain groups or individuals – displacing their anger onto vulnerable but structurally irrelevant targets.

On the other hand, some individuals might realize that they are victims of injustice, and therefore deny the legitimacy of the social order. They might then adopt a radical political position, engage in political action to change society, or attempt to create new ones. They might emigrate to other societies that seem more just or where there is a greater potential for a new social order. Although for Durkheim such radicalism would most likely involve the demand that the egalitarian promises of the French Revolution should be realized, Durkheim's discourse acknowledges that whole categories of individuals who are denied an active role in the organizational life of social institutions could make a significant contribution to them, particularly under equal material conditions (which would require collective control of large-scale production). The meritocratic principle does not exhaust the criteria for determining whether a society is just or not. Once the citizenry has reached a minimally adequate level of culture and education, democratic control and active participation can become two sides of the same coin. But what will happen to those who pessimistically, but by no means irrationally, think it is impossible to change the system? Suicide might well be the logical consequence. Fatalistic suicide, then, would be a common phenomenon in societies with a forced division of labour. It is therefore related to forced solidarity which, from the point of view of the disaffected, means an anomic situation since they do not subscribe to, and are indeed opposed to, many of the dominant social norms.

From this discussion it is clear that Durkheim included under 'fatalistic suicide' somewhat disparate phenomena with diverse and complex social causes. His discussion of the concept of 'fatalistic suicide' was overly cryptic and his examples, though seemingly empirical, were in fact abstract, since he did not use concrete historical or social data. There is indeed a poor fit between the concept and the examples that were meant to illustrate it. This is partly owing to the inadequacy of the concept itself, but also because some elements of more useful concepts need to be teased out of these examples. In other words, Durkheim's discussion of fatalistic suicide is itself incoherent and the category itself needs to be reformulated. The overall conclusions of this discussion can be summarized as follows: *a society based upon a forced division of labour will survive in that form only in so far as it relies upon a combination of force and mechanisms of ideological obfuscation, i.e. in so far as it creates a 'forced solidarity'; thus fatalism hides anomie under conditions of forced solidarity.*

Conclusion

Douglas showed how fatalism could be related to Durkheim's three other suicidogenetic social currents. He also demonstrated that Durkheim's conceptual schema was tautological and that the four kinds of social currents functioned as one of the conceptual links in his spurious arguments. Once he had demolished Durkheim's pretensions to an empirically grounded, testable theory, Douglas simply rejected *Suicide* in its entirety. A less dogmatic and more constructive approach is to assess the coherence of the theory by analysing its different elements, rejecting some, retaining others, making up deficiencies where necessary and then reformulating it. In the case of social currents it might be asked what kind of phenomena are they and what kind of events are they meant to explain?

Durkheim used the concept of social currents in a vitalist manner. In his view the social is an irreduceable essence, a phenomenal level, a distinctive and continuous realm, which constitutes the subject matter of sociology. This can be identified with the 'horde', and as readily with social currents. This actually produces a superficial coherence in his conceptual schema but also, as shown in Chapter 2, makes it vulnerable to penetration by the transposed concepts of positions that he had elsewhere explicitly rejected – Bergsonian mysticism for example (Durkheim, 1951, p. 320). On the other hand, my earlier discussion of Durkheim's analysis of charismatic phenomena and of his relationship to post-structuralism shows how dynamic his representation of social reality could be.

Douglas improved upon Durkheim's discussion of social currents because he rendered it more formally symmetrical. But this is only the first phase in a complex task because the phenomena interpreted as expressing, registering or produced by the movement of social currents are heterogeneous and often complex. For example, anomie refers primarily to a state of the social system, and egoism and altruism primarily to the orientations of actors. Fatalism relates to disparate phenomena and requires, for its exploration, reference to a range of different types of structures. The concept of 'social current' is not relevant in this context (although elsewhere it can be used to communicate some of the dynamism of social life) and the main task to be confronted in reformulating *Suicide* is the exploration of the nature of and relationships between these different types of structures. We begin this task in the next chapter.

Notes

1 Since there are many surveys of the sociological writings on suicide and particularly on Durkheim's analysis (Douglas, 1967; Giddens, 1971c; Pope, 1976; Taylor, 1982; etc. etc.), there is little point in duplicating this work and/or becoming involved in the minutiae of the disagreements between these commentators, for example Taylor and Pope.

2 The word 'objectivation', found in Berger and Pullberg (1966), has

been used quite deliberately since Nisbet's comments are so compatible with such a view of the nature of language and of social life. Lichtman (1971) and Geras (1971) have both criticized such analyses of social life and Caughie (1981) has edited a collection of texts critical of the view that texts can be understood as the expresssion of authorial intention.

3 Parodi had taken the Enlightenment position that there is an intimate connection between religion and despotism, but Durkheim dismissed the idea that the 'universal inequalities of caste and class . . . could have become established and been maintained by artifice and ruse' (Pickering, 1979, p. 71). The kind of inequalities that were found in caste societies were rational because they accurately reflected differences in the value of various activities. They were functional, 'founded in the nature of things' and would have been supported by the rational and perspicacious members of the societies.

Parodi replied that while members of a caste society might accept its inequalities they would only do this

> in so far as the members were governed by the practice of tradition or custom – in so far as they would not wonder about the wherefore of the institutions they accept. The existing order of things would seem natural rather than rational and in actual fact the problem would not even occur to them. . . . One can only conclude, it seems to me, that the rational need does not exist, or that it is entirely devoid of force, whether because, in certain cases, habit deadens or smothers it, or because in other cases, habit deceives and mystifies it.
>
> (Pickering, 1979, pp. 73–4)

4 Indeed early in his article, Lockwood denies the relevance of the 'coercion theory' of social order for understanding societies of any size or complexity, and instead looks to ideological factors. This is a false dichotomy. In recent years there has developed a corpus of Marxist writing, grounded in Gramsci's writings, which has acknowledged the complexity and importance of ideology and has attempted to theorize the articulation of the ideological with other elements of the social system (Gramsci, 1971; Sassoon, 1982; Mouffe, 1979). Althusser's focus on the relationships between various 'instances' and 'apparatuses', whatever its inadequacies, has made it possible to think about this issue without necessarily giving primacy to the experience and consciousness of individuals or to interpersonal relations (Althusser, 1971).

5 In addition to Finley it is well worth consulting the work of Geoffrey de Ste Croix, where there is an appreciative but critical assessment of Finley's work (de Ste Croix, 1981, 1984).

6 The work of the psychologist Zimbardo is of relevance here. He demonstrated in an experiment that two groups of individuals all with psychologically normal personality profiles when assigned the roles of

prisoners and guards developed the behaviour patterns, attitudes and sets of emotions often associated with prisoners and guards – a craven individualism on the one hand and extreme authoritarianism on the other. These are often assumed to express the intrinsic personality of these groups and to explain why they became prisoners or guards (Zimbardo, 1971, 1972).

There is a complex discussion of the role of torture in political conflict, its functions and its effects on both torturers and victims in Ruthven (1978).

7 This discussion owes a great deal to Genovese (1965, 1969, 1971, 1974). Genovese has played a key role in recent debates about the nature of the old South, the relationship between the White aristocracy and the slaves, and their respective cultures. Parish (1979) provides a useful summary of these debates, which also involved, amongst others, Stampp (1956), Elkins (1968), Blassingame (1972), Fogel and Engerman (1974) and Gutman (1976).

8 Weber might have been able to develop such a position but failed to follow through his own insights. In his analysis of 'legitimate domination', he first defined power in a manner compatible with the theoretical position that we have been exploring here. He then simply dismissed this as 'sociologically amorphous' and narrowed his focus to 'domination'. This 'is the probability that a command with a given specific content will be obeyed by a given group of persons' (Weber, 1978, vol. 1, p. 53). He suggested that there are a number of reasons why people might obey such commands – opportunistically or for material self-interest; weakness, helplessness and fear; and out of a sense of duty. Again, he then focused only on the latter, simply assuming that it is the 'essential' motive within a society. The dutiful, by definition, believe in the 'legitimacy' of the 'domination' to which they are subjected. Logically there are three different grounds for claiming and conceding legitimacy – rational, traditional and charismatic.

> 'Obedience' will be taken to mean that the action of the person obeying follows in essentials such a course that the content of the command may be taken to have become the basis of action for its own sake.
>
> (Weber, 1978, vol. 1, pp. 212–15)

Here we find Weber providing a potentially complex set of categories for analysing stable social systems but wasting its potential because of an unargued conservative belief that any society that persists does so because its institutions can be assumed to express the *will* of its members.

9 For a detailed analysis of Durkheim's understanding of the nature and social positioning of women see Gane (1983a).

10 Warner (1962) and Hofstadter (1967) show how in the case of Lincoln this myth was constructed. More generally as Marx argued much 'primitive accumulation' was the result of various forms of 'force and fraud' (Marx, 1965; see also Pearce, 1976).

7   A reformulation of Durkheim's Suicide

Introduction

In this chapter I reconsider the four major forms of suicide and the major themes implicit in Durkheim's text, *Suicide*, in order to generate a new set of concepts. *Suicide* is not only an exploration of social pathology but also a resource for developing a sophisticated account of the relationship between certain kinds of rational individuals and certain kinds of rational social orders. Durkheim himself believed that his work had far broader implications than merely the provision of an aetiology of suicide.

> There will even emerge from our study some suggestions concerning the causes of the general maladjustment being undergone by European societies and concerning remedies which may relieve it.
>
> (Durkheim, 1951, p. 37)

Durkheim's specification of the determinants of suicide and the evidence he used, however, have little credibility. For Durkheim, the cause of any social fact is always another social fact and the same kind of social fact is always the effect of an identical cause – 'since there are different causes of suicide, different suicidogenetic impulses, there must be different kinds of suicide . . . defined in terms of different causes' (Keat and Urry, 1975, p. 85). In contrast, realists seek to discover underlying structures that may then explain what can be observed:

> while Durkheim links together a single cause and a single effect, the realist argues that *any such effect results from the complex interrelations between mechanisms, structures and background conditions*.
>
> (Keat and Urry, 1975, p. 85)

In other words, any particular suicidal act will be the combined effect of a complex of causal chains. It is a register of the mediated effects of the 'social'. Many suicides happen because one or more of the conditions of existence of a particular kind of social subject is not secured. There are a variety of forms of subjectivity – different kinds and degrees of rationality, responsibility, spontaneity, etc. – each of which has complex foundations. By focusing on the structural level one can best explore how such subjectivities are constituted. *Suicide* itself is like a photographic negative: its text is more illuminating when its implicit elements are highlighted and brought to the foreground. When this has been done it can then be used, in conjunction with other of his texts, to investigate aspects of one personality/society configuration – the spontaneous, active, rational, socially constructive actor in a democratic egalitarian socialist society.

Fatalism and anomie

Durkheim's discussion of fatalism is confused and incoherent, yet by reading it aporetically it became clear that his discourse was, in part, *a trace of elements of the concept of 'the forced division of labour' and an effect of the process of its suppression.* This is not to deny that there is a sense in which it can in part be counterposed to the concept of anomie. If the lives of individuals are totally controlled – regulated by detailed abstract rules or supervised by the continuous critical gaze of another – then there will be no space for them intelligently to interpret their social role in a way that will fulfil their own needs as well as society's.[1] *This* suicidogenetic situation is the opposite of anomie. Anomic suicide 'results from man's activity lacking regulation and his consequent sufferings' (Durkheim, 1951, p. 258). The desires of human beings are potentially insatiable so must be subject to normative constraint. Members of the different social strata must accept society's right to determine the resources allocated to them and then to ensure that these are used responsibly by using the power of society to discipline the passions. In a rapidly changing world with continuous changes in people's fortunes a coherent but flexible normative system is necessary.

There is little doubt that Durkheim's exploration of anomie in *Suicide* is extraordinarily complex and fruitful. On the other hand, if one compares the discussion of it in *The Division of Labour in Society* there are interesting differences. According to the earlier work there is an anomic division of labour if the social relations within an enterprise or between social groups lack normative regulation; or if individuals are neither clear about nor committed to these regulative rules or to the fulfilment of their social role. One way of developing the commitment of individuals is to appeal to their reason by making clear to them the goals of the enterprise in which they are involved and by showing them their contribution to it. It is, of course, only one of the 'pathological forms of the division of labour'. The other, the 'forced division of labour', suggests that such 'pathology' can only be overcome if this normative order is a rational one, so that individuals can rationally commit themselves to it. In this earlier view the subject is potentially a rational subject, one who transcends the immediate social environment, in contrast to the socially determined, 'behaviourist' subject of *Suicide*.[2] Both views, however, have strengths, and later will be drawn upon to explore the kind of social relations that could produce and be energetically sustained by rational, active and creative subjects. But first let us return to *Suicide*, where some of the issues formerly raised under the rubric of 'the forced division of labour' are subsumed in a truncated form under 'anomie'.

A genuine regimen exists . . . which fixes with relative precision the maximum degree of ease of living to which each social class may legitimately aspire. . . . This relative limitation and the moderation it involves make men contented with their lot while stimulating them moderately to improve it.

But it would be of little use for everyone to recognize the justice of the hierarchy of functions established by public opinion, if he did not also consider the distribution of these functions just. . . . Once it regarded birth as the almost exclusive principle of social classification; today it recognizes no other inherent inequality than heredity, fortune and merit.

Some, to be sure, have thought this moral pressure would become unnecessary if man's economic circumstances were no longer determined by heredity. If inheritance were abolished, the argument runs, if everyone began life with equal resources and if the competitive struggle were fought out on a basis of perfect equality, no one could think its results unjust. . . .

Truly the nearer this ideal equality were approached, the less social restraint will be necessary. But it is only a matter of degree. One sort of heredity will always exist, that of natural talent. . . . A moral discipline will therefore still be required to

make those less favoured by nature accept the lesser advantages
which they owe to the chance of birth.

(Durkheim, 1951, pp. 249–51)

Durkheim himself had believed (and continued to believe) that
beneficial effects would follow 'if inheritance were abolished'.
Although in his later years he was somewhat equivocal,
nevertheless in *Professional Ethics and Civic Morals* he still argued
that contracts cannot be truly just if the contracting parties have
radically unequal material circumstances. In this passage in *Suicide*
he does not so much refute his own earlier argument as so qualify
it that the 'abolition of inherited wealth' seems a marginal issue.
Indeed, he shifted the whole terrain of the argument by
introducing something of a 'red herring' – the problems of
'persuading a naturally talented elite to submit to an absolutely
egalitarian society' – a proposal that neither Durkheim nor, for
example, Marx, had made, at least when discussing socialism,
although communism was a different matter (see Chapter 8). He
thus avoided the problem of the forms of social relationships that
would make a society and a meritocratic *conscience collective*
structurally congruent.

However, by stating that the regulative power in society must
'be obeyed through respect not fear' (ibid., p. 252), Durkheim
acknowledged that there are a number of different ways in which
social stability may be achieved. If order is the effect of 'custom
and force' (ibid., p. 251) or 'force or fraud', then the regulative
authority is not worthy of obedience. In these same pages he
defines the 'good citizen' in such a way that he is able to avoid
these issues. This citizen will limit his aspirations because 'he
respects regulations and is docile to collective authority, that is has
a wholesome moral constitution, he feels that it is well not to ask
more' (ibid., p. 25). *Thus a rather abstract general problem – how to
achieve a stable social order in any society – displaces the anterior question
of whether all societies have general characteristics and what these might
be and of exploring the nature of the different kinds of social order that do
or can exist and of determining upon what their stability depends.* His
conservatism is untheorized, and expressed in a commitment to
order for its own sake, thereby pre-empting a more complex
development of his ideas.

Reintroducing the issues posed by the concept of the 'forced
division of labour' allows the reformulation of these arguments. If
we assume that the social order is just and democratic and that
there is an equality of condition, then it will be reasonable for

individuals to limit their expectations to those that can be satisfied by the resources made available to them. Some might argue that it is only the capitalist order that incites individuals to endless consumption, greed, etc. Thus the individual's inherent goodness is distorted by the negative effects of social institutions. Durkheim certainly believed that employers

> are probably most stricken by the state of anomy. The enormous [suicide] rate of those with independent means (720 per million) evidently shows that the possessors of most comfort suffer most. Everything that enforces subordination attenuates the effects of this state. At least the horizon of the lower classes is limited by those above them, and for this same reason their desires are more modest. Those who have only empty space above them are almost mentally lost in it, if no force restrains them.
>
> (Durkheim, 1951, p. 257)

Thus one perfectly plausible explanation of the high suicide rate of such individuals is that their economic activity is oriented to the pursuit of profit ever-renewed and ever expanding:

> industry, instead of being still regarded as a means to an end, transcending itself, has become the supreme end of individuals and societies alike. Thereupon the appetites thus excited have become freed of any limiting authority.
>
> (Durkheim, 1951, p. 255)[3]

This endless pursuit of money continually excites the passions: 'From top to bottom of the ladder, greed is aroused. . . . Nothing can calm it, since its goal is far beyond all it can attain' (ibid., p. 256). But if this is a generalized criticism of capitalism, it is for *stimulating* the appetites and passions not for creating them. All human beings in all societies are subject to these and they have their own inherent tendency to excess.

As we can see, at times, when writing about the appetites of working-class people, Durkheim suggested a fundamental opposition between their satisfaction and the possibility of normal social relations. Social order requires their repression. Nevertheless, the term 'appetites and passions' communicates the ambiguous nature of the emotions, since in themselves they are neither good nor bad. The same emotion can be the source of both virtue and vice. Indeed, our appetites must be to some extent looked after in order for us to survive. We are, after all, both biological entities rooted in the material world and social beings with complex needs. Each of our passions must be allowed some satisfaction, but in a controlled way. In an anomic situation the suicidal individual suffers because

> Unregulated emotions are adjusted neither to one another nor to the conditions they are supposed to meet; they must therefore conflict with each other most painfully.
>
> (Durkheim, 1951, p. 285)

Elsewhere, in *Moral Education*, Durkheim spelt out the consequences of such a condition, particularly the debilitating effects of unlimited excess.

> A need, a desire freed of all restraints, and all rules, no longer geared to some determinate objective, and through this same connection limited and contained, can be nothing but a source of constant anguish for the person experiencing.
>
> (Durkheim, 1961, p. 40)

In this telling passage we are given not only a picture of the destructured personality but also one of a healthy personality, which he believed was created by discipline (ibid., p. 48).[4]

In many ways *Moral Education* is one of the most conservative of Durkheim's works. Not only did he concentrate on the adjustment of the individual to society, but, as in much of *Suicide*, his ideal human being seems to have been somebody so moderate that they would have been decidedly dull, unlikely to take intellectual or emotional risks. Yet , as we have just seen, he believed that discipline helps create a 'reflective consciousness', which by definition must allow the individual to transcend his or her immediate social environment. Although conformity in some things is necessary,

> . . . it does not follow from a belief in the need for discipline that discipline must involve blind and slavish obedience.
>
> (Durkheim, 1961, p. 52)

Durkheim believed in a great deal of conformity, but that everything else – including critical thinking – should be in moderation. He was so fearful of the dangers of the working class positing and pursuing disruptive demands that he saw their acquiescence to the *status quo* as an unqualified good. He failed to develop the concepts to explore adequately the different ways of guaranteeing conformity. He did not explain how working-class people could alone or collectively develop and exercise their 'reflective individual will', nor was he willing to confront the likely consequences if they did. Nevertheless his concepts can be reworked so that these issues can be examined.

He has described some of the conditions of existence of any active, rational human subject. After all, even the revolutionary is subject to the play of appetites and passions, and he or she cannot be effective unless these are controlled (in part through a relationship with a real or symbolic community) and they are compatible with the requirements of a politically committed life. The demand 'for an equilibrium' between the various needs and desires leave open the question of their overall intensity and which particular configuration is apposite. There is nothing in Durkheim's concepts that prescribes stolidity; they merely *receive* such an inflection because of his own temerity. Moreover, Durkheim is not simply describing the genesis of personality, rationality, etc., but also their reproduction. Educational disciplines and the later disciplines of everyday life are 'constitutive'. The involvement in collective social actions produces the emotional energy needed for constructive social action. It was for this reason that Durkheim conceived of religion as a set of representations of 'collective realities *and* a set of rites which arose

> in the midst of the assembled groups and which are destined to excite, maintain or recreate certain mental states in these groups.
>
> (Durkheim, 1976, p. 10)

An individual's capacity to be rational is intimately linked with his sociality and therefore

> necessarily presupposes a society which he expresses and serves. If this dissolves, if we no longer feel it in existence and active about and above us, whatever is social in us is deprived of all objective foundation. All that remains is an artificial combination of illusory images, a phantasmagoria, vanishing at the least reflection: that is, nothing which can be a goal for our action.
>
> (Durkheim, 1951, p. 213)

This consideration of anomie and fatalism is suggestive of what may be some of the conditions of existence of a rational human subject within at least one kind of arguably rational society. These have been derived from a concern with the nature of social rules and the actor's relationship to them, and with the role of social discipline in the constitution and reconstitution of the rational subject. A clear and reasonable normative structure and meaningful social rituals are required to create contexts both where internal emotive commitments develop to social norms and where external social obligations pattern action in predictable ways. Most adults are responsible for the well-being of at least some other people and, inevitably, plan their own actions in the anticipation that others will act in a relatively predictable way. The binding nature of the contract came about in part because of this:

I may engage to sell or lend to you a certain object, and on such terms that once the undertaking is made I have no longer the right or means to break it. If I do this, I arouse in you by this very action a state of mind equally decided and in line with the certainty you are justified in assuming about my action. . . . You may make a certain decision or decide on a certain sale or purchase, by reason of this legitimate certainty. If I then suddenly withdraw and deprive you of this certainty. . . . I bring about a change in your established position and I render any transactions you may have engaged in on the good faith of the given word, ineffectual.

(Durkheim, 1957, p. 192)

Specific obligations, too, concretely constitute individuals within relationships as certain kinds of people. It is, for example, the sum total of specific rights and duties within the family that determines the modes of relationships within it, the affect with which it is invested and its moral foundations (Durkheim, 1933, p. 419). Such normative systems, however, should not be overwhelming; they should leave the individual some space to improvise, to be questioning, and even to initiate change.

Furthermore, on occasion, Durkheim recognized that the balance between emotions that he sought could occur on a more collective level. In one discussion of the workings of 'occupational corporations' he recognized that, within it, emotions could be distributed amongst the different individuals and interest groups and temporarily become their exclusive property, thus creating an emotional balance within the group:

> Whenever excited appetites tended to exceed all limits, the corporation would have to decide the share that should equitably revert to each of the co-operative parts. . . . By forcing the strongest to use their strength with moderation, by preventing the weakest from endlessly multiplying their protests, by recalling both to the sense of their reciprocal duties and to the general interest, and by regulating production in certain cases so that it does not degenerate into a morbid fever, it would moderate one set of passions by another, and permit their appeasement by assigning them limits.
>
> (Durkheim, 1951, p. 383)

In this discussion of the 'appetites and passions' Durkheim advocates a low-energy stasis, but, once again, there is no reason why the same concepts should not be used to understand and create far more dynamic environments. Indeed, it is in relationship to the dynamic movement of emotions within collectivities that the term 'social currents' is an apposite metaphor.

> all sorts of currents come, go, circulate everywhere, cross and mingle in a thousand different ways, and just because they are constantly mobile they are never crystallized in an objective form. Today, a breath of sadness and discouragement descends on society; tomorrow, one of joyous confidence will uplift all hearts.
>
> (Durkheim, 1951, p. 315)

Some of these collective emotional phenomena will be examined later when discussing the the 'large group'.

Causes and occasions

The discussion of the conditions that make it possible for a social actor to be reflective might imply that Durkheim was overly rationalistic. At times his concerns certainly seem juridical and, as Edelman (1979, pp. 146–69) has argued, legal categories (particularly of continental law) are decidely Kantian. Consider Durkheim's definition of his object of analysis:

suicide is applied to all cases of death resulting directly or indirectly from a positive or negative act of the victim himself, which he knows will produce this result.

(Durkheim, 1951, p. 44)

The lawyer is similarly concerned with *mens rea* and believes that the defendant's moral or political stance is irrelevant because the law is an absolute – the focus is on establishing an *actus reus* and the defendant's guilt and responsibility. Durkheim, too believed that the subjective reasoning of the actor is irrelevant, but for other reasons.

Intent is too intimate a thing to be more than approximately interpreted by another. It even escapes self-observation. How often we mistake the true reasons for our acts! We constantly explain acts due to petty feelings or blind routine by generous passions or lofty considerations.

(Durkheim, 1951, p. 43)

We rationalize our activities; our deliberations

are often purely formal, with no object but confirmation of a resolve previously formed for reasons unknown to consciousness.

(Durkheim, 1951, p. 297)

We imagine, because we can reflect upon our conduct, that we can gain access to all that is needed to explain why on some occasion we have acted in a particular way. But, Durkheim argues,

psychical life, far from being directly cognizable has on the contrary profound depths inaccessible to ordinary perception, to which we attain only gradually by devious and complicated paths like those employed by the science of the external world.

(Durkheim, 1951, p. 311)

Jacobs (1967) has argued that a study of the 'reasoning processes' of suicides will show that these are relatively uniform within the 'same cultural environment' and that they *explain* the suicidal act. They may be uniform but there is something of a problem in that 'religious dogma, specifically intended to prevent suicide can, with the proper "rationalization", serve to encourage suicide' (Jacobs, 1967; reprinted in Giddens, 1971, p. 347). This suggests that some other processes are also at work – those determining the emotional condition of the individual, making them both receptive to thoughts of suicide and willing to engage in 'rationalization'.

Thus one implication of Durkheim's argument is that, whilst individuals might be able to describe the circumstances that made them feel suicidal, they would be unlikely to be able to say why, on that occasion, these feelings were so overwhelming. If, for example, a bachelor has been jilted a number of times but only attempts suicide on the third occasion, we might ask why only then? It might be assumed that it was simply because the misery was cumulative and had eventually overwhelmed him – his cup runneth over! However, if the suicide attempt, though unsuccessful, was genuine and when subsequently jilted again he accepted this without too much difficulty, then his earlier vulnerability may have been less a function of the number of rebuffs that he suffered than an effect of the social relationships in which he was imbricated. This, admittedly hypothetical, example illustrates the potentially complex implications of Durkheim's statement that

> The incidents of private life which seem the direct inspiration of suicide and are considered the determining causes are in reality only incidental causes. The individual yields to the slightest shock of circumstances because the state of society has made him a ready prey to suicide.
>
> (Durkheim, 1951, p. 215)

Durkheim's scientism, however, led him to conclude that for a scientific explanation of the incident the actor's understanding of his own motives is not merely inadequate but also irrelevant. True he cites the work of Brierre de Boismont, who developed a morphological classification of suicides based upon an examination and summary of 1,328 cases where the suicide had left letters or other records, but only to dismiss it:

> first this summary is much too brief. Then the patient's revelations of his condition are usually insufficient, if not suspect. He is only too apt to be mistaken concerning himself and the state of his feelings . . . besides being insufficiently objective, these observations cover too few facts to permit definite conclusions . . . proper observations are next to impossible.
>
> (Durkheim, 1951, p. 146)

Valid as these comments might be, they do not provide support for the view that it is possible and desirable to understand suicidal acts without reference to the actor's subjective experiences and motives – what counts in a particular culture as an adequate and relevant motive for suicide depends upon its specific 'vocabulary of motives' (Mills, 1940; Blum and McHugh, 1971).

This is a sociological position and differs from the psychologism of, for example, Stengel (1973). He too distinguishes between 'motives and causes' but, whilst his analysis of the psychodynamics of suicide is instructive, he works with a somewhat correlative concept of the relationship between social structures and individual action. He therefore does not develop a causal analysis specifying what structures and mechanisms, under what conditions, affect (and constitute) the individual – the Oedipal triangle, for example, is itself *a set of social relationships* (Lévi-Strauss, 1969, pp. 490–1).

Nevertheless, the issue is not whether one is concerned with structural *or* subjective/psychological factors but how to theorize the relationship between socio-structural factors and the ways in which individuals are socially constituted and how motives and meanings are socially provided. There is an additional *empirical problem* of establishing quite what the subject is going through/what is happening to the subject – and some kind of subjectivist methodology seems an indispensable aid in discovering this. Thus, whilst both Benton (1977) and Keat and Urry (1975) wish to argue that motives are causes, they have no doubt that they play a role both in human action and in its explanation.[5]

Durkheim, in fact, begrudgingly admits elsewhere that the experience of misfortune and disappointment might sometimes be the major reason for suicide:

> if it really sometimes occurs that the victim's personal situation is the effective cause of his resolve, such cases are very rare indeed and accordingly cannot explain the social suicide rate.
>
> (Durkheim, 1951, p. 298)

Durkheim's argument is fallacious. The dilemma is not whether to opt for an individualistic or a sociological explanation but rather how one integrates the different modes of sociality in the explanation of this, or any other, social act. To analyse a social act it is necessary to establish the nature of the subjective orientation of actors, the vocabulary of motives and modes of reasoning that are current within their society, the major forms of social relationships and their mode of articulation with the major, particularly the hegemonic, ideologies (see Benton, 1977, p. 127).

Despite his strictures about the unreliability of common sense, 'pre-conceptions', 'rationalizations', etc., Durkheim acknowledged unique features of the human subject when he argued *contra* Tarde that human behaviour depends upon an active interpretive and reflective consciousness.

> Our way of conforming to the morals or manners of our country has nothing in common, therefore, with the mechanical ape-like repetition causing us to reproduce emotions which we witness. Between the two ways of acting, is all the difference between reasonable, deliberate behavior and automatic reflex. The former has motives even when not expressed in implicit judgements. The latter has not; it results directly from the mere sight of an act, with no other mental intermediary.
>
> (Durkheim, 1951, pp. 127–8)[6]

It would then be necessary to integrate this conceptualization of the nature of human subjectivity with an analysis of the ways that social relationships constitute individuals with different kinds of emotional economies. It is this latter set of issues that will now be addressed.

Egoism and altruism

Anomie and fatalism primarily concern the coherence, relevance and flexibility of the normative system and its relationship to the rhythms of everyday activity, the social space available to social actors, and their capacity to assess the legitimacy of the social order to which they are subject. 'Egoism' and 'altruism' concern subjective orientations more, for in much of his work Durkheim does not so much dismiss subjective motives as redefine their meaning and significance, albeit crudely but productively, in terms of altruism and egoism. These are to be found in all societies.

> No moral idea exists which does not combine, in proportions varying with the society involved, egoism, altruism and a certain anomy. For social life assumes both that the individual has a certain personality, that he is ready to surrender it if the community requires, and finally, that he is to a certain degree sensitive to ideas of progress. This is why there is no people among whom these three currents of opinion do not co-exist,

bending men's inclinations in three different and even opposing directions. Where they offset one another, the moral agent is in a state of equilibrium which shelters him against any thought of suicide. But let one of them exceed a certain strength to the detriment of others, and as it becomes individualized, it also becomes suicidogenetic, for the reasons assigned.

(Durkheim, 1951, p. 321)

Simple egoism is not unlike Freud's primary narcissism (Laplanche and Pontalis, 1973, pp. 337–8) – 'Its object is the pleasure of the agent' (Durkheim, 1961, p. 208). It is ever-present as a permanent regressive tendency in even the most socialized of human beings. Individualism is not the same as this simple egoism and, indeed, has different roots. In order to be a member of even the most primitive society we must develop states of consciousness that 'turn us towards ends that we hold in common with other men; it is through them and them alone that we can communicate with others' (Durkheim, 1951, pp. 127–8).

The ability to communicate is intimately linked with the development of a reflective consciousness and of the ability to control ourselves. Subsequently the division of labour differentiates these already reflective people; it individualizes them with a concomitant public valorization of the individual. In many ways this has been historically progressive, producing creative energetic societies (see 'Individualism and the Intellectuals' in Bellah, 1973). But

When morality consists primarily in giving one a very high idea of one's self, certain combinations of circumstances readily suffice to make man unable to perceive anything above himself. Individualism is, of course, not necessarily egoism, but it comes close to it; the one cannot be stimulated without the other being enlarged.

(Durkheim, 1951, p. 364)

Individualism and egoism are intimately related. There is the continuous danger of a slippage from the first to the second. This may not be a total regression but the individual may become detached from group life, self-involved and selfish (ibid., p. 209). Such a narcissistic absorption in his thoughts and feelings may mean that

The individual no longer cares to live because he no longer

cares enough for the only medium which attaches him to reality, that is to say for society. Having too keen a feeling for himself and his own value, he wishes to be his own goal, and, as such an objective cannot satisfy him, drags out languidly and indifferently an existence which henceforth seems meaningless to him.

(Durkheim, 1951, p. 356)

Under such conditions the individual's feelings and fortunes become the touchstone of reality and its sole measure. When he or she feels depressed the world *is* a depressing place. The boundary between internal experience and external, independent reality has been erased. The same set of events usually do not affect everybody in the same way; they may be matters of sorrow, indifference or jubilation for different people. A setback for oneself may not have negative consequences for someone else whom one loves, for example a child. Their good fortune may occur independently of ours. Similarly the progress of some cause in which one believes, perhaps a religious or political movement, will be determined by many other factors than one's own activities. If we have such external involvements, then even our most harrowing experience will no longer seem so overwhelming, nor will it colour all of reality. People

> cling to life more resolutely when they belong to a group they love, so as not to betray interests they put before their own. The bond that unites them with the common cause attached them to life and the lofty goal they envisage prevents their feeling personal problems as deeply. There is, in short, in a cohesive and animated society, a constant interchange of ideas and feelings from all to each and to all, something like a mutual moral support, which instead of throwing the individual on his own resources, leads him to share in the collective energy and supports his own when exhausted.
>
> (Durkheim, 1951, pp. 209–10)

An altruistic orientation, sustained by participation in an egalitarian collective life, can act as a prophylactic.

Nowhere does Durkheim explore in more depth the positive and indeed constitutive effect of the social than in *The Elementary Forms of the Religious Life*. Echoing Pascal, he pointed out that participation in social rituals often calls forth the beliefs and emotions that the rituals supposedly express – experiences may be produced, emotions invoked and explanations provided by involvement in religious activity (Durkheim, 1976, p. 408).[7] And, more generally,

> When a society is going through circumstances which sadden, perplex or irritate it, it exercises a pressure over its members to make them bear witness, by significant acts, to their sorrow, perplexity or anger. It imposes upon them the duty of weeping, groaning or inflicting wounds upon themselves or others, for these collective manifestations and the moral communion which they show and strengthen, restore to the group the energy which circumstances threaten to take away from it, and thus they enable it to become settled. This is the experience which men interpret when they imagine that outside them there are evil beings whose hostility, whether constitutional or temporary, can be appeased only by human suffering. These beings are nothing other than collective states objectified; they are sociality itself seen under one of its aspects.
>
> (Durkheim, 1976, p. 412)

If one disregards his angelicism, Durkheim presents here a powerful argument as to how our experiences are the effects of an interaction between social forces and our (socially constituted) individual sensibilities. Moreover, the worship of a god, the fear of evil, the belief in an immortal soul, are all 'real', collectively produced phenomena that are misrecognized. Religious rites usually energize people in a socially constructive way, and through 'catharsis' may produce a measured relationship between a person's feelings and the tasks they confront in their lives (Aristotle, 1920).

Yet, as Durkheim also makes clear, without the balancing force of egoism, individuation would not occur and the individual would not survive. Altruism has its own dangers. If there is nothing to act as a countervailing power to the collectivity's demand that its members subordinate themselves to its rhythms, then they will be swamped. Their lives will be so ordered by its dictates that they will neglect their own needs and be out of touch with their feelings, and then their emotions will be both unsatisfied and undirected. This of itself can disorient the individual and produce a volatile situation. Consider the typical private soldier, whose first quality

is a sort of impersonality . . . in the regular exercise of his profession, discipline requires him to obey without question and sometimes without understanding. For this an intellectual abnegation hardly consistent with individualism is required. He must have but a weak tie binding him to his individuality to obey external impulsion so docilely.

(Durkheim, 1951, p. 234)

the soldier kills himself at the least disappointment, for the most futile reasons, for a refusal of leave, a reprimand, an unjust punishment, a delay in promotion, a question of honor, a flush of momentary jealousy, or even simply because other suicides have occurred before his eyes or to his knowledge.

(Durkheim, 1951, p. 239)

Indeed, if he is a a member of an elite corps, *its* well-being and the question of *its* honour may become more important than his own survival, and thus the sacrifice of himself may seem desirable or a (collectively enforced) duty.

For society thus to be able to compel some of its members to kill themselves, the individual personality can have little value. For as soon as the latter begins to form, the right to existence is first conceded to it or is at least only suspended in such circumstances as war. For the individual to occupy so little place in the collective life he must be almost completely absorbed in the group and the latter accordingly very highly integrated.

(Durkheim, 1951, pp. 220–1)

Both egoism and altruism must be construed, in part, in terms of duties to oneself and to others. Furthermore, as Durkheim argued in *Professional Ethics and Civic Morals*, egoism and altruism and the related sets of obligations are themselves the effects of the organizational features of society. Each will have a greater or lesser significance according to the degree of effective authority with which such duties are invested (Durkheim, 1957, pp. 113–20). At any particular time it is the relationship between secondary associations and the state, a relationship itself dependent upon the given social conditions (i.e. war or peace, etc.), that helps determine the orientations of individuals and their significance.

The argument can be summarized as suggesting that elements of both egoism and altruism and their related conditions of existence are necessary for a society of rational, active, social subjects. In order to avoid both anomie and fatalism it is necessary to create a clear and coherent normative system with some flexibility to allow for individual interpretation and a social space for the individual to 'set up an environment of his own in the shelter of which he may develop his own nature and form a physiognomy that is his exclusively' (Durkheim, 1951, p. 221).

A Durkheimian perspective on the 'large group'

The argument so far has been primarily theoretical. An empirical dimension is added by Turquet's recent research on 'Threats to identity in the large group' (1975). The 'large group' comprises forty to eighty people who have come together to learn about group behaviour by studying their own reactions to this somewhat unusual setting. Two or more of its members are consultants and have a different relationship to the group, the exact nature of which is not articulated to its other members. The group meets six to twelve times and the members' accounts of their subjective experience are used as empirical evidence of the group processes. Turquet argues that one can specify three different ways in which individuals relate to the group. A 'singleton' is a potential participant who, as yet, has made no relationship with it. To move from this position to some form of participation is not easy and some, indeed, never actually do so. One possible alternative is for the individual to immerse himself or herself in the group to the point where the demands of group membership block out the individual's independent self-definition and sense of one's own needs, to become a 'membership individual' (MI). Another is to become an 'individual member' (IM), achieving a precarious equilibrium 'as between personal needs and roles and group needs and roles', to be a participant with some independent sense of self, some individuality. In this anonymous 'society' 'singletons', i.e. initially everybody except perhaps the consultants, face the problem of what to do:

> Given the size of the large group, the singleton has this special problem how to put his mark on the situation, to become and remain an I.M. but at the same time to resist the large group's attempts at putting its own particular stamp on him by turning him into an M.I. Nor is this problem made easier by the distinctive tone of the large group, especially compared with

the very small family group, where the singleton has had his training and where by primary experience he is rooted.

(Turquet, 1975, p. 95)

It is also unsafe to remain a 'singleton' since this, as Foulkes argues, puts the personality at risk – the individual may regress to a narcissistic passivity with an objectifying sadistic stance towards others (Foulkes, 1975, p. 54). Since none of these states is stable and movement between them is perilous, individuals are vulnerable to 'deskilling', 'disarroy' and alienation. There is no need to detail these arguments in full; let us merely note that this kind of research has usefully investigated some of the conditions of existence of adult personalities.[8]

Such research on group processes can be understood as the sociological equivalent of an experiment. In so far as the 'large group' is structurally similar to social groups in society as a whole, then the events that occur and the processes, structures and mechanisms identified within it can also be assumed to occur more widely; in 'realist' terms one would be entitled to generalize from the 'closed' system to 'open' systems (Bhaskar, 1978, p. 32). In that sense sociology is similar to astronomy (and meteorology) since they also explore relationships between phenomena under uncontrollable conditions and where only some of the processes that are occurring have been and could have been investigated experimentally.

Rationalities, personalities and social orders

Nisbet (1975) and Coser (1960), from different political positions, have contributed to the orthodox view that Durkheim was a conservative. Llobera (1981a,b) agrees and believes that Durkheim and his followers collectively 'misrepresented Marx'. Zeitlin's position (1981) is more qualified in that, whilst he accepts that some of Durkheim's thought is complex and fruitful, he believes that its potential is vitiated by a concern with adapting the 'individual to society'. Whilst both Lukes (1975) and Hunt (1978) acknowledge that his work contained socialistic elements, they imply that these are of little intrinsic interest or importance. For Pels (1984) on the other hand whatever Durkheim's protestations about the scientific nature of sociology, much of his work showed him to be little more than a 'fellow traveller' of socialism. The position argued in this chapter, whilst not absolutely opposed to these views, is somewhat different and more akin to that of Gane (1984), Filloux (1971, 1977) and Lacroix (1978), namely, that throughout his career Durkheim utilized and developed essentially valid socialistic concepts and drew upon socialist ideals but at the same time truncated their development. In much of his work the implications of his more radical concepts were unrealized but, although they were suppressed, this act of suppression produced aporias in his texts, traces of the suppressed concepts and of the act of suppression but in a displaced and condensed form – as in the case of the relationship between 'fatalistic suicide' and the 'forced division of labour'.

A consideration of this relationship has helped me to reread *Suicide* and thereby tentatively to generate some arguably useful concepts. Thus I have suggested that a dynamic differentiated socialist society would need to be well-organized and also sustain a high degree of individuation. This would require the presence of a state and relatively autonomous secondary associations, both subject to legal regulation, and a general agreement on the overall nature of social relationships and a possibility of interest groups emerging either to consolidate as secondary associations or to dissolve. Citizens would be subjected to a series of social obligations but at the same time would have rights *vis-à-vis* the collectivities – they would have a private sphere where they could become aware of their needs, satisfy them within reason and keep them under control. Individuals would also participate in social rituals, and on occasion *subordinate themselves to* and identify with the fortunes and needs of society as a whole, its sub-collectivities and its individual members (political movements, community groups, friends, lovers, children, etc.). Through their participation in social life, they would both contribute to and benefit from collective energy.

Institutions would be democratically organized – with some kind of functional representation (Durkheim, 1957; Hawkins, 1981; Hirst, 1986) – and with individuals encouraged to *interpret* their tasks creatively. Some organizational forms, however, even if fewer than today, would require hierarchical relationships and positions of power and authority, which would be filled by meritocratic recruitment. In Durkheim's view, individuals who occupy such posts ought to receive higher monetary remuneration than other individuals. Whilst his justification for such inequity is unconvincing – i.e. that they make a greater contribution to social well-being – there is, nevertheless, a problem of motivating individuals to undertake onerous, responsible (and also particularly unpleasant) work but one that might be solved by the possibility of supplementary income or paid leave. The rationale for abolishing inherited wealth would also indicate that relatively privileged individuals should not be able to 'buy' advantage for their children and thus that the provision of equal conditions for citizens in the areas of education, health care, housing, etc. should be a social responsibility.

In *Professional Ethics and Civic Morals* Durkheim explicitly questions the belief that meritocratic arrangements are, on their own, an adequate solution to the problem of justice.

> To us it does not seem equitable that a man should be better treated as a social being because he was born of parentage that is rich or of high rank. But is it any more equitable that he should be better treated because he was born of a father of higher intelligence or in a more favourable moral milieu. It is here that the domain of charity begins. Charity is the feeling of human sympathy that we see becoming clear even of those last remaining traces of inequality. It ignores and denies any special merit in gifts of mental capacity acquired by heredity. This, then, is the very acme of justice.
>
> (Durkheim, 1957, p. 220)

Thus the principle that individuals should be rewarded unequally because of the unequal contributions that they make to society may eventually be *superseded* by one based on charity. Even in the foreseeable future, as 'the depth of feeling of human fraternity will go on increasing . . . the best amongst men' will be 'capable of working without getting an exact recompense for their pains and services' (ibid., p. 220).

This notion of supersession overstates the case. The crucial question is what role can 'charity' play in a society that requires a complex form of economic organization and that needs to motivate the average individual to work well in his or her chosen occupation? The average individual must be the analyst's reference point since, as Durkheim argued elsewhere, not all praiseworthy conduct can realistically be made obligatory; some is exemplary but exceptional (Durkheim, 1933, pp. 428–9) – one could not *base* a social order on the conduct of exceptional individuals. But Durkheim's own professional associations could, on particular occasions and under certain circumstances at least, develop norms that could pressurize their members to prioritize the needs of their clients and the public as a whole over their own personal 'rights'.

This in combination with an institutional commitment to the right of individuals to satisfy certain of their needs would help produce an equality of condition. In other words, a sophisticated socialist society might be organized according to a complex of different, even conflictual, normative systems and principles – both a legitimate egoism and a countervailing altruism.

Citizens could then be expected to operate within the general framework of the normative order and to restrict their expectations to what is legitimate for them within the constraints imposed by the availability of resources. Under such conditions most individuals could lead meaningful and productive lives, with a capacity to confront and deal with the inevitable setbacks and frustrations of life. It is, however, unlikely that suicide could be completely eliminated. In the first place, it may be rational for some individuals to choose the moment of their own death, particularly since it is inescapable. They may be ill, or wish to die because they have accomplished all they feel they can, because their faculties are fading fast and because they do not wish to be a burden on society.[9] In the second, this model of a rather resilient social actor assumes that he or she is produced and reproduced by opposing social forces that are in equilibrium, whilst at the same time both the individual and society go through dynamic transformations. Some casualties of such an unpredictable and unstable situation might still become suicidal. After all, as Durkheim pointed out in *The Rules of Sociological Method*, a certain level of disorder, deviance and distress is the inevitable concomitant of a dynamic society and can also be seen as one index of the society's flexibility and dynamism.

Conclusion

A consideration of Durkheim's concept of fatalism led us back to his discussion of the 'forced division of labour' and then to partially deconstruct and reconstruct *Suicide*, to make it signify something more or something other than was Durkheim's original intention. A careful consideration of his concepts *and* of the examples that are meant simply to illustrate these concepts allows us to retheorize much of the text and to theorize some of the social conditions of existence of potentially rational subjects and the kind of social order to which they might commit themselves – i.e. to a pluralistic democratic socialist society. In Chapters 8 and 9 certain of its features are discussed in somewhat more detail.

Notes

1 In so far as individuals are always to some extent held responsible for their actions (see Chapter 5 above) and that this is particularly true in modern western societies, suicide would probably be frequent in panopticon-like contexts (Foucault, 1979b).

2 Neale (1977) has begun to explore the different ways in which the relationship between individuals and their situations are represented. Whilst he is concerned with how cinematic experience is conceptualized, his comments have wider implications. He suggests that some subjects are represented as totally socially determined, the behaviourist subject; and others as absolutely transcendental-autonomous, and fully rational, outside of ideology. But there is a third form of conceptualization, which recognizes that:

> to speak of representation in discourse in relation to ideology is also to speak of subject positions: each discursive utterance constitutes a subject position, a place for the production and configuration of meaning, for its coherence, or, occasionally, for its critical rupture.
> . . . the subject is psychoanalytic – a heterogeneous subjectivity in a constant process of (re)constitution through discourse and meaning . . . dependent upon the modality of address . . . audiences are determined economically, politically *and ideologically*.
>
> (Neale, 1977, pp. 19–20)

He is suggesting that, whilst we are never completely outside of ideology, we have a complex relationship to it which we may be able to use in a critical and 'demystifying' way.

3 There are good conceptual and empirical reasons to be sceptical of Weber's idealistic characterization of the ascetic entrepreneur. If profits grow at a high enough rate there is no necessary contradiction between increasing personal consumption and increasing investment. (On the lifestyles of early American entrepreneurs see Zeitlin, 1981, pp. 137–42.) Moreover, wealth has rarely been simply a matter of conspicuous consumption – wealth brings power, which includes the ability to bend others to one's will and also to feel *affirmed* by the accompanying sense of potency.

4 In Chapter 4 there was a brief discussion of the relationship between Durkheim and Lacan. Here it is worth noting how similar are Durkheim and Foucault (Foucault 1978, 1979) – both argue that subjectivation and responsibility are produced by social practices, including educational ones:

> the capacity for containing our inclinations, for restraining ourselves – the ability that we acquire in the school of moral discipline – is the indispensable condition for the emergence of reflective, individual will. The rule, because it teaches us to restrain and master ourselves, is a means of emancipation and freedom.
>
> (Durkheim, 1961, p. 48)

The argument in this book, however, is that Durkheim's positive evaluation of these processes is far more persuasive than Foucault's somewhat blanket dismissal (see Dews, 1984).

5 For radically different arguments as to why subjective meanings must be taken into account see Fenton (1968) and Dawe (1970).

6 This Durkheim is related to the positivist Durkheim as the Lacanians are related to the cruder Freudians. The latter see the real determinants of human behaviour as unconscious forces – primeval emotions of rage, fear, rivalry, partially contained within an unstable Oedipal complex – which they counterpose to the 'screening' chatter of the patient's superficial discourse. But when Lacan argues that the 'royal road to the unconscious' is through *The Interpretation of Dreams* (Freud, 1976a) rather than through the *Three Essays on the Theory of Sexuality* (Freud, 1962) this is because the first is a paradigm of investigative analysis (as opposed to a lexicon): dreams are related to dream texts and to unconscious complexes through threads of meaning the transformations of which need to be actively deciphered (Thom, 1976, pp. 434–69).

7 Durkheim, for example, argues that:

> even when religious ceremonies have a disquieting or saddening event as their point of departure, they retain their stimulating power over the affective state of the group and individuals. By the mere fact that they are collective they raise the vital tone. When one feels life within him – whether it be in the form of painful initiation or happy enthusiasm – he does not believe in death; so he becomes reassured and takes courage again, and subjectively everything goes on as if the rite had really driven off the danger which was dreaded.
>
> (Durkheim, 1976, p. 408)

8 (a) Garfinkel (1967) developed the method of disruption to uncover invariant features of social interaction. McHugh (1968), however, has pointed out the limitations of this technique and argues that it is also necessary to study the process of social interaction when it seems normal to the participants. In a sense this methodology synthesises both of these approaches. (b) This concept of an 'adult personality' is clearly normative in that it is positively evaluated. It can nevertheless be defined conceptually in a neutral manner – see Bazelgette (1971). (c) There is a further interesting point: Turquet states that his work is 'A study in the phenomenology of the individual's experience' and there is no doubt that he reinterprets members' accounts of their experience within such a framework. I have no quarrel with sensitive empirical strategies determining the content of experience. I would, however, stress that these are both an element of, and traces of, some of the dynamic processes that take place within the group and that many of these are 'emergent', irreduceable to these experiences.

9 In some societies where there is little surplus – an example might be the Chukchee (Gibbs, 1971, p. 284) – those who are no longer productive might be encouraged by the dominant ideology to kill themselves. It might even provide an appropriate vocabulary of motives. Whilst this would include genuine cases of 'voluntary suicide', most of Durkheim's examples of 'obligatory altruistic suicide' are of a radically different nature. They occur in class societies where there is a surplus that is used to support the privileged rather than those who are incapacitated. Sexist and elitist ideologies decree that those who are dependent on the more powerful should be subsumed by them and hence expected to follow them in death. This is the fate of many widows and of the soldiers and retainers of dead chiefs (Durkheim, 1951, p. 219). In the latter case, of course, the elimination of the armed band benefits the rivalrous oligarchy of the remaining chiefs.

8 Durkheim and Marx: A dialogue

Introduction

The argument of earlier chapters has been that Durkheim's work is rich and fruitful, particularly when liberated from some of its more dubious assumptions. In his texts there is a somewhat underdeveloped set of concepts associated with a radical socialist vision which, if elaborated and integrated with certain other of his concepts, produces a 'reconstituted' Durkheimism that has much to say about the characteristics of a *feasible* democratic socialist society, one where some kind of organic solidarity might truly be possible. In this chapter this version of Durkheim's theories is used to critique but then build upon the work of Marx, exploring the meaning and importance of equality of opportunity and condition, the constraints imposed by economic and ecological factors, the role of democratic forms and the kinds of social conflicts that might develop between different groups and interests. I then briefly discuss the significance of juridical relations and the conditions of existence of a rational subjectivity.

Organic solidarity

Durkheim's understanding of the potential inherent in modern complex societies is interesting and complex but this 'promise' could not be realized, as he sometimes believed, if they remained capitalistic. The inherently contradictory and exploitative foundations of the capitalist mode of production – continuous economic crises and wage labour used by capital in a careless and authoritarian manner – place a fetter not only on the overall development of the forces of production but also upon the development of rational, creative individuals and a dynamic and supportive society, that is one truly based upon 'organic

159

solidarity'. Furthermore, the disparity between the legitimating ideologies of capitalism (that there is an equality of opportunity, a just distribution of rewards, a democratic and impartial state dedicated to the commonweal) and capitalism's necessary conditions of existence (privilege, inequality, and a coercive state dedicated to the reproduction of these class relations) means that social conflict is always generated, and has to be contained and explained away. This is one reason why simplistic individualistic ideologies are invoked to justify the relative fate of both the privileged and the unsuccessful. Mystification and repression are endemic to class societies.

Many of Durkheim's explicit political arguments were in a socialist mould: he believed that efficient production requires democratic planning and control; that property relations should change since the inheritance of wealth and the private ownership of productive resources are anachronistic; that the distribution of income should be determined consensually; and that the care of the unproductive – the old, the sick, children, the unemployed – is a collective responsibility. However, he was also committed to constitutionalism, to the need for juridical relations and law, to giving to the state real but limited power; thus he argued for the social and political necessity of 'intermediate associations' and for the importance of the individual. These were not only liberal or conservative concerns but also grew out of the strong French libertarian socialist tradition which can provide a useful corrective to Marxism.

I used an analysis of Durkheim's discussion of 'the forced division of labour' to elaborate and develop many of Durkheim's concepts in order to explore the nature and social foundations of a dynamic, non-coercive society. Such a society, I argued, would be differentiated and complex, with its members acknowledging the collective nature of human activity and the mutual interdepedence of human beings. Many intimate needs would be satisfied within diffuse *reciprocal* and relatively egalitarian interpersonal relations. Since both individuals and organizations also satisfy some of their needs through a general exchange of services, goods and information, reciprocity would also often be achieved by more impersonal means. For this to be non-exploitative there would have to be a public commitment to the equality of condition and opportunity – of access to the same quality of education and health care, and an adequate level of accommodation and transportation. The society would need to be an active democracy – individuals would need the rights, capacities and opportunities to organize themselves, to develop their understanding, to communicate their viewpoint and effectively to pursue their interests when negotiating with other individuals, groups and institutions. True, Durkheim's own understanding of the working of the economic sphere in capitalist and 'post-capitalist' societies was inadequate and needs to be supplemented by that of Marx but, in the same way that Durkheim has been criticized and reconstituted, aspects of Durkheim's arguments can be used to reformulate aspects of Marx's work.

Marxism: A Durkheimian critique

Although in Chapter 3 it was argued that Durkheim underestimated the complexity of Marxist thought, here it will be shown that his distinction between and criticisms of 'socialism' and 'communism' help to locate significant weaknesses in Marxism, for the last hundred years the major source of the socialist critique of capitalism. In its concept of state, economy and society it is deficient in ways that can be highlighted and hopefully corrected by this (reconstituted) Durkheimism.

Durkheim argued that for communists the ideal society would be ascetic and radically egalitarian with subsistence living and a minimal amount of activity geared to economic production. They assume that there will be a general uniformity of interest and that economic differences should not and will not affect political decisions:

> In utopia each works in his own way, as he thinks proper, and is simply obliged not to be idle. . . . There is no common rule which determines relationships among the different workers, or the manner in which these diverse activities should co-operate for collective goals. . . . He brings [his products] to the community and consumes them only when society itself makes use of it collectively.
>
> (Durkheim, 1962, p. 71)

This communist image of an alternative social order is Utopian because it is abstract, unrelated to extant societies and shows no sense of the exigencies of *social organization*. Communism functions as a *moral* critique of any differentiated, organized society but provides no real guidance for social reconstruction or for practical political action in the here and now. Aspects of

Marx's concept of communism fit this model only too well and, however dismissive Marx may have been of Utopianism, it is precisely a moralistic anti-materialism and a radical egalitarianism that has inspired many Marxists to oppose and denounce capitalism.

Socialists, on the other hand, Durkheim argued, believe that the major motivation of human action springs from their economic interests – there are no 'social interests outside of economic interests' – and economic transformation precedes moral transformation. They are committed to organizing economic activity and other social relations in a way that will maximize production. They believe that the productive members of society will control the state, a major function of which will be collectively to control production. Implicit in the socialist analysis is the problematic belief that

> the way to realize social peace is to free economic appetites of all restraints on the one hand, and on the other to satisfy them by fulfilling them . . . but such appetites cannot be appeased unless they are limited and they cannot be limited except by something other than themselves.
>
> (Durkheim, 1962, p. 242)

This something is a 'moral authority' respected by individuals who are content because they accept that 'they have no right to more' than they already have (Durkheim, 1962, p. 242). All societies and all individuals, Durkheim argued, must be regulated by some moral authority.

Marx (and Engels) refused to provide detailed blueprints of either socialism or communism but retained throughout most of their lives a certain attachment to some of their early romantic ideas. Their discussion of post-capitalist societies is to be found mainly in *The Economic and Philosophic Manuscripts* (1844), *The German Ideology* (1845), *The Manifesto of the Communist Party* (1848), *Critique of the Gotha Programme* (1875) and Engels' *Anti-Duhring* (1891). Marx argued that in post-capitalist societies production would be under the collective control of the 'associated producers' and geared to the satisfaction of their needs rather than the creation of profit. In socialist societies the state would play the major role in planning and coordinating an economy still based upon the circulation of commodities. There would be no exploitation, so workers would receive a return for their labour proportionate to its intensity and duration, although a certain percentage of what was produced would be diverted to the satisfaction of collective needs. The capacities of individuals to work effectively differ, so there would be some inequality of income; the circumstances of individuals vary, so all needs would not be met to the same extent.

> The right of the producers is proportional to the labour they supply. . . . This *equal* right is an unequal right for equal labour. . . . It is, therefore, a right of inequality, in its content, like every right.
>
> (Marx, 1875, in Tucker, 1978, p. 530)

Socialism will be put on the agenda by the structural contradictions of, and social crises in, capitalist societies, but it will be achieved only when the working class takes economic and political power. The capitalist class, even when displaced, will not abandon its attempts to regain its power and immediately after the revolution society will still contain remnants of the previous era – individuals, organizations and ideologies. A 'revolutionary dictatorship of the proleteriat' – of the majority over the minority – organized in and through the state will therefore be necessary. The state will coordinate economic activity and impose socialist legality, which, like all law, is coercive and, ultimately, partisan.

Socialism is a transitional form, 'stamped with the birthmarks of the old society' (Marx, 1875, in Tucker, 1978, p. 529). 'Communism' appears when all vestiges of class relations have vanished and there is an end to structurally generated social conflict and social inequality. As a result, 'the government of persons' will be 'replaced by the administration of things' (Engels, 1878, in Henderson, 1967, p. 221), 'the public power will lose its political character' (Marx and Engels, 1948, p. 31) and be 'transformed into the simple administrative function of watching over the true interests of society' (Engels, 1874) and, as Pashukanis later argued, the legal form will disappear (Pashukanis, 1978, p. 64).[1] Work will no longer be oppressive and restrictive, it will be 'possible for me to do one thing today and another tomorrow, to hunt in the morning, fish in the afternoon, rear cattle in the evening, criticise after dinner' (Marx and Engels, 1845 in 1976, p. 467):

> after labour has become not only a means of life but life's prime want; after the productive forces have also increased with the all-round development of the individual, and all the springs of

co-operative wealth flow more abundantly – only then can the narrow horizon of bourgeois right be crossed in its entirety and society inscribe on its banner: From each according to his ability, to each according to his needs.

(Marx, 1875, in Tucker, 1978, p. 531)

One interpretation of Marx's vision, supported by much of *The Economic and Philosophical Manuscripts*, is that in communist societies individuals will not be particularly concerned with the accumulation of material things; they will be somewhat ascetic and concerned with creative and expressive labour (Marx, 1844, in Marx and Engels, 1975, p. 274). Another is that production will be so efficient that all needs can be satisfied with relatively little effort. In either case the commodity form and the legal form will be eliminated, all will subscribe to the same Universal Form of Reason – consciousness will determine being and for the first time men will make history.

Marx and Engels, then, believed that there are two different forms of post-class societies. One, socialism, is statist: the state organizes and attempts to maximize production and enforces a socialist law and, although Marx was sceptical of abstract moralism (Wood, 1981, pp. 123–56), a socialist morality. In the second, communism, the state will have withered away and production will be organized 'from each according to his ability, to each according to his needs'; people will be more concerned with expressive activity than the accumulation of objects. In *Socialism* Durkheim questioned the feasibility of absolute egalitarianism and asceticism, criticized socialist cornucopias, argued that desire is both socially constituted and insatiable, and was sceptical about economic determinism.

In Marx and Engels there is no adequate account of how to get from socialism to communism – from a world still subject to economic determination to one where consciousness determines being. Marx provides us with few tools for avoiding the tyranny of statism or the irrelevance of Utopianism. The contrast between the two radically different kinds of society is elided by treating them as distinct phases in an evolutionary relationship to each other. Here in one thinker there are the concerns of two different and somewhat contradictory schools (Durkheim, 1962, p. 237). Marx's understanding of the mechanisms of social change is generally complex and far superior to that of Durkheim, but this is an example of pure evolutionism. This evolutionism contains a number of implicit assumptions, which include: that the only differences of interest that generate conflicts that are irresolvable without altering fundamental social relations are those associated with class; that the needs, desires and rationalities of those actively employed in socialist societies are so homogeneous that they will have the same priorities; overall that either communism will be a non-materialistic society or there will be such material abundance that there need be no conflict over resources; that in communism there is an unambiguous 'general interest' and no group suffers because of the the realization of the goals of another.

Central to the whole of Marx's argument is a concern with needs, which he viewed from both a societal and an individual viewpoint. A society's existence depends upon its continuity and hence its reproduction, and this in turn depends upon the allocation of sufficient resources for the reproduction of its means of production and administration and its economically active members. From the point of view of the system, this minimally means that sufficient funds are made available to take care of their basic physical needs and to allow them to develop appropriate levels of skill. From the individual's point of view the means of subsistence must be

> sufficient to maintain him in his normal state as a labouring individual. His natural wants such as food, clothing, fuel and housing, vary according to the climate, and other physical conditions of his country. On the other hand, the number and extent of his so-called necessary wants, as also the modes of satisfying them, are themselves the product of historical development and depend themselves to a great extent on the degree of civilisation of a country, more particularly on the conditions under which, and consequently on the habits and degree of comfort in which the class of free labourers has been formed.
>
> (Marx, 1965, p. 171)

An important cause of class struggle is that proleteriat and capitalists compute the former's needs in different ways – the workers relative to their level of 'civilization', capitalists in terms of the minimal costs of reproducing labour.

Under socialism and communism needs must also be computed from the point of view of society and of the individual. But how determine the needs of individuals? One answer given by Marx is that in communist society they will be reconciled since production is organized 'from each according to his ability, to each according to his needs'. This is only plausible if the level of production is sufficient to satisfy individual *and* collective (reproductive) needs relatively easily. Under these conditions, according to a contemporary 'defender' of orthodox Marxism, G. A. Cohen,

> activity under communism, both within and outside its economy, is not unstructuured, but it also is not prestructured. No social form is *imposed* upon it, but it does have a form. One might say: *the form is now just the boundary created by matter itself.* The structure displayed by communism is no more than the outline of the activities of its members, not something into which they must fit themselves.
>
> (Cohen, 1978, p. 131)

It would be difficult to find a clearer example of a putative communist Utopia in which 'each works in his own way, as he thinks proper' with 'no common rule which determines relationships among the different workers, or the manner in which these diverse activities should co-operate for collective goals' (Durkheim, 1962, p. 71). This atomism is taken even further by Cohen when he claims that, under communism,

> the state is not the only structure due for retirement. The social structure will also subside. The liberated association of individuals is less a new social structure than freedom from social structure.
>
> (Cohen, 1978, p. 133)

Leaving aside Cohen's bizarre conception of production (and his theoretically regressive prioritization of the forces over the relations of production – Callinicos, 1982, p. 145; Hirst, 1985, p. 39), let us simply note that social continuity requires social reproduction and this in turn necessitates social organization. Social structure generates social order and constitutes human subjects and, as Durkheim and Foucault have both rightly stressed, power and social organization are productive as well as repressive. In so far as Cohen accurately represents part of Marx's arguments when he claims that 'Marx's freely associated individuals constitute an alternative to, not a form of society' (Cohen, 1978, p. 37), these are manifestly flawed.

   As even Cohen acknowledges, there remains another and significant problem. Given that the future supplies of natural resources and energy are limited and that, at last, the devastating effects on the environment of ever expanding production are beginning to be acknowledged, it is clear that there are 'real limits to growth'. A socialist cornucopia, where everybody's desires can be accommodated, seems no longer a feasible goal. What consequences does this have for 'communist society'? A partial answer to this problem is provided by the argument that capitalism is so inequitable, wasteful and inefficient that a more rational productive and distributive system would place fewer demands on the world's resources. But these fewer consumer demands may still be well in excess of the capacity of the productive forces. Another answer is that advertising, in particular, has developed within us false needs – both Marcuse (1955, p. 86; 1966, pp. 4–5) and Macpherson (1979, p. 49) distinguish between true needs and manipulated or self-indulgent desires. Marx certainly sometimes argued that under communism there will be a modification in the perception of the nature of human needs. Labour itself will become 'not only a means of life but life's prime want' and as an activity it will be inherently satisfying in part because only a limited amount of labour would be required to produce the objects to satisfy physical needs. This may be because individuals are somewhat ascetic with modest needs, i.e. 'natural needs' plus those collectively and consensually defined by individuals who 'recognize' their true nature is that of *homo faber*. It is only if one assumes that they would be relatively modest that one can assert that production would be sufficient for them. Such ontological arguments, grounded as they are in a philosophical anthropology, are untenable and pre-emptive (Althusser, 1969; Ranciere, 1971; Jones, 1982). One cannot assume that the desire for and satisfactions from meaningful labour will automatically *displace* other kinds of felt needs.

If Marx's ontology is abandoned then it is necessary to seek out the other basis of restraint – and in this Durkheim seems correct – it would have to be a morality socially constituted and collectively imposed. Marx assumed that under communism the collective morality would be in accord with the individual's true interest but this would only be concievably true if, on the one hand, there was a consensus on what needs should be acknowledged and, on the other, individual desires were relatively uniform. Since desires are socially constituted, this presupposes a small homogeneous population. Durkheim seems correct – communism presupposes an ascetic morality and the kind of undifferentiated population only conceivable in a small-scale radically egalitarian society (Durkheim, 1962, p. 237). Moreover, despite Marx's (and

Cohen's) optimism about the end of the state, the enforcement of such homogeneity would require a repressive morality and, in any large-scale society, a repressive state. Such a denial of difference would create a form of 'forced solidarity' (and would be associated with its correlative amount of 'fatalistic suicide'). In practice, then, much of Marx's writing on communism has little to tell us about how to organize the kind of complex, differentiated, dynamic socialist society that would produce and sustain the 'all-round development of the individual' (Marx, 1875, in Tucker, 1978, p. 531). Whilst there is indeed good reason to be wary of the state, to believe that it will simply wither away is wishful thinking.[2]

Socialism

Schmidt, in his book *The Concept of Nature in Marx* (1971), shows that, whilst Marx's conception of the nature of communism and of human needs is often problematic, on occasion he recognized that there is an inescapable tension between the development of human needs (or desires) and the capacity to act upon nature in a way that will satisfy them.[3] Thus, in an important and interesting passage in the third volume of *Capital*, he points to the material constraints on social activity, thereby dismissing cornucopic fantasies:

the realm of freedom actually begins only where labour which is determined by necessity and mundane considerations ceases; thus in the very nature of things it lies beyond the sphere of actual material production. *Just as the savage must wrestle with nature to satisfy his wants, to maintain and reproduce life, so must civilised man, and he must do so in all social formations and under all possible modes of production.* With this development this realm of physical necessity expands as a result of his wants; but at the same time, the forces of production which satisfy these wants also increase. Freedom in this field can only consist in socialized man, the associated producers, rationally regulating their interchange with Nature, bringing it under their common control, instead of being ruled by it as the blind forces of Nature; and achieving this with the least expenditure of energy and under conditions most favourable to, and worthy of, their human nature. But it nonetheless still remains a realm of necessity. Beyond it begins that development of human energy which is an end in itself, the true realm of freedom, which, however, can blossom forth only with this realm of necessity as its basis.

(Marx, 1972, p. 820).

Bearing this point in mind and building upon this passage, Marxian *and* Durkheimian concepts can be combined to suggest that the major determinants of the forms and levels of production in a complex socialist society would be the relationships between the following:

1 The gross level of production possible if all resources were used with maximum efficiency.
2 The general standard of life – for those in paid employment, for those engaged in socially necessary but unpaid tasks, and for those unable to make an active contribution to the commonweal – and the demographic distribution of individuals within these various categories.
3 The balance between the public and private provision of needs.
4 The ecologically sound use of resources.
5 The balance between achieving the maximally efficent organization of labour and developing conditions that are 'worthy of human nature', i.e. criteria of 'instrumental' efficiency and 'human dignity' may be at odds.[4]
6 The relative balance that people wish to establish between the time they spend in 'the realm of necessity' as opposed to 'the realm of freedom' – of *paid work* as opposed to self-directed but not necessarily individualistic or unproductive activity. In his book *Ecology as Politics* (1980), Gorz has argued that a socialist economy should combine commodity production for certain essentials with more self-directed activity where people might themselves produce useful objects or services for themselves or others, to exchange them or – as Mauss (1984) might argue – to offer them as gifts. The nature and level of contrast found here will depend in part upon the kind of decision made in (5) above.
7 The limitations produced by the existence of other states and economies – political and economic competition may have an extensive structuring effect on social priorities.

Thus constraints imposed by the relationship of human beings to the material world, those that derive from the imperatives of social organization and others that are a function of the conditions of existence of the human personality, limit the forms of social order possible in a socialist society.

Let us return briefly to the issue of morality and restraint. Durkheim did not deny that people's desires are manipulated. He agreed with Ihering that the continuous wasteful changes in clothing due to fashion happened because of 'the need of the superior classes to externally distinguish themselves from the inferior' who 'tend ceaselessly to imitate the first' and since 'it loses all its value once it is adopted by everybody . . . it is bound to change continually' (Durkheim, 1886, p. 353; and see Gorz, 1980, pp. 30–1). Furthermore he was aware that appetites are 'excited' by capitalism and that the wealthy and powerful are only too likely to be subject to an anomie of 'affluence' since

> wealth by the power it bestows deceives us into believing that we depend upon ourselves only. Reducing the resistance we encounter from objects, it suggests the possibility of an unlimited success against them.
>
> (Durkheim, 1951, p. 254; and see Simon and Gagnon, 1977, p. 372)

As well as this somewhat specific incitement to excess owing to a socio-structually generated ideological misunderstanding of the relationship between particular individuals and the material world, there is also a more pervasive and less remediable social problem.

> how fix the quantity of well-being, comfort, luxury, that a human being ought to possess? . . . Picture the most productive economic organization possible and a distribution of wealth which assures abundance to even the humblest – perhaps such a transformation, at the very moment it was constituted, would produce an instant of gratification. For desires, though calmed for an instant, will quickly acquire new exigencies. . . . excited desires will tend naturally to keep outrunning their goals for the very reason that they have nothing before them which stops them.
>
> (Durkheim, 1962, p. 241)

Since 'needs' develop historically there seems no *a priori* reason to believe that new needs and therefore new demands will cease to be continually and spontaneously made on the productive system. The construction and imposition of a morality that adjudicates on legitimate and illegitimate demands will then always be a necessity for the system and, incidentally, for the individual. For if no limits are placed upon the development of needs and if none is placed on the pursuit of gratification of specific needs, the individual personality cannot survive. Durkheim anticipated Lacan in arguing that 'passions and appetites', or better desires, are in principle insatiable and therefore must, in some way, be limited and balanced.

If Marxism has been criticized here, it is not to suggest that either Marx himself or some Marxists have failed ever to confront some of these critical points. The argument that socialism must prioritize certain systemic and individual needs is not necessarily romantic or reductionist. As Doyal and Gough (1984) have argued, a necessary goal of socialist planning is the production and reproduction of the rational subjects that individuals need to be and society needs them to be if they are rationally to assent to and abide by the normative order. This would require a high aggregate level of production and therefore an extensive use of social resources and would provide a serious constraint on what was produced, how it was produced and how distributed within any particular society and even more so if the reference point was the world system as a whole. One would expect tensions within society about the use of resources but the implication is that they would be due to sectional demands for an ultimately unjustifiable proportion of resources (a point to which I return below). The imposition of a collective morality in this case would be in the name of the higher rationality. However, even in a rationally organized socialist or communist society, since even rational individuals are not rational all the time, there would still be the need for a collectively produced and occasionally coercively enforced morality.

> The end of the state as a coercive apparatus need not imply the complete termination of public coercion as such. Communist societies need not be perfectly cooperative associations, but only communities based on rational cooperation. A community of rational cooperators could decide, as it were, to use force against itself.
>
> (Levine, 1987, p. 136; and see Geras, 1985)

These comments certainly show an awareness of and a capacity to resolve at least some of the problems raised by Durkheim. Nevertheless there is no 'socialist calculus' that can be used to provide definitive solutions to the choices that confront a socialist society.

To see why this is the case we need to turn to Marx's discussion of socialism. Whilst the elimination of class relations would remove exploitation and the major structural basis for conflict, Marx implied that these are not the only source of social and political inequality. In *The Critique of the Gotha Programme* (1875) he argued that, under socialism, different forms of labour would be seen as equivalent and that the income of individuals would be related to the 'duration and intensity' of their labour, but since individuals have different needs (number of dependants, etc.) this is 'a right of inequality in its content like all rights' (Marx, 1875, in McLellan, 1977, p. 569). Marx assumed that all members of society have the same 'general interest' and thus that this method of distributing resources will be universally acceptable. On the other hand, he also argued that such income would be subject to a 'tax' – to replace, expand and insure the means of production, to cover the costs of administration not related to production and the costs of the common satisfaction of needs, of schools, health services, unemployment benefit, etc. (Marx, 1875, in Tucker, 1978, pp. 528–9). There are other functions that might be collectively financed – for example, maternity leave and child care, and the costs of retraining workers. Furthermore, as Marx pointed out, the differences in the ecological context within which individuals or communities operate might lead them to claim a greater share of the collective funds than others not so disadvantaged. The communal provision for needs, however, partially subverts the principle that right is solely connected to the performance of labour – and this is without moving to the Utopianism of Marx's conception of communism. There are good historical reasons to believe that societies can and indeed do function with more than one mode of distributing income – in part according to right, in part according to need.

In a socialist society, the distribution of resources in a manner proportionate to the quanta of labour contributed by particular individuals would both facilitate the organization of production and function to motivate the individual. But there are a number of problems unresolved in Marx's formulation. First it is clear that much of production under socialism would inevitably be hierarchically organized (even if democratically controlled). What kind of 'right' would motivate an individual to accept the burden of a position of responsibility in such an organization? Durkheim can be followed here in that the importance of their particular contribution to the organization and society as a whole could be recognized in part by some financial reward. This might seem just to others if there was an open meritocratic form of recruitment

(Durkheim, 1933, pp. 374–88). But these comments of Durkheim's only partially resolve the problem.

The difficulty lies in distinguishing between those situations where individuals and groups receive extra resources because of their greater contribution to the commonweal and to reward them for the particular efforts they have made and those where they have used their power to extract concessions from the system as whole. Marx is quite equivocal about this, as can be seen in his discussion of the relative rewards that skilled workers should receive. In *The Critique of the Gotha Programme*, he treated all labour as equivalent and used a universal measure of labour. But earlier, in *Wages, Prices and Profit* (1865, reprinted in Marx and Engels, 1968), he argued that under socialism skilled workers would receive a higher wage than others because of the cost of reproducing their skills. This was in part an oversight – under socialism such costs would be socialized – but also probably a recognition on his part that such workers have the power to demand higher remuneration. Under socialism there is always the danger that in addition to 'legitimate' inequalities others will be produced by 'skills and organizational exploiters' (Levine, 1987, p. 147). Wide and open access to the training required for both skilled work and administrative positions could minimize these problems. Similarly, if particularly unpleasant or burdensome but necessary work was particularly well rewarded, an equitable principle of remuneration, rather than one based upon simple 'muscle' could be established. When Durkheim pointed to a sentiment of 'charity' (Durkheim, 1957, p. 221) he was suggesting a collective pressure to persuade those who might simply be selfish and effectively self-interested to moderate their demands. Nevertheless, since the extent to which the quantity, duration and intensity of labour could act as an unequivocal measure of social input is itself problematic, some negotiation about the relative value of different activities seems inescapable and therefore makes some egoistic self-interest inevitable and disagreements likely. This is also true about what should be done with the surplus over and above that required to reproduce workers and their immediate families. Differing evaluations of worth and self-interested disputes about the use of social resources seem inevitable.

The different structural locations of individuals and the different ideologies by which they are interpellated will inevitably generate a whole series of what Weber characterized as 'material and ideal interests' (1958, p. 280).[5] Although there is a sense in which for both individuals and societies one can specify some 'needs' that must be taken care of, many of the issues that are at stake in this discussion concern the 'desires' of individuals – who may or may not, for example, wish to prioritize meaningful labour over the accumulation of commodities. These desires cannot be objectively assessed and ranked as more or less important; their significance is a matter of negotiation. Elimination of class relations, then, will not automatically produce a consensus – any hegemonic ideology will be the product of negotiation and compromise between differentiated groups and individuals.

Whatever their structural location, individuals will have to surrender some of their desires – some more and some less. What will make them content with their lot

> is not that they have more or less but that they are convinced that they have no right to more . . . it is absolutely essential that there be an authority whose superiority they acknowledge and which tells them what is right.
>
> (Durkheim, 1962, p. 242)

A socialist society like any other society will therefore require a *compromise* hegemonic ideology incorporating some kind of morality.

Whilst Durkheim's discussions of morality often seem overconcerned with the need for individuals to repress their desires, other important issues are raised by his arguments. Thematic in much of his writing was a belief that, when societies developed to the point that a genuine meritocratic system had been achieved, more privileged individuals should surrender some of their advantages in the name of a common humanity. In other words, whilst within the system there would remain some kind of inegalitarian dynamic, this would be countered by the more egalitarian sentiment of charity. This 'altruistic orientation' means that many relatively privileged individuals will be willing to see the attenuation of their economic 'rights'. 'Charity is the feeling of human sympathy' for another as a human person (*la personne humaine*) (Durkheim, 1898, in Traugott, 1978, p. 48), as a member of a particular society *and* ultimately humanity as a whole – 'For it is man as a human being that we should love' (Durkheim, 1957, p. 219). Such a morality would need to be an aspect of the general hegemonic ideology and would be communicated and enforced by the state and by intermediate groups – by professional associations or any other organized groups. Let us reiterate: Marx's fantasy that the state would wither away under communism allowed him to be complacent about its functions and role in socialism. Durkheim's position was more adequate: the state is essential to the functioning of complex societies but its power and authority can and should be constrained by other organizations.

The sentiment of charity is an altruistic counterweight to the inescapable concern with individual rights (both might be necessary to motivate individuals to fulfil their social roles). The concern of individuals that they are receiving just rewards for their efforts is a perfectly reasonable form of egoism. In so far as such individuals feel generally satisfied with social arrangements, then their relationship to morality is less likely to be one of simple subordination, of a sense of external compulsion and dull duty, but rather one of self-realization.

No act has ever been performed as a result of duty alone; it has always been necessary for it to appear in some respect good.
(Durkheim, 1974, p. 45)

Individuals are more likely to experience moral imperatives as good if they are part of a system that acknowledges their interests, nourishes them and facilitates their self-realization. Durkheim has been used to show that justice, charity, desire and self-restraint would all need to be aspects of a socialist morality.

What then would be the relationship between the organization of such an egalitarian socialist system and the individual subjects within it? From this reformulation of the concepts developed in Durkheim's *Suicide* it is clear that it would be legitimate in such a society to ask individuals to restrict their expectations to those that can be satisfied by the resources that are made available to them and to submit to the overall normative structure. Significant parts of this – at a somewhat abstract level – would be rendered as explicit as possible, although leaving adequate room for individuals both to interpret its meaning and to develop their own more private realm of activity. Both anomie and fatalism could largely be avoided by the correct combination of regulation and flexibility.

Whilst anomie and fatalism relate primarily to the coherence, relevance, flexibility and legitimacy of the normative system and the way in which everyday life is organized, it is also necessary to examine how individuals would orient themselves to the needs of others and of themselves. Each individual's orientation to the world needs to include both altruistic and egoistic elements. Individuals will need the right to a private realm where they can become aware of and organize their lives so as to satisfy, within reason, their 'appetites and passions'. At the same time a more social, altruistic orientation will help them to identify with the interests of other individuals and collectivities – interpellations at times produced by social rituals – thus providing them with an external reference point that will energize them and render them less liable to the vagaries of their own moods. In this rereading of Durkheim, then, it becomes clear that rational subjects need to find in themselves elements of egoism and altruism and their social environment organized so that it avoids both anomie and fatalism.

Conclusion

A major concern of this work has been to develop concepts that make it possible to grasp adequately those elements of social life that seem intrinsic to any society, those that seem to be associated only with specific forms of social relations and how then these ubiquitous and more localized features are articulated together – juridical relations, law and class for example. If there are universal elements of social life and others that are found only in certain kinds of society and if, as it could be argued, their mode of articulation (and level of development) determines their relative roles and significance, then superficially and on a deeper 'structural' level there will be significant elements of continuity and discontinuity between different kinds of society. Our major concern here is with the relationship between the organization of capitalist societies and of a feasible form of socialist society and particularly the role of law in the latter. This is to question the use of Utopian communist images of the future as moral critiques of contemporary societies. If socialists seek power and wish to retain it *democratically* it is important that they do not make impossible promises. To do so would be to guarantee that many in the disillusioned populace would seek alternatives. A socialism that seeks to rule, to govern society rather than to be in opposition to it, must accept that it will face difficulties and prepare to deal with these; only then could it stay in power.

Notes

1 Pashukanis, in his reading of Marx, explicitly constructs such an image of the communist future (Pashukanis, 1978, pp. 47–64, see also the editor's introduction to the same book).

2 Mauss's 'sociological assessment' of Bolshevism (Mauss, 1984) follows similar lines. Gane demonstrates that this

> is a consistent development of Durkheim's critique of revolutionary communism from the position of evolutionary organic socialism. Fundamentally, he argues, the Bolsheviks remained trapped within a primitive revolutionary individualist conception of communism, an ascetic communism to be imposed by a minority from above by a mixture of decree and violence. . . . [But] Politics, law, violence, cannot create socialist institutions.
>
> (Gane, 1984, p. 327)

3 There is a significant overlap between the arguments of this book and Schmidt's work, much as earlier there was some overlap with that of Habermas, and this despite the fact that they are both 'critical theorists'.

4 Despite its tone, in many ways Engels was making a somewhat similar point when he argued that factory technology imposes important constraints on the organization of production and that even if questions

> concerning the mode of production, distribution of materials etc., which must be settled at once on pain of seeing all production immediately stopped; whether they are settled by decision of a delegate placed at the head of each branch of labour or, if possible, by a majority vote, the will of the single individual will always have to subordinate itself, which means that questions are settled in an authoritarian way.
>
> (Engels, 'On Authority', in Tucker, 1978, p. 731)

5 For the implications of such points for Cohen's (1978) work see Hirst (1985). Earlier (Hirst, 1980), he addressed this issue in the context of political demand for 'unconditional abortion'. This, he argues, is untenable:

> abortion is not a 'private' act but involves the consumption of medical resources, the provision of facilities and questions of alternative forms of provision. These questions of provision are not a matter of *a* woman's choice, but a general social question of health policy.
>
> (Hirst, 1980, pp. 100–3)

Conflicts over the use of resources, problems over levels of competence, disputes about the rights of individuals (as 'woman', 'husband', 'foetus', etc.), whether enshrined in the law or not, the conscientious objection of professionals to fulfilling certain tasks may all occur in any conceivable society.

The problems do not end here. There may be disputes about what kind of private practices individuals are entitled to engage in – drug use/abuse for escapist, hedonistic or religious reasons, sado-masochistic sexual practices, etc. These are difficult issues because the age of those engaging in the practice may be an important consideration as may the degree of choice and the social consequences of these actions. For example, if drugs debilitate their users, their consumption ceases to be a private matter; similarly, if drug users or sado-masochists proselytize (and in the latter case rear children to be sado-masochists), there is clearly a moral issue (see Young, 1971, 1974; Dorn, 1980, Nagel, 1969).

9 The state, law and order in complex societies

Introduction

In their work *The Crisis of Democracy* (1975), Crozier, Huntingdon and Watanuki make explicit and implicit use of Durkheimian concepts to present a pessimistic picture of western society and to develop some rather conservative solutions to its political problems. Many such societies have become characterized by an 'anomic democracy' owing to a 'delegitimation' of authority, the 'excessive' demands made by 'disaggregated interests' and a 'parochialism' in international affairs. Their rather banal solutions – which are more concerned with ruling these societies than with democracy as such – are in line with the ideology of the body that sponsored the study, namely the 'Corporate Liberal' Trilateral Commission, and are of little intrinsic interest.[1] Of more moment is that, although elements of Durkheim's thought can easily be deployed in such a study, a careful reading of *Professional Ethics and Civic Morals*, the text in which he most explicitly addressed the nature of the state and of democracy, generates a more radical and socialist (see Filloux, 1971), indeed a more interesting, set of concepts.

In Durkheim's view, for an advanced complex society to work effectively and reproduce itself it must be able to develop and sustain an autonomous political identity. A political society is 'one formed by the coming together of secondary social groups, subject to the same one authority which is not itself subject to any other superior authority duly constituted' (Durkheim, 1957, p. 45). There must be clear structures of rights and obligations, codified in law and rigorously enforced, which govern the conduct of individuals, secondary associations and government agencies. In such a society subject to the rule of law both individuation and cooperation are encouraged without falling into the excesses of egoism or obligatory altruism. The importance of

179

the individual, of particularistic collectivities such as secondary associations and the necessary coordinating role of the state can then all be recognized.

The state must be separate from the rest of society as an effective 'organizing centre'. It must be clear what it is doing, what is occurring within society as a whole and what needs to be done to make society function adequately. It must produce collective representations that are truly distinguishable 'from the other collective representations by their higher degree of consciousness and reflection' (ibid., p. 50). In fact, for Durkheim the state is ultimately defined by this deliberative role and its essence is to be found in whatever assemblies carry this out. But rational deliberation requires accurate information and in Durkheim's view this would be produced by a dialogue between the state, sub-collectivities and individual citizens. The imperative need for such a dialogue is heightened if the state is genuinely striving to act in the collective interest, since this can only be discovered by taking account of what different groups know and want. This can only happen if there exist institutions in which groups and individuals can effectively participate and it is only under these conditions that it becomes rational for the generality of citizens willingly to cooperate with the state.

> Here, the particular advantage of democracy is that, owing to the communication set up between those governing and the citizens, the latter are able to judge of the way in which those governing carry out their task, and knowing the facts more fully, are able to give or withhold their confidence.
>
> (Durkheim, 1957, p. 108)

For Durkheim, democracy, as opposed to other political systems, is less defined by its specific voting arrangements than by the fact that it is based upon the maximum openness of dialogue between the state and its subject populations. Whilst he acknowledged the importance of a general, individuated franchise, he believed that such an electorate is atomized. It is also necessary to develop mechanisms that allow for the representation of sub-collectivities as such, since secondary associations are essential components of any healthy complex society. A plurality of forms of representation will maximize communication.

Hirst has also recently argued for the need to institutionalize pluralist diversity and to develop corporatist mechanisms for 'the institutionalized representation of organized interests' so that 'those interested in an area or service may have a say in how it is run or performed even if they are not directly involved in producing or delivering it' (Hirst, 1986, p. 121).

For Durkheim a precondition for democracy is open and rational debate, which requires an openness of information and a political community composed of autonomous and informed sub-collectivities. His criticism of plebiscitary politics was based upon his belief that under such conditions demagogic manipulation is likely. His stress on the need for the relative autonomy of the state, secondary associations and the individual from each other was based upon his recognition that otherwise the state would be subject to the sway of a reactionary, unreflective conservativism and the individual to the tyranny of a forced altruistic solidarity. The experience of both capitalist and socialist societies suggests that such fears are well founded.

From this discussion and that in the previous chapter it is clear that large-scale socialist societies, although integrated under a hegemonic ideology incorporating certain substantive principles (e.g. equality of condition, rational rule-making procedures and a collective morality), cannot be homogeneous but comprise many different groups that will all have some success in pursuing their interests. This is not too dissimilar a picture to that painted of America by pluralists in the 1950s. This was criticized by the left on a number of grounds. First, if there are social conflicts in a capitalist system, the owners and controllers of capital both individually and collectively have disproportionately large resources to call upon and these may also be used to pre-empt. the emergence of conflict. Second, the very logic of the economic system as a whole works in their favour and reproduces inequality. Third, the state and political and legal forms support and presuppose capitalistic forms of social relations and actively marginalize and delegitimate certain forms of political ideology and organization. Fourth, pluralism itself therefore serves as a legitimating ideology and contributes to the concealment of class relations (Gittlin, 1965; Bachrach and Baratz, 1962; Hayes, 1972; Wolfe, 1973). In his more recent work even Dahl has deployed his own pluralistic categories to criticize both the political and economic organization of contemporary America (Dahl, 1985).

The absence of class relations in a socialist society – and of some aspects of 'skills and organizational' exploitation (Levine, 1987) – would remove major systemic mechanisms for distributing disproportionate power and influence to minorities. The radical democratization of all institutions could make democracy more substantive and less formal and enhance the power and importance of the producers. Nevertheless, some of the issues raised by both pluralists and their radical critics retain some pertinence for a socialist society.

To argue that a society, at a national and local level, could and should be actively democratic is to suggest that all organizations should be subject to some kind of democratic control with individuals enfranchised as citizens, as workers within organizations, or as recipients of services. But democracy has no one form since many different relationships between nation and region, all-embracing organizations and more particularistic ones, modes of recruiting and controlling personnel, voting systems, etc., are compatible with its principles (Hindess, 1983). There are limitations to both popular participatory democracy and representative democracy. The former is only really viable for small-scale organizations, the latter only meaningful if elected bodies are of some consequence. Even then, many administrative decisions inevitably remain the virtual monopoly of personnel with high levels of skill and competence, who thereby exert a disproportionate influence upon social life, and this is true even if their decisions are more contestable than is usually the case now. This does not mean that since 'government . . . is always in the hands of a minority' (Durkheim, 1957, p. 85) democratic elections are 'but a means of providing personnel to bodies that serve definite functions' (Hirst, 1986, p. 46). Nor is it realistic to believe that some time in the future 'the appointments necessary to control political organs may come about . . . automatically, by the pressure of public opinion, and without . . . any definite reference to the electorate' (Durkheim, 1957, p. 108). Democratic theory has always functioned on the one hand as a critique of arbitrary power and a specification of the mechanisms by which it might be refused and, on the other, as a means of assessing legitimacy, i.e. when we should subordinate ourselves to 'power' – that of norms, laws or individuals. As both Durkheim and Hirst acknowledge elsewhere, the capacity to have some kind of veto over unacceptable arrangements is an equally essential element of democracy.

Corporatism is not without problems either. True it can complement the universal franchise (Hirst, 1988, p. 201) and overcome the atomization of its participants, but corporatism tends to acknowledge only already established and legitimated groups. The legitimacy of a system is associated with the development of a hegemonic ideology, which is always something of a compromise (articulation or conglomeration of diverse fragments from previous and more local ideologies) and thus the legitimacy of *any* socio-political order is always somewhat conditional. An advanced complex society – no matter how egalitarian – will inevitably contain diverse organizations, social categories and groups. The commitment of individuals and groups to the social order will bear some relationship to whether it realizes what they see as their legitimate interests and to the extent that they believe it to be generally valid and fair. If they feel alienated and politically ineffective they may well use deviant and even illegal methods to pursue their goals.[2]

The state and the law in socialist societies

Durkheim was understandably somewhat distrustful of the state; he did not believe that it should monopolize too many social functions or exercise too much power. It has been shown that on occasion he conceptualized the state not as an expression of a unified society but rather as separate from it with possibly different but not necessarily contradictory interests. This view seems correct but it is necessary to add that no complex society, whether capitalist or socialist, can be assumed to be unified around shared interests; nor can it be assumed that the state is itself unitary and united in the pursuit of its goals. The implication of these comments is that there is inevitably something of a tension between state and society and that it is always possible that state functionaries will pursue interests that are counter to those of some or most of the other members of society, and for that matter other elements of the state. Durkheim, like such social democratic Marxists as Renner (1949), was clear that the state and its functionaries should be subject to the 'rule of law', but he recognized that this did not automatically occur (Durkheim, 1973). It can perhaps be put more strongly: since the state is itself a source of, and the effective agency for implementing, the law, it is itself, in part, outside of the law. It is only likely to remain within the 'rule of law' if it is subject to external pressures and if each of its component elements is subject to scrutiny by other relatively autonomous elements – there is something to be said for the liberal theory of checks and balances.

If in his explicit definition of law Durkheim focused on its repressive role and ignored its formal properties in his elaborated discussion and substantive analyses, he did recognize its facilitative and even constitutive role. Moreover, it was shown earlier that the juridical relation that occurs in all societies can be distinguished from legal rules, which have certain formal properties. In Hirst's recent work there is a discussion of law that is similar to but in some ways goes beyond Durkheim's, foregrounding issues that are of immediate relevance. For Hirst, law refers to forms of definitive/regulatory rules produced by certain institutions presented as a sovereign power and enforced by specific state agencies (Hirst, 1980, p. 64). 'Sovereignty' is a necessary 'fiction', which allows for the exploration and resolution of disputes between law-issuing institutions, thereby producing some consistency within its discourses. It thus

> resolves in doctrine the paradox . . . how 'law' (legal agencies) can at once be above the activities it regulates and yet subject itself . . . It . . . prioritizes certain agencies and activities within the apparatuses of the state; these are held to express the will of the sovereign.
>
> (Hirst, 1980, p. 69)

Sovereignty is a 'symbolic function' but in reality the paradox remains. The state has no essence, no clear organizing centre that is the source of law and order; the totality of the state is not intrinsically and spontaneously limited by law. On the other hand, social order, justice and liberty depend upon the existence of a relatively consistent and predictable legal system and the effective regulation of state activities.

How then is the legal system articulated with the non-legal aspects of social relations since the nature of the state and the economic system and the forms of interpersonal relationships will surely affect its form and substantive content? Marxists, for example, would argue that in class societies the law is an element of a repressive and mystificatory system (Marx and Engels, 1845, in 1976, pp. 89–93) – legal categories, the content of laws, the forms of organization and access to legal institutions are all marked (and often materially affected) by class relations (Burton and Carlen, 1979). Against such views Hindess and Hirst (1977) have asserted the virtual autonomy of law and in particular its 'necessary non-correspondence' with economic relations. For Durkheim, on the other hand, law is an index and source of different kinds of solidarity and therefore is both determined by other social relations and also has its own causal efficacy. But, whatever the problems in Durkheim's overall conceptual schema, the combination of elements of his work with aspects of Marxism has a great deal of potential.

Woodiwiss (1985) has argued that, whilst law does not have the absolute autonomy attributed to it by Hirst and it often helps maintain oppressive class relations, nevertheless it is not simply an expression of class interests. It is better understood as

a set of state enunciated and enforced discourses, which interpellate the subjects they address in such a way that they will be law-abiding, provided that the same subjects do not successfully resist this disciplining because of prior or other interpellations originating in and articulated within counter discourses . . . the law may be understood to produce a background ideology-effect that helps to maintain the security of the social relationships that the state also and in other ways reproduces . . .

. . . the law places the subjects it addresses in particular positions relative to one another according to the schema to be found in its component discourses. These positions are constituted by the rights and duties that define them and which therefore determine the relations that can and should exist between them; e.g. husband/wife, employer/employee and citizen/state . . . such positions and such relations are also defined and confined by other discourses and intrinsic technologies apart from those specific to the law.

(Woodiwiss, 1985, pp. 72–3)

For Woodiwiss, like Durkheim, law is both an effect of and affects other fundamental social relations. Its development and substantive concerns depend upon its own internal logic, the specific (possibly conflictual) social relations that are present within a society, and their (possibly contradictory) articulation with both each other and the law. Provided that there are adequate institutional resources through which it can be 'realized', the legal recognition or creation and enforcement or denial of capacities, powers or duties will have significant social effects. Law can be constitutive, enabling and coercive.

If social formations are conceived of as mobile, articulated combinations of elements, which have as one effect the interpellation of subjects by complementary or (possibly) contradictory discourses, then the interaction between the dynamics of the social relations and the forms of collective social organization, discourses, interpersonal relationships and ideologies will determine the form, substantive content and significance of the law. These will determine what interests are secured by it and the relative ease with which individuals will wish to, or be able to, submit themselves to the exigencies of social life and the lawful authority of the state. In a socialist society the production of a formal and substantive equality for individuals would be a major social goal realized in and, in part, through the law.

Juridical relations – i.e. the existence of structures of rights and obligations and modes of attributing responsibility to individuals or collectivities – are an endemic feature of any society. Exchange relationships of various kinds – particularly the 'equitable' exchange of goods and services – can contribute to social solidarity. One of the most significant features of these forms of relationship is that the mutual interest of the parties in current and future transactions motivates them to honour their obligations. Legal recognition and control may facilitate these relations. True, it may, on occasion, enforce obligations primarily as Durkheim argued, in a 'restitutive' manner. However, once rights and obligations become subject to legal discourse they will be evaluated according to its substantive criteria of equity and of the kind of rights and duties it recognizes and prioritizes. With the development of 'organic solidarity' only certain kinds of contracts would be recognized – those between substantively equal partners.

Since Durkheim's economics are somewhat inadequate, organic solidarity would only be achieved with a more complex system like that of the Swedish Meidner plan. This, in making socialist producers' associations the basic unit of the economy, gave some indication of a more adequate legal and economic framework. Thus the socialist jurists Abrahamson and Bromston argued for the establishment

> of a set of labour rights, which should be privileged relative to private property rights . . . with such an amendment in place the contract of employment itself would be radically changed as well as the distribution of rights within it. Moreover, remembering Marx's strictures against 'equal rights' this would be profoundly unequal since if enforced they would gradually undermine any rights of capital, in the pursuit of the material equality of need-fulfillment.
>
> (Woodiwiss, 1985, p. 64)

The valorization by the law of any specific rights means that other rights and interests may suffer; from their point of view such law is not enabling but punitive. The disadvantage that they thereby experience and the threat of sanctions if they actively oppose the operation of lawful relations vindicate the Austinian–Durkheimian view that an essential (although by no means the sole) quality of law is its potential coerciveness (Skillen, 1977, p. 100). Nevertheless, legal forms may be constitutive. They may provide the rules to determine who is qualified to fulfil which tasks and to exercise which powers. They may help organize the means by which individuals are held accountable for the fulfilment of their role-related responsibilities.

The rule of law and socialism

Durkheim argued that the development of the state, if it is itself subject to law, can increase liberty, and Hirst has argued that socialism will probably see an extension of legally regulated intervention into social life. Such an extension of state activities would only be 'progressive' if there are social forces that can control the state and if the legal institutions have some real autonomy, i.e. if they are relatively independent of other state institutions and have their own bases of power (Hirst, 1980, pp. 77–88). Such socialist constitutionalism is still somewhat limited. If the structure, ordering and priorities of the state and the content of the law are the effect of a struggle between shifting heterogeneous forces and of the attempt to produce within it one or other form of coherence, then it will not work to the benefit of everybody to the same degree. It will be unlikely spontaneously to take cognizance of the interests of newly emerging groups. Whatever efforts are made to give all interests political representation within the dominant political and legal discourse, there will probably be very little understanding of the goals or the determinants of the action of the more marginal groups and individuals. As a matter of course, at times one would expect from them some illegal behaviour, some of which would be simply criminal and some proto-political. The latter might subsequently be legitimated in the same way that Socrates' conduct came to be interpreted as based upon a higher morality (Durkheim, 1938, pp. 71–2).

Moreover, it is not necessary to subscribe to any iron 'law of oligarchy' to believe that, even with sophisticated methods of supervision, powerful functionaries can rarely be totally controlled. They are under various pressures – the exigencies of office (national security, for example), contradictory demands from different groups, etc., which usually lead them to adopt a somewhat managerialist view of the world, leading in turn to their developing separate interests from the ruled. Given the resources at their disposal, this allows them to act in a partisan way. In so far as the law does not acknowledge all interests equally and since the state may act in a partisan way then, whilst a policy of legally enforced 'social defence' may be inescapable, law-abiding behaviour cannot be seen as unquestionably good, nor law-breaking behaviour as 'reactionary', 'selfish', 'anti-social', 'pathological' or 'wicked'.

The 'constitutionalist' view was put well by US Supreme Justice Fortas when he claimed that 'Just as we expect the government to be bound by all laws, so each individual is bound by all of the laws under the Constitution' (Fortas, 1968, p. 65). To which Zinn responded:

> the government being bound by law is an expectation, while the citizen's being bound by law is a fact. . . . The government does pick and choose among the laws it enforces and the laws it ignores. . . . Furthermore, when the government does violate the law . . . – it has no punishing body standing over it as does the citizen; it does not and cannot accept the rule of law as final. National power prevails.
>
> (Zinn, 1968, pp. 23–4)

For, if the law is somewhat partisan, if one cannot be confident that state functionaries will stay within the law and if sovereignty is a 'fiction' (however necessary), then the 'rule of law' cannot simply be invoked – as it often was by Durkheim – to justify subservience to the state. (Subsequently, 'when his links with a notorious financial wheeler dealer in Florida were revealed' (Chambliss, 1982, p. 175) Fortas was forced to resign from the Supreme Court!) In any society, individuals may rationally choose, for moral or political reasons, to engage in illegal acts in the context of political strugggle rather than as a moral gesture – Socrates' mode of civil disobedience is only one option! A legal system based upon an adequate analysis of the nature of social order will recognize the category of political crime (Moran, 1981).[3]

Capitalism, socialism and the criminal law

This section will examine law in its most coercive form, as criminal law. Now Marxists have argued that crime – whether it is overridingly destructive or a form of 'primitive rebellion' – is primarily an effect of the forms of social organization and ideologies found within class societies. Poverty and egoistic ideologies help generate street crime and greed, and the defence of privilege leads the ruling class and the state to break the law, usually with impunity (Bonger, 1916; Pashukanis, 1978, p. 212; Taylor, Walton and Young, 1973; Hirst, 1972). Since class relations have been considered the most fundamental aspect of the social order, there has been a tendency to believe that the end of class inequality will see the virtual end of anti-social behaviour of crime and the criminal law (Engels, 1845, in Marx and Engels, 1975, pp. 248–9).

In an earlier work, *Crimes of the Powerful* (1976), I also argued that inequality generates conflicts that may be expressed in criminal activity. Although that text operated with an overly instrumentalist view of the state (Jones, 1982), much of its analysis of the sources and significance of crime within capitalist societies is still sound. *Inequalities of power and wealth generate criminal conduct and provide differential protection from the criminalizing power of the state.* Moreover, whilst class relations play a major role in generating and sustaining inequalities other relatively autonomous aspects of social organization (those associated with race and gender) also generate their own forms of social inequality and anti-social conduct. Thus an equality of condition (and power) between men and women and the development of different forms of personal relations and modes of eroticism would make crimes like rape less likely, since this is, in part, *an expression of and a support for male dominance* (Clarke and Lewis, 1977; Barnet, 1974; Schwendinger and Schwendinger, 1983; Henriques *et al.*, 1984, p. 251–60).

Nevertheless, it is necessary now to reject the thesis implicit in much Marxist writing, including my own, that crime will be completely eliminated from a socialist society. There will still be criminogenic situations and the socialist position on crime must be rethought. The elimination of certain kinds of inequality may itself produce problems for the elimination of others: the extent to which individuals have their desires satisfied within socialist societies will vary considerably. Moreover in areas like drug use and drug abuse (from cigarettes to marijuana, from alcohol to heroin) where there are different forms of calculation, priorities and moralities, conflict between different groups is likely and indeed virtually unavoidable.

A useful way of considering these issues is by a brief consideration of the work of Jock Young, a sociologist who has made a significant contribution to the development of criminology and who has been strongly influenced by both Durkheim and Marx. In the *The Drugtakers* (1971) he demonstrated the relevance of a transactionalist approach to the British context. *The New Criminology* (1973), which he wrote with Ian Taylor and Paul Walton, helped transform the level of theorizing in the area. His articles on 'Working class criminology' (1974) and on 'Left idealism, reformism and beyond: from new criminology to Marxism' (1979) forced many radical criminologists to confront the destructiveness of much crime. In his recent empirical studies using crime victimization surveys (Jones, Maclean and Young, 1986) and in his related development of a 'realist criminology' (Lea and Young, 1984; Kinsey, Lea and Young, 1986; Matthews and Young, 1986) he has shown that socialists must try to discover what actually are the patterns of criminal activity and victimization. They must also be willing to assess empirically the effectiveness of different crime pre-emption, crime prevention and crime control strategies by monitoring their effects. A socialist response to crime cannot be built upon principled positions and abstract theorizing alone. Nevertheless, it is possible and useful to criticize much of his work from the perspective of a reconstituted radical Durkheimism.[4]

In his earlier writings, Young argued that capitalistic social relations are a major cause of criminal activity, that much criminal activity is proto-political and that 'the task is to create a society in which the facts of human diversity, whether personal, organic or social, are not subject to the power to criminalize' (Taylor, Walton and Young, 1973, p. 282). Subsequently, whilst retaining the first proposition, he stresses rather the destructive consequences of present-day working-class crime on working-class people (Young, 1975, 1979; Lea and Young, 1984; Kinsey, Lea and Young, 1986; Matthews and Young, 1986). In a recent book co-authored with John Lea, he has developed a somewhat unreconstituted Durkheimian characterization of criminal activity. Working-class criminals, he argues, have an egoistic orientation and have adopted 'capitalistic' values.

    . . . street crime itself, far from being different in terms of values from the crimes of the powerful, displays precisely the same ethos of competitiveness and machismo.

(Lea and Young, 1984, p. 74)

These individuals may experience relative deprivation but they choose to become involved in crime, 'an egoistic response to injustice' that itself 'perpetrates injustice' (ibid., 1984, p. 91). Instead of engaging in 'collectivist' political action, criminals are committed egoists, willing agents of capitalistic values, who should be caught and *punished* for the protection of working-class people. Presumably if socialistic rather than capitalistic values ('altruistic rather than egoistic values') became dominant, crime would be an unlikely – but not an impossible – option for individuals to 'choose'.

These arguments of Young can be criticized for their tendency to rely upon a culturalist neo-classicism. Frequently the assumption is made that the author has an adequate understanding of the meanings that criminals give to their activities and how they interpret their interests. There is a presupposition that a rational response would be collectivistic and that all individuals are equally able to refuse the egoistic alternative. Such arguments are voluntaristic, often overly moralistic and grounded in a negative conception of freedom.[5] What freedom we have lies not only in the possibility of refraining *from action* but also in being able *to act*, of being able to work towards one's projects (Merleau-Ponty, 1962, pp. 438–9).

It is also necessary to understand how social relations affect the possibility of the realization (or displacement) of the projects and desires of individuals and hence the degree of frustration that such individuals may experience. How stark are the choices that confront them? Must they either live a lawful frustrated life or realize their goals illegally or, for that matter, relieve some of their frustration irrationally? Are they working with sensibilities, moralities and rationalities and in social milieux that we do not grasp (Foucault, 1979a)? Whilst the ideology the individual uses to interpret his/her own activity (and by which he/she is interpellated) must be a component of any explanation of human conduct (individuals must be motivated to act), it is unlikely to provide an *adequate* explanation of the determinants of their actions. Accounts are often mere glosses and at best partial explanations (Mills, 1940; Blum and McHugh, 1971). The full determinants of an individual's activities in concrete social settings are never known.

For Freud and Lacan although the conscious/preconscious/

unconscious system can never be grasped in its totality, this does not rule out all forms of individual responsibility. The individual human subject operates at the point of intersection of social pressures and also possibilities; of ideologies that he or she may be able to, in part, analyse; of a socially constituted unconscious and desire; *and* at the same time he/she has some capacity to control conduct. Freud formulated the issue in the imperative statement '*Wo es ist, so ich wollen*', which was interpreted by Lacan to mean

'There where IT WAS ITSELF, it is my duty that I come to be.'

The I of the formula refers to an ideal concept of a harmonious accord between subject c (the conscious) and subject u (the unconscious).

(Bar, 1971, p. 260)

Duty here means a responsibility to avoid situations known to precipitate conduct that is harmful to self or others and implies *a limited freedom to seek those where the effect of the constitutive play of differences is likely to be personally and socially constructive*.

Egoism and altruism should not be viewed as mutually exclusive orientations. Individuals need to take cognizance of egoism too. Their capacity to order their conduct bears a direct, albeit complex, relationship to their ability to develop, acknowledge and satisfy their (socially constituted) 'appetites and passions'. Their socio–structural location, their emotional investments and their value commitments (McCabe, 1974, 1976; Henriques *et al.*, 1984) affect the degree to which they *need* to control their desires and particularly to control them by suppression as opposed to simply organizing their lives to satisfy them in an ordered way. The logic of these comments is that a major aim of a sophisticated socialist response to crime is *to open up the socially constructive and personally fulfilling options for those who are so often faced with the stark choice between criminal activity through which they can realize their desires (or at least release tension) and an overly repressive self-denying lawfulness*.

Now implicit in much of Young's work is a somewhat Rousseauian conception of the human subject as a fundamentally good, perfectible entity. Negative traits or activities are construed as perversions of the human essence and explained either as the effect of some outside agency, i.e. of an exploitative and oppressive society, and/or as the result of a perverse choice by the individual. Young would not deny that there is some tension between the essential nature of human beings and attempts to control them, but believes that this is generally due to the contradictions between their essential humanity and the inhumanity of capitalism. In a socialist society man's nature and social relations could be in accord. Young implies that rational individuals will be able and willing to submit themselves to a socialist normative order.

For Durkheim, the rationality of the human subject is produced and sustained by society. Society is not an expression or an extension of the subject's ontological attributes; rather it provides individuals with the capacity to follow its rules and the ability to engage in meaningful and orderly social interaction. If one can *follow a rule*, by definition one can break it. Any normative order requires of its subjects that their 'appetites and passions' be controlled and ordered. 'A community of rational co-operators' may need 'to use force against itself' (Levine, 1987, p. 136) so that its members are the rational subjects they desire to be.

A Critique of judicial ideology

Before returning to the issue of the role of law and the likelihood of crime under socialism, let us explore some of the implications of these remarks. Those of high social status and income have a radically different life experience from most others. This is particularly true of the very poor, who are the most likely to be convicted of crimes. The possession of wealth guarantees that an individual can feed, clothe and shelter himself or herself more than adequately. The wealthy are able to choose the activities in which they engage and plan their participation in them in ways that are likely to match their moods and thus *although they may work hard and be disciplined nevertheless they will be able to satisfy many of their desires.* Their contacts with others will rarely if ever produce anything but the self-affirming respect of equals or the deference of inferiors. In contrast, individuals of low social status can rarely plan their lives in a satisfying way and frequently do not experience social contact of a kind that might energize them to control themselves and conform to social norms. The everyday experience of the capitalist or professional academic or judge is radically different from that of the unskilled, particularly when unemployed.

Weber argued that those with access to honour, power,

possessions and pleasure were seldom satisfied with the fact of being fortunate:

> he needs to know that he has a *right* to his good fortune. He wants to be convinced that he 'deserves' it and above all in comparison with others. He wishes to be allowed the belief that the less fortunate also merely experiences his due.
>
> (Weber, 1958, p. 271)

Such a concern with the 'legitimacy' of their fortune represents not so much an aspect of human ontology as an ever-present 'political' problem: how can the 'fortunate' justify themselves to the less fortunate? One function of law enforcement in capitalist societies is the legitimation of privilege.

The legal category of 'mitigating circumstances' to some extent acknowledges that the conditions under which people live affects their ability to live lawful lives (Stevens, 1863). This poses the question: if the 'fortunate' are subject to less pressure to steal than the poor, how is it then that they feel free to condemn the lower-class criminal? Foucault paraphrases the reasoning behind their answer as follows:

> He steals because he is poor; certainly we all know that not all poor people steal. So for this individual to steal there has to be something wrong with him, and this is his character, his psyche, his upbringing, his unconscious, his desires.
>
> (Foucault, 1980b, p. 44)[6]

The argument is that, since there are poor people who do not steal, it is possible to be poor and law-abiding. And further that, if the privileged were poor themselves, they would still be law-abiding. Thus the 'deserving poor' and the privileged are supposed to have similar 'moral fibre', although the latter have additional qualities that explain their relative worldly success.

'Character' then, or some other quality of the individual that transcends social contexts, is invoked to explain and justify the different trajectories of people's lives. The category of the 'deserving poor' is more a convenient legitimating and obfuscating category than a substantive reference to a specific group of people (Palmer and Pearce, 1983). Such individualistic and 'abstract' (non-materialist) (Burton and Carlen, 1979) explanations of social action are untenable. Subjects are socially constituted and continually reconstituted through their current social relations.

For example, a High Court judge with a net salary in excess of £45,000 p.a. would be unlikely to know how he would feel and act if he had the life experiences and prospects of an unemployed Black youth on £1,500 or less p.a.[7] How would he cope with insufficient money for even the bare necessities of life, with a frequent lack of fit between his desires and his opportunities, with the contempt of lower-middle-class bureaucrats, with the media's portrayal of him and 'his kind', etc? What grounds would he have to assume that if he were one of the poor he would not develop and display their qualities (or values)? In his discussion of 'the forced division of labour' Durkheim argued that in any society with inherited privileges there could not be equality of opportunity, yet the idea that in capitalist societies positions of high social status are primarily achieved in a meritocratic manner is still promulgated. This discussion of course accepts at face value the claim of the privileged that their own fortune and current conduct are lawful but it has been shown elsewhere that this can by no means be assumed (Pearce, 1976; Reiman, 1979).[8]

The implications of the above discussion are manifold. The outraged self-righteous language of the privileged when they condemn the criminality of the poor is offensive because it is misleading and ultimately self-serving. But to recognize the importance of structural factors is not to argue that criminality is always the only possible outcome of criminogenic situations. Nor does one accept at face value the idea that the law-abiding poor are merely (diluted) versions of privileged role models. Some kinds of crime and types of criminal have always been tolerated by working-class people (Foucault, 1979b; Palmer, 1976).

Crime in socialist societies

Whilst a formal legal system involves some self-consciousness about at least some elements of the normative system, the extent to which the content of legal norms is subject to collective critical scrutiny depends upon the forms of political organization and the distribution of power within a society. The more egalitarian and democratic they are, the more likely it is that the legal system will function to benefit all groups and thus win their loyalty. In everyday interaction, however, new definitions of norms are constantly generated. Even when individuals and groups have roughly equivalent power, and thus engage in non-repressive communication and negotiation (Mueller, 1970), some of their activities may become defined as deviant, leading to the frustration of some of their goals. This is particularly true in a dynamic society where new activities, norms and social organizations are continually generated. Since some of these are probably mutually incompatible, the legal valorization of some entails the suppression of others. In any society this inescapable aspect of societal management will on occasion confront criminal resistance. As Durkheim argued, a high degree of social dynamism creates the possibility of a high rate of crime.

In the same way that a society of saints is more scrupulous about its members' conduct than are laymen (Durkheim, 1938, pp. 68–9), a humane society is more demanding of its members than an inhumane society. The overriding commitment of a socialist society to an equal and humane life for *all* would mean that higher standards of performance and conduct would be expected than is true under capitalism. A genuine respect for the individual might mean more rigorously imposed safety regulations (Hirst, 1980, p. 103), and a greater respect for the collectivity might mean that:

> Frauds and injustices, which yesterday left the public conscience almost indifferent, arouse it today, and this sensitivity will only become more acute with time.
>
> (Durkheim, 1973, p. 307)

The elimination of the ruling class and of many structural contradictions would make certain kinds of destructive criminal activity and the creation of a *forced solidarity* through moral panics, scapegoating, etc. less likely. But it is clear that there are features of social life as such and particularly of a dynamic society that make it inevitable that some forms of diversity will be defined as deviant and/or criminal (*contra* Taylor, Walton and Young, 1973, p. 282). Whilst a general equality of condition would be a goal in a socialist society, the existence of diverse organizations, social categories and groups would still create variations in income and differences in life chances. A lack of social homogeneity and the existence of a plurality of values in the community mean social priorities and the content of the law will always remain contentious. (Young argues a somewhat similar position to this in *Losing the Fight against Crime* – Kinsey, Lea and Young, 1986.) Furthermore, it is clear that in many areas of social life the development of skills and capacities will be uneven and some individuals will be relatively deficient and therefore disadvantaged.

I have argued that a rational orientation to the world must include, and be sustained by, both 'egoistic' and 'altruistic' elements. But there is no simple calculus determining their relative proportions, so on occasion an imbalance between them may lead to excessive individualism (cynicism, careerism, crime, 'egoistic' suicide') or excesssive 'collectivism' (over-conformity, a militant search for homogeneity, altruistic suicide). Thus many problems would not simply disappear with the demise of capitalism.

Durkheim argued that for individuals to develop any form of rationality they must control, limit and order their 'appetites and passions' to what those in their social position can realistically and legitimately expect. They are aided in achieving this by the various systems of social constraint, from the most intimate and concrete nexus of rights and obligations to the most abstract system of social norms – the legal system. Constraint may be exercised by a fear of sanctions, by a somewhat compulsive sense of duty and/or by a belief in social norms grounded in desire – in a sense of self-realization based upon an identification with the collectivity. On the other hand, society can only function and be reproduced if individuals contain their appetites and passions and submit to the dynamic of social life and its regulative norms. Durkheim argued rightly that because the despot is unconstrained he is as much at the mercy of his desires as is the untutored child (Durkheim, 1961, p. 45). In a society that developed true organic solidarity individuals would be expected to demonstrate a socially responsible concern with the actual consequences of their actions and a willingness to recompense anybody suffering because of them. Similarly, if 'charity' is an aspect of the dominant ideology and it is recognized that it is not individuals alone who author actions, one would expect 'victims' to be more interested in restoring their own fortunes and in understanding how harmful acts come about than in punishing their perpetrators. In the 'Two laws of penal evolution' Durkheim argued that the increase in secularism has meant that the humanity of individuals is not so readily forgotten. Those found guilty of crimes are punished more humanely (Durkheim, 1973). As an overall characterization of the history of penal practice this is undoubtedly overly optimistic – but as a prescripive argument it has a great deal of power. If a social order valorizes all of its members and recognizes that their actions are, in large part, an effect of social forces over which they have little control, then to respond to their criminal acts in a vindictive and overly moralistic manner is illogical.

Crime: Some modest socialist proposals

Since, as I have argued, a crime-free society is a Utopia, the criminal law and its enforcement apparatuses have a role to play in both capitalist and socialist societies. There is some continuity in the dilemmas faced by all complex societies. In Durkheim's terms, capitalism and socialism are of the same *genus*. The extent to which individuals are authors of their actions can vary substantially and some recognition of this should inform socialist strategies of 'social defence', in both class and non-class societies. Durkheim not only stressed the need to control the 'passions and desires' but he also recognized that they needed some gratification. A useful *initial* assumption in reacting to criminals is that they engage in crime largely because few other courses of action that allow them to gratify their desires are open to them. This neither reduces them to the status of purely behaviourist subjects – as in the work of Pashukanis, for example[9] – nor 'elevates' them to purely transcendental subjects – as in Lea and Young (Neale, 1977).

What, then, should be the socialist attitude to crime in capitalist and post-class societies? First, there is no need to accept that all acts currently defined as crimes should be prosecuted. The repeal of some legislation may be more important than its effectiveness. Second, the whole judicial system and its panoply of coercive institutions need to be reorganized, democratized and the 'powers of the judiciary . . . redefined and redistributed' (Carlen, 1983, p. 210; Taylor, 1981). Every effort should be made to reduce the role of imprisonment. It should rarely be used, except for detention – if it is literally the only way to protect people's life and limbs – or in a denunciatory manner to demonstrate the seriousness of an offence, for example in cases of rape. If prison is not generally used for other offences it is the fact of imprisonment rather than longevity of stay that demonstrates social abhorrence (Box-Grainger, 1986, pp. 49–51).

If an anti-social crime has been perpetrated, then the state should intervene in an individual's life if he or she was *its* author. Prosecution should occur if the defendant is sane and does not successfully plead 'necessity'. If guilt is established then the individual should suffer some specified penalty, although mitigating circumstances should be able to modify a sentence. The criminalizing of certain kinds of conduct and the punishment of its perpetrators publicly signals that it is anti-social and not a viable solution to personal problems, and specifies, for example in situations of interpersonal conflict such as wife battering (and crimes such as rape, see above) that there is a criminal and a victim. A scale of penalties shows the relative seriousness of different crimes and aims to deter the more serious. It can also thereby help to reinforce positive forms of social relationships – e.g. approprately framed and enforced laws against sexual violence can help sustain sexual equality (Taylor, 1981, pp. 191–200).

Punishment allows the criminal to expiate his or her crime and therefore to become a citizen again, i.e. to return to life as a legitimate subject in a way that pre-empts the development of vigilantism and lynch law. Furthermore, a general assumption that a defendant is a responsible juridical and legal subject limits the *right* of the state to interfere in the lives of criminals inside and outside of detention. This must imply that subjectifying disciplinary and 'therapeutic treatment' has to be in some sense voluntary – criminals ought to have enforceable rights, including the right to refuse 'treatment'.[10] However, this is not to deny that other strategies might be relevant – currently, for example, in Holland and the Scandinavian countries many offenders can avoid trial and conviction if they acknowledge their guilt and attend treatment programmes for drug abuse, alcoholism, etc. (Carlen, 1983, p. 213).

Nevertheless, a socialist response to criminals and to crimino-genic situations must involve the search for ways of opening up the individual's possibilities of engaging in more constructive and satisfying activities. For example, it can be argued that some criminals do suffer from an 'educational problem' – they commit offences largely out of ignorance of the way in which society operates and of their own role and motives. Although often not the case (Muncie, 1984, p. 172–8), group work with young people can be non-authoritarian, equipping them with the social skills and personality attributes to cope more adequately with their environment and to make their own decisions more rationally (Bazelgette, 1971, Jones and Kerslake, 1979). Violent men are often consumed by some kind of destructive rage and/or are interpersonally inept and should be offered the possibility of some kind of therapeutic treatment, for example that which Jimmy Boyle received in Barlinnie (Boyle, 1977). Wife batterers, rapists and child molesters should be offered contexts to develop the understanding and social skills needed for a reciprocal egalitarian sexuality (Abel *et al.*, 1976; Yaffe, 1981). As in China during the 'cultural revolution', criminal activity should be seen not as authored exclusively by the individual but as an effect of general social relationships and often of an 'underdeveloped perspective' (Pepinsky, 1978). What is needed is a neo-classicism that is able to live up to its promise and recognize its limitations, as opposed to one that functions as a support and mask for 'disciplinary processes' (Foucault, 1978b, pp. 87–8; 1979b, pp. 183, 223).

On a more structural level an understanding and/or modification of the social contexts in which potential criminals live can make crime less likely. Thus 'resource-oriented' strategies developed to deal with criminogenic situations are worth maintaining and developing. Whilst a general improvement in living conditions and sexual equality would limit the incidence of wife battering, the continued provision of accommodation for battered women could prevent its repetition (Binney et al., 1981; Wilson, 1983). Mathiesen (1976), amongst others, explains the genesis of crime and the existence of prisons primarily in terms of the production and control of surplus populations and therefore believes that the replacement of capitalism by socialism would render imprisonment anachronistic. Others such as Christie (1976) and Hulsman (1986) argue that many offences should be decriminalized and conflicts should be resolved by the protagonists rather than punished by the state.[11] There is little doubt that much would improve if these changes came about. What cannot be treated as an axiom, however, is that the role of the prison as a mode of detention, of protecting society from people who are currently dangerous, will automatically disappear. It is difficult to see what alternative there would be to preventive detention for such mass murderers as Brady and Hindley (Williams, 1968), Peter Sutcliffe (the Yorkshire Ripper – Yallop, 1981; Bland, 1984), Nielsen (Masters, 1986), or David Berkowitz (the Son of Sam – Willeford, 1980).

Even if the major aim of a sophisticated socialist response to crime is to open up constructive options for those in criminogenic situations, we cannot presume to know with *scientific* certainty why (and indeed sometimes whether) an individual committed a crime or if in future they will be a law-abiding citizen or not. Some individuals commit crime when subject to no obvious overwhelming internal or external pressure, as in the case of much white-collar crime. Since all subjects are socially constituted, even in these cases it is important for socialists to remember that criminals remain part of society. As individuals they should have the right to a fair trial. If found guilty they should not be treated vindictively – like all of us, they are only in part responsible for their own desires and actions and should never lose the right to humane treatment.[12] At the end of this chapter it is worth reiterating Durkheim's arguments why a genuinely civilized society, as well as sympathizing with victims, would also care about offenders.

> What tempers the collective anger, which is the essence of punishment, is the sympathy which we feel for every man who suffers, the horror which all destructive violence causes us; it is the same sympathy and the same horror which inflames this anger. And so the same cause which sets in motion the repressive apparatus tends also to halt it. . . . But there is a real and terrible contradiction in avenging the offended human dignity of the victim by violating that of the criminal.
>
> (Durkheim, 1973, p. 303)

Notes

1 The policies and politics of the Trilateral Commission are assessed in Sklar (1980) and Van der Pijl (1984).

2 I have criticized Hirst (1986) for the implicit evolutionism that he shares with Durkheim in Pearce (1987a). Recently Hirst (1988) has elaborated his arguments on the need to complement the universal franchise with corporatist institutions.

3 Whilst Hirst is critical of Thompson's naive trust in the 'rule of law' (Hirst, 1980, p. 199), he does not seem adequately to think through the implications of his own comments for a socialist society.

4 Young with Taylor and Walton was involved in a somewhat acrimonious debate with Paul Hirst (see Taylor, Walton and Young, 1975; and Pearce, 1985a). Hirst (1980) sharply attacked Greenwood and Young (1976), although in Hirst (1986, p. 67) there is a strong endorsement of Young and Lea (1985). Young and Lea (1984) and other recent works have been strongly criticized by Gilroy (1982, 1987), Sim (1982), Gilroy and Sim (1985), Scraton (1985).

5 In this text, Lea and Young's analysis of social milieux is sometimes somewhat empiricist (Lea and Young, 1984, pp. 76–104; Willer and Willer, 1973, pp. 88–95).

6 James Watson drove a car along a pavement crowded with Christmas shoppers, knocking down one elderly Tottenham woman, Wood Green Crown Court heard last week.

   He was jailed for reckless driving and a string of other offences, for a total of four years and nine months after admitting he turned to crime when he lost his job.

   Recorder Douglas Blair pointed out that while many people were unemployed, they did not break the law.

Watson (31), from West Hampstead, pleaded guilty to five burglaries, four offences of deception, one of handling stolen goods and two of taking cars without consent in addition to reckless driving. He asked for another ten deceptions and two burglaries to be taken into consideration.

(The Haringey Independent, 27 August 1987)

7 In 1988, when a High Court judge earned £68,500 p.a. (£45,633 after tax), an unemployed 18–24 year old on social security received £1,355 p.a. (*Guardian* 22 April and 19 May 1988).

8 This is not the place to explore these issues in any great depth but it is worth reiterating the point that this abstract concept of the juridical subject can function in judgements about the venality of the powerful and privileged too. They may be roundly condemned for setting a bad example, *but*, more often, the fact that judge and defendant share similar lives and 'temptations' may create an empathic understanding of the complex pressures to which individuals are subject and hence to a non-essentializing view of the relationship between these criminals and their acts. Chapman (1968, pp. 54–96) provides many examples of this differential response to criminal activity.

9 For Pashukanis the science of Marxism shows that crime and/or destructive deviance are the direct consequence of class relations, particularly capitalistic ones. *Mens rea*, motives, degrees of guilt, etc. – in short, *the juridical subject* within law – are therefore ideological constructs that have real enough effects but are of little relevance in explaining how and why people become criminals or how to deal with them. Crime is caused by class inequality and they will therefore disappear together. If individuals commit crimes in a socialist society, then this is because it still contains 'dangerous situations' owing to an incomplete social transformation or, alternatively, because such individuals are 'medical–educational' problems. Criminality that can not be diagnosed as a symptom of social contradictions or of a lack of 'education' would then have to be a 'medical problem' needing a 'medical' response (Pashukanis, 1978, p. 187). From a neo-Durkheimian viewpoint there are two obvious problems with this position. First, as was argued in Chapter 5, no society can exist that did not develop ways in which individuals (or collectives) are made responsible either to others or to themselves for their actions. Such 'juridical relations' are pervasive throughout social life, although the attribution of responsibility for behaviour has various meanings and consequences. Second, an essential component of the explanation of human conduct is the motives that individuals attribute to themselves and others; whilst the understanding that subjects have of their action is insufficient to explain it adequately, it is certainly not irrelevant.

10 Without such 'rights' psychoanalysis could not be meaningfully used. 'Transference', the 'treatment contract' and the moment of individuation and separation from the analyst are all important elements of the

therapeutic process. In a prison setting it would be virtually impossible for the analysand and the analyst to work out when 'insight' was a function of transference, an unconscious wish to be agreeable in order to get out of prison, or a sign of 'individuation'. Thus, *contra* Foucault, subjectifying 'disciplines' are not *per se* modes of coercive social control; in the case of psychoanalysis at least, this is so only when they are abused. Conventional psychoanalysts have, of course, often presumed that criminal acts are necessarily symptoms of a defective personal structure and that criminals seek to be caught and punished to assuage guilt. However, even one such author, Franz Alexander, acknowledged the existence of 'normal non-neurotic criminals – professional delinquents whose superegos have criminal tendencies . . . with a moral code different from that of the rest of society' (Alexander and Straub 1956, p. xi).

Foucault has been criticized by Hirst for his ultra-leftist libertarianism, for presenting 'normatising individuation' as if disciplinary practices had some 'unity of object, content or effect' and for counterposing legal and disciplinary regulation. He thereby fails to recognize that

> law defines the status of the specialist practices . . . and sets limits to the powers of the agents and institutions involved in forms of discipline, doctors, teachers, reformatories, hospitals etc. . . .
>
> (Hirst, 1980, p. 92)

Whilst some of Hirst's criticisms are powerful, he does not recognize that a major thrust of Foucault's argument is that formal definitions of status and capacity tell us little about *how* disciplinary practices are organized and how their 'objects' – mental patients, prisoners, schoolchildren, etc. – are in practice 'subjectified'. Moreover the language of rights, duties and capacities is not adequate to describe or control what occurs, it legitimates disciplinarity and itself needs to be redefined (Foucault, 1980c, p. 105). The crucial problem then is how institutions are organized, monitored and controlled.

Foucault himself fails to discriminate between different forms of organizational structure – for him they are all equivalent because they all require the disciplining and subjectivation of their members. He thus ignores the significant differences between different kinds of subjectivities and how they allow individuals to relate to themselves and the world. A capacity for self-reflection and self-control is a precondition for any kind of rational activity and any kind of social order (Dews, 1984, pp. 94–5). Foucault's over-valorization of non-reflective modes of pursuing desire is either inherently elitist – some people will inevitably be constrained by discipline in 'the realm of necessity', and let us not forget that de Sade was a marquis and von Sacher-Masoch a count! – or it is associated with a romantic nostalgia about the world of non-commodity or petty-commodity producers. In a system of petty-commodity production there would be no 'exploitation', no 'organizational oppression' and an equality of condition. Despite the far more sophisticated concepts of which he was surely aware – he was a student of Althusser's (Althusser and Balibar, 1970, p. 323) – Foucault uses concepts akin to those of the young Marx to describe exploitation and struggles against it.

> Generally, it can be said that there are three types of struggles: either against forms of domination (ethnic, social and religious): against forms of exploitation *which separate individuals from what they produce: or against that which ties the individual himself and submits him to others in this way (struggles against subjection, against forms of subjectivity and submission).*
>
> (Foucault, 1982, p. 212)

Thus he often uncritically accepted the classical concept of law and crime (Foucault, 1979b, pp. 221, 223), which after all implicitly presupposed something like petty-commodity production. Such conditions do not obtain in capitalist societies. Therefore, by default, Foucault gave support to a 'formal and inequitable egalitarianism of the deed' (Rose, 1984, p. 175).

The argument of this book has been that in a socialist society there would be many large-scale democratic organizations, which, with other pressures, would create some inequalities of income. Therefore such an absolute equality of condition could be approximated to only by a totalitarian deadening of social energies, i.e a form of 'forced solidarity'. The construction of a mode of punishment that had equivalent effects on all offenders would remain a problem. The deprivation of liberty in humane conditions provides the one universal and quantifiable system. This might be a relevant mode for a society still dominated by commodity production – but its manifold problems are only too well known.

11 See the comments on Christie and Mathiesen in Taylor (1981) and on Hulsman in Lea (1987).

12 Thus in developing a policy for sentencing rapists one needs the humane but unsentimental assessments of someone like Jill Box-Grainger, who is both a feminist and involved in radical alternatives to prison. In the case of trying and sentencing individual corporate criminals, Braithwaite (1984) and Box (1987) are to be preferred to Box (1983) – see Pearce (1987b).

10 Conclusion

In the early part of this book Marxism was used to criticize much of Durkheim's work. There it functioned primarily as a resource, as a sophisticated alternative discourse that helped to liberate a radical set of neo-Durkheimian concepts. In Chapters 4–7 these concepts were developed to explore the exigencies of social organization in complex societies and particularly the continuities and discontinuities between societies based upon a capitalist mode of production and those based upon an egalitarian and democratic socialism. In the last two chapters these issues were pursued but with a reversal of the earlier procedure, since Durkheim's reconstituted concepts were used to criticize the Utopian elements within Marxism.

One can only agree with Steven Lukes (1975, p. 248) that Durkheim's writings on socialism (particularly the book of his lectures, published as *Socialism*, 1962) are of interest as an exploration 'of the technocratic strand in socialist thought'. I hope that I have shown how *Socialism* also tells us a great deal about the cornucopian romanticism and the, somewhat chilling, monolithic moralistic asceticism that runs through much socialist and communist thought, including that of Marxism. That Durkheim's *Socialism* should function so well as a critique is in one sense surprising in that he makes continual references to 'discipline' and 'morality'. However, some level of self-control is a precondition for human subjectivity and effectiveness, even for the revolutionary, and Durkheim is correct about the need for a socialist morality. From other elements of his work it is clear that a version of morality can be constructed that not only would entail some abstinence but would also take cognizance of the legitimate desires of individuals and function to balance self-interest with altruism or 'charity'. *Socialism*, like the 'Two laws of penal evolution' (1973), is not subtended (and limited) by the assumption that society is an 'expressive totality' and can therefore be used in a relatively unreconstituted form.

Ernest Mandel has pointed out that socialism would solve only two or three of the problems that confront mankind. These are not trivial. It is possible to create a society where there would be a genuine equality of condition, with an end to exploitation and waste; an actively democratic society within which organic solidarity could be realized; a society where there would be *relatively* little of the destructive criminal behaviour that we now confront. No doubt life in such a society would be infinitely preferable to anything that exists today. Nevertheless, many of our desires would still be thwarted, at least sometimes – perhaps because some are inherently unrealizable, or because from the point of view of the individual or society the achievement of one set precludes the achievement of others. This seemingly trivial point has devastating implications. Not only can we not blame all of our disappointments upon the existence of a particular system or systems but we must accept that as human beings we are condemned to a certain level of frustration and discomfiture and that this will have organizational consequences.

We will not escape the state, law enforcement or crime! However, to invert and modify an earlier comment, we can perhaps console ourselves with the thought that our frustrations, destructive rages and jealousies are the *recto et verso* of our capacity to imagine alternative forms of life, to pursue them creatively and to love and respect other human beings, even those who are venal. Good or bad, constructive or destructive, we are all socially constituted, we are all socially produced. The kind of socialist society discussed throughout this book is no 'New Jerusalem' but it is realizable and does provide a meaningful and realistic standard by which to judge current forms of social relations and some guidance on moving from one to the other. A recognition and acceptance of what cannot be changed and that certain goals are mutually incompatible makes it easier to achieve what is possible.

Bibliography

1 Writings of Emile Durkheim Cited and Consulted

These are listed in chronological order of original publication date in France, which is indicated in brackets after the work.

Durkheim, E. (1887) 'La Science positive de la morale en Allemagne', *La Revue Philosophique*.

Durkheim, E. (1898) 'The nature of society and causal explanation', Letter to the Editor, *American Journal of Sociology*, 3. Reprinted in Lukes, S., (ed.) (1982) *Durkheim: The Rules of Sociological Method and Selected Texts on Sociology and Philosophy* London, Macmillan (Halls translation).

Durkheim, E. (1986) 'The positive science of morality in Germany', *Economy and Society* (translated by Pearce). See also Pearce (1986).

Durkheim, E. (1933) *The Division of Labor in Society*, New York: The Free Press (Simpson translation). [1893]

Durkheim, E. (1984) *The Division of Labour in Society*, London: Macmillan (Halls translation). [1893]

Durkheim, E. (1938) *The Rules of Sociological Method*, New York: The Free Press (Solovay and Mueller translation). [1894]

Durkheim, E. (1951) *Suicide*, New York: Free Press of Glencoe [1897]

Durkheim, E. (1963) 'Incest: the nature and origin of the taboo', in Ellis, E. and Ellis, A. (1963) *Incest*, New York: Lyle Stuart.

Durkheim, E. (1982) 'Marxism and sociology: the materialist conception of history', in Lukes (1982). [1898]

Durkheim, E. (1984) Review article, *Economy and Society*, 13 (translation of 1899 review of Merlino's *Formes et essences du socialisme*).

Durkheim, E. (1973) 'Two laws of penal evolution', *Economy and Society*, 2(3), August. [1901]

Durkheim, E. (1976) *The Elementary Forms of the Religious Life*, London: Allen & Unwin [1912].

Durkheim, E. (1964) 'The dualism of human nature and its social conditions', in Wolff, K.H. (ed.) *Essays on Sociology and Philosophy by Emile Durkheim et al*, New York: Harper Torchbooks. [1914]

Durkheim, E. (1974) *Sociology and Philosophy*, New York: Free Press of Glencoe. [1924]

Durkheim, E. (1961) *Moral Education: a study in the theory and application of the sociology of education*, New York: Free Press of Glencoe. [1925]

Durkheim E. (1962) *Socialism*, New York: Collier Books. [1928]

Durkheim, E. (1960) *Montesquieu and Rousseau: Forerunners of Sociology*, Ann Arbor: University of Michigan Press. [1937]

Durkheim, E. (1977) *The Evolution of Educational Thought*, London: Routledge & Kegan Paul. [1938]

Durkheim E. (1957) *Professional Ethics and Civic Morals*, London: Routledge & Kegan Paul. [1950]

Durkheim, E. (1983) *Pragmatism and Sociology*, New York: Cambridge University Press. [1955]

Durkheim, E. (1898) 'Individualism and the intellectuals', *Revue Bleue*, série 10. Reprinted in Bellah (1973).

Durkheim, E. and Mauss, M. (1963) *Primitive Classification*, Chicago: University of Chicago Press. [1903]

2 Collections of Durkheim's Writings Consulted

Bellah, N. (ed.) (1973) *Emile Durkheim on Morality and Society*, Chicago: University of Chicago Press.

Durkheim, E. (1973) *Textes*, 3 vols, Paris: Les Editions de Minuit.

Giddens, A. (ed.) (1986) *Durkheim on Politics and the State*, Cambridge: Polity Press.

Lukes, S. (ed.) (1982) *Durkheim: The Rules of Sociological Method and Selected Texts on Sociology and its Method*, London: Macmillan (Halls translation).

Lukes, S. and Scull, A. (eds) (1983) *Durkheim and the Law*, Oxford: Martin Robertson.

Nandan, Y. (ed.) (1980) *Emile Durkheim: Contributions to L'Année Sociologique*, New York: Free Press of Glencoe.

Pickering, W. S. F. (1975) *Durkheim on Religion*, London: Routledge & Kegan Paul.

Pickering, W. S. F., (ed.) (1979) *Durkheim: Essays on Morals and Education*, London: Routledge & Kegan Paul.

Traugott, M. (ed.) (1978) *Emile Durkheim on Institutional Analysis*, Chicago: Chicago University Press.

Wolff, K. H. (ed.) (1964) *Essays on Sociology and Philosophy by Emile Durkheim et al.*, New York: Harper Torchbooks.

3 Other Relevant Texts Cited and Consulted

Abel, G. G., Blanchard, E. B., and Becjer, J. V. (1976) 'Psychological treatment of rapists', in M. J. Walker and S. L. Brodsky (eds) *Sexual Assault*, Lexington, Mass.: Lexington Books.

Alexander, F. and Straub, H. (1956) *The Criminal, the Judge and the Public: A Psychological Analysis*, New York: Free Press of Glencoe.

Alpert, H. (1939) *Emile Durkheim and his Sociology*, New York: Columbia University Press.

Alpert, H. (1965) 'Durkheim's functional theory of ritual', in R. A. Nisbet (ed.) (1965) *Emile Durkheim*, Englewood Cliffs, NJ: Prentice Hall.

Althusser, L. (1969) *For Marx*, London: Allen Lane.

Althusser, L. (1971) *Lenin and Philosophy and other Essays*, London: New Left Books.

Althusser, L. (1984) *Essays in Ideology*, London: Verso.

Althusser, L and Balibar, E. (1970) *Reading Capital*, London: New Left Books.

Aristotle (1920) *On The Art of Poetry*, London: Oxford at the Clarendon Press.

Atkinson, D. (1971) *Orthodox Consensus and Radical Alternative*, London: Heinemann.

Austin, J. (1955) *The Province of Jurisprudence Determined and the Uses of the Study of Jurisprudence*, London: Weidenfeld & Nicholson, first published 1832.

Bachrach, P. and Baratz, M. S. (1962) 'Two faces of power', *American Political Science Review*, 56(4), December.

Bar, E. (1971) 'The language of the unconscious according to Jacques Lacan', *Semiotica*.

Barnet, H. (1974) 'The political economy of rape and prostitution', *Review of Radical Political Economy*.

Barrett, M. (1980) *Women's Oppession Today: Problems in Marxist Feminist Analysis*, London: Verso Books.

Bazelgette, J. (1971) *Freedom, Authority and the Young Adult*, London: Pitman.

Becker, H. (1963) *Outsiders*, New York: Free Press of Glencoe.

Beetham, D. (1974) *Max Weber and the Theory of Modern Politics*, London: Allen & Unwin.

Bennett, T. (1979) *Formalism and Marxism*, London: Methuen.

Bennett, T., Boyd-Bowman, S., Mercer, C. and Woollacott, J. (1981) *Popular Television and Film*, London: British Film Institute.

Benoit-Smullyan, E. (1969) 'The sociologism of Emile Durkheim and his school', in H. E. Barnes (ed.) *An Introduction to the History of Sociology*, Chicago: University of Chicago Press.

Benton, T. (1977) *The Three Sociologies*, London: Routledge & Kegan Paul.

Benton, T. (1984) *The Rise and Fall of Structural Marxism: Althusser and his Influence*, London: Macmillan.

Berger, P. and Luckman, T. (1967) *The Social Construction of Reality*, London: Allen Lane.

Berger, P. and Pullberg, S. (1966) 'Reification and the sociological critique of consciousness', *New Left Review*, 35, January–February.

Bergson, H. (1958) *Les deux sources de la moral et de la religion'*, 88e edition, Paris.

Bernstein, R. J. (1976) *The Restructuring of Social and Political Theory*, London: Methuen.

Besnard, P. (ed.) (1983) *The Sociological Domain: The Durkheimians and the Founding of French Sociology*, Cambridge: Cambridge University Press.

Bettelheim, B. (1984) *Freud and Man's Soul*, New York: Vintage Books.

Bhaskar R. (1978) *A Realist Theory of Science*, Hassocks, Sussex: Harvester.

Binney, V., Harkell, G. and Nixon, J. (1981) *Leaving Violent Men: A Study of Refuges and Housing for Battered Women*, London: Women's Aid Federation.

Bland, L. (1984) 'The case of the Yorkshire Ripper: Mad, bad, beast or male', in P. Scraton and P. Gordon (eds) *Causes for Concern: British criminal justice on trial?*, Harmondsworth, Middx: Penguin.

Blassingame, J. W. (1972) *The Slave Community: Plantation Life in the Ante-Bellum South*, New York: Oxford University Press.

Blum, A. and McHugh, P. (1971) 'The social ascription of motives', *American Sociological Review*, 36.

Bonger, W. (1916) *Criminality and Economic Conditions*, New York: Little, Brown & Co.

Bottomore, T. and Goode, P. (eds) (1978) *Austro-Marxism*, Oxford: Oxford University Press.

Bottomore, T. and Nisbet, R. A. (eds) (1978) *A History of Sociological Analysis*, London: Heinemann.

Box, S. (1983) *Power, Crime and Mystification*, London: Tavistock.

Box, S. (1987) *Recession, Crime and Punishment*, London: Macmillan.

Box–Grainger, J. (1986) 'Sentencing rapists', in R. Matthews and J. Young (eds) *Confronting Crime*, London: Sage.

Boyer, P. and Nissenbaum, S. (1974) *Salem Possessed: The Social Origins of Witchcraft*, Cambridge, Mass.: Harvard University Press.

Boyle, J. (1977) *A Sense of Freedom*, London: Pan Books.

Braithwaite, J. (1984) *Corporate Crime in the Pharmaceutical Industry*, London: Routledge & Kegan Paul.

Bukharin, N. (1969) *Historical Materialism*, Ann Arbor: The University of Michigan Press.

Burton, F. and Carlen, P. (1979) *Official Discourse*, London: Routledge & Kegan Paul.

Callinicos, A. (1982) *Is There a Future for Marxism?*, London: Macmillan.

Carlen, P. (1983) 'On rights and powers: some notes on penal politics', in D. Garland and P. Young (eds) *The Power to Punish*, London: Heinemann Books.

Caughie, J. (1981) *Theories of Authorship*, London: Routledge & Kegan Paul and the British Film Institute.

Chambliss, W. (1982) *On The Take*, Bloomington: Indiana University Press.

Chapman, D. (1968) *Sociology and the Stereotype of the Criminal*, London: Tavistock Publications.

Christie, N. (1976) 'Conflicts as property', *British Journal of Criminology*, 17(1), January.

Clarke L. and Lewis, D. (1977) *Rape: The Price of Coercive Sexuality*, Toronto: The Women's Press.

Cohen, A. P. (1985) *The Symbolic Construction of Community*, London: Tavistock.

Cohen, G. A. (1978) *Karl Marx's Theory of History: A Defence*, Oxford: Clarendon Press.

Coser, L. (1964) 'Durkheim's conservativism and its implications for his sociological theory', in K. H. Wolff (ed.) *Essays on Sociology and Philosophy by Emile Durkheim et al.*, New York: Harper Torchbooks.

Coser, L. (1977) *Masters of Sociological Thought*, New York: Harcourt Brace Jovanovich.

Coulanges, F. de (1972) *The Ancient City*, Garden City, NY: Doubleday-Anchor.

Cousins, M. (1980) '*Mens Rea*: A note on sexual difference, criminology and the law', in P. Carlen and M. Collison (eds) *Radical Issues in Criminology*, Oxford: Martin Robertson.

Cousins, M. and Hussain, A. (1984) *Michel Foucault*, London, Macmillan.

Cowie, E. (1978) 'Woman as sign', *M/F*, no. 1.

Crozier, M., Huntingdon, S. P. and Watanuki, J. (1975) *The Crisis of Democracy: Report on the governability of democracies to the Trilateral Commission*, New York: New York University Press.

Dahl, R. A. (1985) *A Preface to Economic Democracy*, Cambridge: Polity Press.

Danto, A. C. (1968) *Analytical Philosophy of History*, Cambridge: Cambridge University Press.

Dawe, A. (1970) 'The two sociologies', *British Journal of Sociology, 21.*

Derrida, J. (1976) *Of Grammatology*, Baltimore, Md.: Johns Hopkins University Press.

Descombes, V. (1980) *Modern French Philosophy*, Cambridge: Cambridge University Press.

Dews, P. (1984) 'Foucault's theory of subjectivity', *New Left Review*, no. 144, March–April.

Diamond, A. S. (1935) *Primitive Law*, London: Longman, Green & Co.

Diamond, S. (1971) 'The rule of law versus the order of custom', in R. P. Wolff (ed.) *The Rule of Law*, New York: Simon & Schuster.

Donzelot, J. (1979) *The Policing of Families*, New York: Pantheon.

Dorn, N. (1980) 'The conservativism of the cannabis debate: its place in the reproduction of the drugs problem', in National Deviance Conference, *Permissiveness and Control: the Fate of the Sixties Legislation*, London: Macmillan.

Douglas, J. (1967) *The Social Meanings of Suicide*, Princeton: Princeton University Press.

Douglas, M. (1982) *Essays in the Sociology of Perception*, London: Routledge & Kegan Paul.

Doyal, L. and Gough, I. (1984) 'A theory of human needs', *Critical Social Policy*, 10.

Dreyfus, H. L. and Rabinow, P. (1982) *Michel Foucault: Beyond Structuralism and Hermeneutics*, Brighton, Sussex: Harvester Press.

Eagleton, T. (1983) *Literary Theory: an Introduction*, Minneapolis: University of Minnesota Press.

Edelman, B. (1979) *Ownership of the Image: Elements for a Marxist Theory of Law*, London: Routledge & Kegan Paul.

Ehrman, J. (1970) *Structuralism*, New York: Doubleday-Anchor.

Elkins, S. (1968) *Slavery*, Chicago: Chicago University Press.

Engels, F. (1845) *The Condition of the Working Classes in England*, London: Panther (1969).

Engels, F. (1874) 'On authority', reprinted in Tucker, 1978.

Engels, F. (1878) *Anti-Duhring: Herrn Eugen Duhring's Revolution in Science*, Moscow: Progress Publishers (1959).

Erikson, K. T. (1966) *Wayward Puritans*, New York: Wiley.

Eve, M. and Musson, D. (eds) (1982) *The Socialist Register 1982*, London: Merlin.

Fenton, C. S. (1968) 'The myth of subjectivism as a special method in sociology', *Sociological Review*, 16(1).

Fenton, C. S. (1980) 'Race, class and politics in the work of Emile Durkheim', in UNESCO, *Sociological Theories: Race and Colonialism*, London: UNESCO.

Fenton, C. S. (1984) *Durkheim and Modern Sociology*, Cambridge: Cambridge University Press.

Filloux, C. (1971) 'Democratie et société socialiste chez Durkheim', *Cahiers Vilfredo Pareto*, 25.

Filloux, J.-C. (1977) *Durkheim et le socialisme*, Geneva: Librairie Droz.

Filmer, P., Walsh, D., Phillipson, M. and Silverman, D. (1972) *New Directions in Sociological Theory*, London: Collier-Macmillan.

Fine, B., Kinsey, R., Lea, J., Picciotto, S. and Young, J. (eds) (1979) *Capitalism and the Rule of Law: From deviancy theory to Marxism*, London: Hutchinson.

Finley, M. I. (1980) *Ancient Slavery and Modern Ideology*, Harmondsworth, Middx: Penguin Books.

Fogel, R. W. and Engerman, S. L. (1974) *Time on the Cross*, Boston: Little Brown.

Fortas, A. (1968) *Concerning Dissent and Civil Disobedience*, New York: Signet Books.

Foster, J. (1985) 'The declassing of language', *New Left Review*, no. 150.

Foucault, M. (1970) *The Order of Things*, London: Tavistock Publications.

Foucault, M. (1973) *Madness and Civilization: A History of Insanity in the*

Age of Reason, New York: Vintage/Random House.

Foucault, M. (1977) *Language, Counter-memory, Practice: Selected essays and interviews by Michel Foucault* (ed. D. F. Bouchard), Ithaca, NY: Cornell University Press.

Foucault M. (1978a) 'The concept of the dangerous individual in the nineteenth century', *International Journal of Law and Psychiatry*, 1(1).

Foucault, M. (1978b) *The History of Sexuality. Volume 1: An Introduction*, London: Allen Lane.

Foucault, M. (1979a) 'The life of infamous men', in M. Morris and P. Patton, *Michel Foucault: Power, Truth, Strategy*, Sydney: Feral Publications.

Foucault, M. (1979b) *Discipline and Punish*, Harmondsworth, Middx: Peregrine Books.

Foucault, M. (1980a) 'Body/power', in Gordon (1980).

Foucault, M. (1980b) 'Prison talk', in Gordon (1980).

Foucault, M. (1980c) 'Two lectures', in Gordon (1980).

Foucault, M. (1982) 'The subject and power', in H. L. Dreyfus and P. Rabinow, *Michel Foucault: Beyard Structuralism and Hermeneutics*, Brighton, Sussex: Harvester Press.

Foucault, M. (1986) 'What is an author?' in P. Rabinow (ed.) *The Foucault Reader*, Harmondsworth, Middx: Penguin.

Foulkes, S. H. (1975) 'Problems of the large group from a group-analytic point of view', in L. Kreeger (ed.) *The Large Group: Dynamics and Therapy*, London: Constable.

Frazier, T. R. (1971) *Underside of American History: Other Readings*, New York: Harcourt Brace Jovanovich.

Frazzetta, T. H. (1975) *Complex Adaptations in Evolving Populations*, Sunderland, Mass.: Sinauer Associates.

Freud, S. (1962) *Three Essays on the Theory of Sexuality*, New York: Avon Books.

Freud, S. (1976a) *The Interpretation of Dreams*, Harmondsworth, Middx: Penguin Books.

Freud, S. (1976b) *The Psychopathology of Everyday Life*, Harmondsworth, Middx: Penguin Books.

Fried, A. and Sanders, R. (eds) (1964) *Socialist Thought: A Documentary History*, New York: Doubleday.

Fried, R. M. (1976) *Men Against McCarthy*, New York: Columbia University Press.

Friedrich, C. J. (1962) *The Philosophy of Law in Historical Perspective*, Chicago and London: University of Chicago Press.

Friedrichs, R. W. (1970) *A Sociology of Sociology*, New York: Free Press of Glencoe.

Fromm, E. (1961) *Marx's Concept of Man*, New York: Ungar.

Gane, M. (1983a) 'Durkheim: the sacred language', *Economy and Society*, 12(1), February.

Gane, M. (1983b) 'Durkheim: woman as outsider', *Economy and Society*, 12(2) May.

Gane, M. (1984) 'Institutional socialism and the sociological critique of communism', *Economy and Society*, 13.

Garfinkel, H. (1967) *Studies in Ethnomethodology*, Englewood Cliffs, NJ: Prentice Hall.

Genovese, E. (1965) *The Political Economy of Slavery: Studies in the Economy and Society of the Slave South*, New York: Vintage.

Genovese, E. (1969) *The World the Slaveholders Made: Two Essays in Interpretation*, New York: Vintage.

Genovese, E. (1971) *In Red and Black: Marxian Explorations in Southern and Afro-American History*, New York: Vintage.

Genovese, E. (1974) *Roll Jordan Roll: the World the Slaves Made*, New York: Pantheon.

Geras, N. (1971) 'Essence and appearance: aspects of fetishism in Marx's *Capital*', *New Left Review*, no. 65, January–February.

Geras, N. (1985) 'The controversy over Marx and justice', *New Left Review*, no. 150, March–April.

Geras, N. (1987) 'Post-Marxism', *New Left Review*, no. 163, May–June.

Gibbs, J. (1971) 'Suicide', in R. K. Merton and R. Nisbet (eds), *Contemporary Social Problems*, 3rd edn, New York: Harcourt Brace Jovanovich.

Gibbs, J. P. and Martin, W. T. (1964) *Status integration and Suicide*, Eugene, Oreg.: University of Oregon Press.

Giddens, A. (1971a) *Capitalism and Modern Social Theory*, Cambridge: Cambridge University Press.

Giddens, A. (1971b) 'Durkheim's political sociology', *Sociological Review*, 19.

Giddens, A. (ed.) (1971c) *The Sociology of Suicide*, London: Frank Cass.

Giddens, A. (1972) *Politics and Sociology in the Thought of Max Weber*, London: Macmillan.

Gilroy, P. (1982) 'The myth of black criminality', in M. Eve and D. Musson (eds), *The Socialist Register 1982*, London: Merlin.

Gilroy, P. (1987) *'There Ain't No Black in the Union Jack'*, London: Hutchinson.

Gilroy, P. and Sim, J. (1985) 'Law and order and the state of the left', *Capital and Class*, no. 25, spring.

Girard, R. (1965) *Deceit, Desire and the Novel: Self and Other in Literary Structure*, Baltimore, Md.: Johns Hopkins University Press.

Girard, R. (1977) *Violence and the Sacred*, Baltimore, Md.: Johns Hopkins University Press.

Girard, R. (1978), interview in *Diacritics*, 8(1).

Girard, R. (1979) 'Myth and ritual in Shakespeare: *A Midsummer Night's Dream*, in J. V. Harari (ed.), *Textual Strategies: Perspectives in Post-Structuralist Criticism*, London: Methuen.

Gittlin, T. (1965) 'Local pluralism as theory and ideology', *Studies on the Left*.

Gluckman, M. (ed.) (1972) *The Allocation of Responsibility*, Manchester: Manchester University Press.

Gordon, C. (1980) *Power/Knowledge: Selected Interviews and Other Writings 1972-1977 by Michel Foucault*, New York: Pantheon.

Gorz, A. (1980) *Ecology As Politics*, London: Pluto Press.

Gouldner, A. (1971) *The Coming Crisis of Western Sociology*, London: Heinemann.

Gramsci, A. (1971) *Selections from the Prison Notebooks*, London: Lawrence & Wishart.

Gramsci, A. (1977) *Selections from Political Writing 1910-1920*, London: Lawrence & Wishart.

Gramsci, A. (1978) *Selections from Political Writing 1921-1926*, London: Lawrence & Wishart.

Greenwood, V. and Young, J. (1976) *Abortion on Demand*, London: Pluto.

Gutman, H. (1976) *The Black Family in Slavery and Freedom, 1750-1925*, New York: Pantheon.

Guttari, F. (1984) *Molecular Revolution: Psychiatry and Politics*, Harmondsworth, Middx: Penguin books.

Habermas, J. (1971) *Toward a Rational Society*, London: Heinemann.

Habermas, J. (1972) *Knowledge and Human Interests*, London: Heinemann.

Habermas, J. (1979) *Communication and the Evolution of Society*, London: Heinemann.

Hall, S. (1985) 'Authoritarian populism: a reply', *New Left Review*, no. 151, May–June.

Hall, S., Hobson, D., Lowe, A. and Willis, P. (eds) (1980) *Culture, Media, Language*, London: Hutchinson.

Harris, M. (1974) *Cows, Pigs, Wars and Witches: the Riddles of Culture*, New York: Vintage Books.

Hart, H. L. A. (1961) *The Concept of Law*, Oxford: Oxford University Press.

Hartz, L. (1964) *The Founding of New Societies*, New York: Harcourt Brace Jovanovich.

Hawkins, M. J. (1981) 'Emile Durkheim on democracy and absolutism', *History of Political Thought*, 2(2).

Hayes, E. (1972) *Power Structure and Urban Policy: Who Rules in Oakland?* New York: McGraw Hill.

Hekman, S. (1983) *Max Weber and Contemporary Social Theory*, Oxford: Martin Robertson.

Henderson, W. O. (ed.) (1967) *Engels: Selected Writings*, Harmondsworth, Middx: Penguin Books.

Henriques, J., Holloway, W., Urwin, C., Venn, C. and Walkerdine, V. (1984) *Changing the Subject: Psychology, Social Regulation and Subjectivity*, London: Methuen.

Hertz, N. (1979) 'Freud and the sandman', in J. V. Harari (ed.) *Textual Strategies: Perspectives in Post-Structuralist Criticism*, London: Methuen.

Hill, C. (1974) *The Century of Revolution*, London: Cardinal.

Hindess, B. (1977a) *Philosophy and Methodology in the Social Sciences*, Brighton, Sussex: Harvester Press.

Hindess, B. (ed.) (1977b) *Sociological Theories of the Economy*, London: Macmillan.

Hindess, B. (1983) *Parliamentary Democracy and Socialist Politics*, London: Routledge & Kegan Paul.

Hindess, B. and Hirst, P. Q. (1975) *Pre-Capitalist Modes of Production*, London: Routledge & Kegan Paul.

Hindess, B. and Hirst, P. (1977) *Mode of Production and Social Formation*, London: Macmillan.

Hirst, P. Q. (1972) 'Marx and Engels on law, crime and morality', *Economy and Society*, 1(1).

Hirst, P. Q. (1975) *Durkheim, Bernard and Epistemology*, London: Routledge & Kegan Paul.

Hirst, P. Q. (1976) *Social Evolution and Sociological Categories*, London: Allen & Unwin.

Hirst, P. Q. (1979) *On Law and Ideology*, London: Macmillan.

Hirst, P. Q. (1980) 'Law, socialism and rights', in P. Carlen and M. Collinson (eds), *Radical Issues in Criminology*, Oxford: Martin Robertson.

Hirst, P. Q. (1985) *Marxism and Historical Writing*, London: Routledge & Kegan Paul.

Hirst, P. Q. (1986) *Law, Socialism and Democracy*, London: Allen & Unwin.

Hirst, P. Q. (1987) 'Retrieving pluralism', in M. Outhwaite and A. Giddens (eds), *Social Theory and Social Criticism: Essays for Tom Bottomore*, Oxford: Blackwell.

Hirst, P. Q. (1988) 'Representative democracy and its limits', *Political Quarterly*, 59(2), April–June.

Hirst, P. Q. and Woolley, P. (1982) *Social Relations and Human Attributes*, London: Tavistock Publications.

Hobbes, T. (1960) *Leviathan*, Oxford: Blackwell.

Hofstadter, R. (1967) *The American Political Tradition*, London: Cape Paperback.

Horowitz, I. L. (ed). (1965) *The New Sociology*, New York: Oxford University Press.

Hulsman, L (1986) 'Critical criminology and the concept of crime', *Contemporary Crises*, 10(1).

Hunt, A. (1978) *The Sociological Movement in Law*, London: Macmillan.

Ihering, R. von (1879) *The Struggle for Law*, Chicago: Callaghan and Co.

Ihering, R. von (1924) *Law as a Means to an End*, New York: Macmillan.

Jacobs, J. (1967) 'A phenomenological study of suicide notes', *Social Problems*, 15, reprinted in Giddens (1971c).

James, L de W. (1971) *William Blake and the Tree of Life*, Berkeley: Shambala.

Jaurès, J. (1895) 'Idealism in history'; translated in A. Fried and R. Sanders (eds) (1964) *Socialist Thought: A Documentary History*, New York: Doubleday.

Jones, G. S. (1983) *Languages of Class: Studies in English Working Class History 1832–1982*, Cambridge: Cambridge University Press.

Jones, K. (1983) *Law and Economy: The Legal Regulation of Corporate Conduct*, London: Academic Press.

Jones, R. and Kerslake, A. (1979) *Intermediate Treatment and Social Work*, London: Heinemann Educational.

Jones, T., Maclean, B. and Young, J. (1986) *The Islington Crime Survey*, Farnborough: Gower.

Keat, R. and Urry, J. (1975) *Social Theory as Science*, London: Routledge & Kegan Paul.

Kelsen, H. (1945) *General Theory of Law and State*, New York: Russell and Russell edn, 1961.

Kinsey, R., Lea, J. and Young, J. (1986) *Losing the Fight against Crime*, Oxford: Blackwell.

Knapp, P. (1985) 'The question of Hegelian influences upon Durkheim's thought', *Sociological Inquiry*, 55, part 1.

Kuhn, T. S. (1962) *The Structure of Scientific Revolutions*, Chicago: University of Chicago Press.

Labriola, A. (1908) *Essays on the Materialist Conception of History*, Chicago: Charles Kerr.

Labriola, A. (1906) *Essays in Socialism and Philosophy*, Chicago: Charles Kerr.

Lacan, J. (1968) *The Language of the Self*, New York: Dell.

Lacan, J. (1977) *Ecrits: A Selection*, London: Tavistock Publications.

LaCapra, D. (1972) *Emile Durkheim: Sociologist and Philosopher*, Ithaca, NY: Cornell University Press.

LaCapra (1987) *History and Criticism*, Ithaca, NY: Cornell University Press.

Laclau, E. (1976 and 1979) *Politics and Ideology in Marxist Theory*, London: Verso.

Laclau, E. and Mouffe, C. (1985) *Hegemony and Socialist Strategy*, London: Verso.

Laclau, E. and Mouffe, C. (1987) 'A reply to Norman Geras', *New Left Review*, no. 166.

Lacroix, B. (1978) 'A propos des rapports entre Durkheim et Marx: de l'analyse de texte à l'analyse sociologique', in Faculté de Droit de Clermont, *Etudes offertes au Professeur Emerentienne de Lagrange*, Paris: Librairie Générale de Droit de Jurisprudence.

Lacroix, B. (1979) '*The Elementary Forms of the Religious Life* as a reflection on power (objet pouvoir)', *Critique of Anthropology*, 5.

Lafargue, P. (1969) *The Right to be Lazy*, Chicago: Charles H. Kerr; reprint of 1907 edition.
Laplanche, J. and Pontalis, J. B. (1973) *The Language of Psychoanalysis*, London: Hogarth Press.
Lasch, C. (1980) *The Culture of Narcissism*, London: Abacus.
Lea, J. (1987) 'Left-realism: a defence', *Contemporary Crises*, 11.
Lea, J. and Young, J. (1984) *Law and Order: Arguments for Socialism*, Harmondsworth, Middx: Penguin.
Lecourt, D. (1975) *Marxism and Epistemology: Bachelard, Canguilhem, Foucault*, London: New Left Books.
Lemert, E. (1972) *Human Deviance, Social Problems and Social Control*, 2nd edn, Englewood Cliffs, NJ: Prentice Hall.
Levine, A. (1987) *The End of the State*, London: Verso.
Levine, A. (1981) 'Althusser's Marxism', *Economy and Society*, 10(3).
Lévi-Strauss, C. (1945) 'French sociology', in G. Gurvitch and W. E. Moore (eds) *Twentieth Century Sociology*, New York: Philosophical Library.
Lévi-Strauss, C. (1963a) *Structural Anthropology*, vol. 1, London: Allen Lane, Penguin Press.
Lévi-Strauss, C. (1963b) *Totemism*, Boston: Beacon Press.
Lévi-Strauss, C. (1969) *The Elementary Structures of Kinship*, Boston: Beacon Press.
Lichtheim, G. (1975) *A Short History of Socialism*, London: Fontana.
Lichtman, R. (1971) 'Symbolic interactionism and Marxism', *Berkeley Journal of Sociology*, 15.
Llobera, J. R. (1981a) 'Durkheim, the Durkheimians and their collective misrepresentation of Marx', in J. S. Kahn and J. R. Llobera (eds) *The Anthropology of Pre-Capitalist Societies*, London: Macmillan.
Llobera, J. R. (1981b) 'Marx' social theory and the Durkheimian School. A note on the reception of Marxism in the *Année Sociologique*', *Etudes Durkheimiennes*, 63.
Llobera, J. R. (1986) 'The socialist Durkheimians', *Critique of Anthropology*, 5(3).
Lloyd, D. (1964) *The Idea of Law*, Harmondsworth, Middx: Penguin Books.
Lockwood, D. (1964) 'Social integration and system integration', in G. K. Zollschan and W. Hirsch (eds) *Explorations in Social Change*, London: Routledge & Kegan Paul.
Lockwood, D. (1982) 'Fatalism: Durkheim's hidden theory of order', in A. Giddens and G. Mackenzie (eds) *Social Class and the Division of Labour: Essays in Honour of Ilya Neustadt*, Cambridge: Cambridge University Press.
Lukacs, G. (1971) *History and Class Consciousness*, London: Merlin Press.
Lukacs, G. (1972) 'Max Weber and German sociology', *Economy and Society*, 1(4).
Lukes, S. (1975) *Emile Durkheim, His Life and Work. A Historical and Critical Study*, Harmondsworth, Middx: Penguin Books.

Lukes, S. and Scull, A. (eds) (1983) *Durkheim and the Law*, Oxford: Martin Robertson.

McCabe, C. (1974) 'Realism and the cinema: notes on some Brechtian theses', *Screen*, 15(2), summer.
McCabe, C.(1976) 'Principles of realism and pleasure', *Screen*, 17(3), autumn.
McIntosh, D. (1983) 'Max Weber as a critical theorist', *Theory and Society*, vol. 12.
McHugh, P. (1968) *Defining the Situation. The Organization of Meaning in Social Interaction*, Indianapolis: Bobbs-Merrill.
McLellan, D. (ed.) (1977) *Karl Marx: Selected Writings*, Oxford: Oxford University Press.
Macpherson, C. B. (1979) 'Second and third thoughts on needs and wants', *Canadian Journal of Political and Social Theory*, 3(1).
Macpherson, C. B. (1980) *Burke*, Oxford: Oxford University Press.
Maine, H. (1861) *Ancient Law*, London: J. M. Dent and Sons.
Malinowski, B. (1926) *Crime and Custom in Savage Society*, New York: Humanities Press.
Marcuse, H. (1955) *Eros and Civilisation*, Boston: Beacon Books.
Marcuse, H. (1963) *Reason and Revolution*, New York: Humanities Press.
Marcuse, H. (1966) *One Dimensional Man*, Boston: Beacon Press.
Marcuse, H. (1968) *Negations: Essays in Critical Theory*, London: Allen Lane, the Penguin Press.
Márquez, G. García (1984) *Chronicle of a Death Foretold*, New York: Ballantine.
Marx, K. (1844) *The Economic and Philosophic Manuscripts of 1844*, reprinted in Tucker 1978.
Marx, K. (1859) *Preface to a Contribution to a Critique of Political Economy*, reprinted in Tucker, 1978 *The Marx-Engels reader*, New York: Norton.
Marx, K. (1875) *Critique of the Gotha Programme*, reprinted in Tucker 1978.
Marx, K. (1965) *Capital*, vol. 1, Moscow: Progress Publishers.
Marx, K. (1972) *Capital*, vol. 3, London: Lawrence & Wishart.
Marx, K. and Engels, F. (1845) *The German Ideology*, reprinted in Marx K. and Engels, F. (1976) *Collected Works, Vol. 5: 1844–45*, London: Lawrence & Wishart.
Marx, K. and Engels, F. (1948) *The Manifesto of the Communist Party*, New York: International Publishers.
Marx, K. and Engels, F. (1968) *Selected Works*, London: Lawrence & Wishart.
Marx, K. and Engels, F. (1975) *Collected Works, Vol 3: 1843–44*, London: Lawrence & Wishart.
Marx, K. and Engels, F. (1976) *Collected Works, Vol. 5: 1844–45*, London: Lawrence & Wishart.
Masters, B. (1986) *Killing for Company*, London: Coronet Books.
Matthews, R. and Young, J. (eds) (1986) *Confronting Crime*, London: Sage.

Mathiesen, T. (1976) *The Politics of Abolition*, London: Martin Robertson.

Mauss, M. (1970) *The Gift*, London: Routledge & Kegan Paul.

Mauss, M. (1979) *Sociology and Philosophy: Essays*, London: Routledge & Kegan Paul.

Mauss, M. (1984) 'A sociological assessment of Bolshevism (1924–5)', *Economy and Society*, 13.

Merleau-Ponty, M. (1962) *The Phenomenology of Perception*, London: Routledge & Kegan Paul.

Merton, R. (1957) *Social Theory and Social Structure*, London: Free Press of Glencoe.

Merton, R. F. (1965) 'Durkheim's division of labor in society', in R. A. Nisbet (ed.) *Emile Durkheim*, Englewood Cliffs, NJ: Prentice Hall.

Mills, C. W. (1940) 'Situated actions and vocabularies of motives', *American Sociological Review*, 5.

Mills, C. W. (1959) *The Sociological Imagination*, New York: Oxford University Press.

Minson, J. (1985) *Genealogies of Morals: Nietzsche, Foucault, Donzelot and the Eccentricity of Ethics*, London: Macmillan.

Moore, S. F. (1972) 'Legal liability and evolutionary interpretation: some aspects of strict liability, self help and collective responsibility', in M. Gluckman (ed.) *The Allocation of Responsibility*, Manchester: Manchester University Press.

Moore, S. F. (1978) *Law as Process: An Anthropological Approach*, London: Routledge & Kegan Paul.

Moran, R. (1981) *Knowing Right from Wrong: The Insanity Defence of Daniel McNaughton*, New York: Free Press.

Morley, D. (1980) 'Texts, readers, subjects', in S. Hall, D. Dobson, A. Lowe and P. Willis (eds), *Culture, Media, Language*, London: Hutchinson.

Morris, M. and Patton, P. (1979) *Michel Foucault: Power, Truth, Strategy*, Sydney: Feral Publications.

Mouffe, C. (ed.) (1979) *Gramsci and Marxist Theory*, London: Routledge & Kegan Paul.

Mouzelis, N. (1978) 'Ideology and class politics: a critique of Ernesto Laclau', *New Left Review*, no. 112.

Mueller, C. (1970) 'Notes on the repression of communicative behaviour', in H. P. Dreitzel (ed.), *Recent Sociology*, no. 2, London: Macmillan.

Muncie, J. (1984) *The Trouble with Kids Today*, London: Hutchinson.

Nagel, T. (1969) 'Sexual perversion', *Journal of Philosophy*, 66(1).

Neale, S. (1977) 'Propaganda', *Screen*, 18(3).

Nisbet, R. (1963) 'Sociology as an art form', in M. Stein and A. Vidich (eds) *Sociology on Trial*, Englewood Cliffs, NJ: Prentice Hall.

Nisbet, R. (ed.) (1965) *Emile Durkheim by Robert Nisbet: with selected essays*, Englewood Cliffs, NJ: Spectrum Books, Prentice Hall.

Nisbet, R. (1967) *The Sociological Tradition*, London: Heinemann.

Nisbet, R. (1975) *The Sociology of Emile Durkheim*, London: Heinemann.
Nizan, P. (1971) *The Watchdogs: Philosophers and the Established Order*, New York: Monthly Review Press.

O'Keefe, D. L. (1983) *Stolen Lightning: The Social Theory of Magic*, New York: Vintage Books.
Outhwaite, M. and Giddens, A. (eds) (1987) *Social Theory and Social Criticism: Essays For Tom Bottomore*, Oxford: Blackwell.

Palmer, J. (1979) 'The dampstones of positivism', *Philosophy of the Social Sciences*, 9(2), June.
Palmer, J. (1976) 'Evils merely prohibited: Conceptions of property and conceptions of criminality in the criminal law reform of the English Industrial Revolution', *British Journal of Law and Society* 3(1).
Palmer, J. and Pearce, F. (1983) 'Legal discourse and state power: Foucault and the juridical relation', *International Journal of the Sociology of Law*, November.
Parish, P. (1979) *Slavery*, Durham: British Association for American Studies.
Parsons, T. (1949) *The Structure of Social Action*, New York: Free Press of Glencoe.
Parsons, T. (1964) 'Durkheim's contribution to the theory of integration of social systems', in K. H. Wolff (ed.) *Essays on Sociology and Philosophy by Emile Durkheim et al.*, New York: Harper Torchbooks.
Pashukanis, E. B. (1978) *Law and Marxism*, London: Ink Links.
Pasquino, P. (1984) 'De la modernité', *Magazine Littéraire*, no. 207, May.
Pearce, F. (1976) *Crimes of the Powerful: Marxism, Crime and Deviance*, London: Pluto Press.
Pearce, F. (1984) review of Jones (1982), *International Journal of the Sociology of Law*, vol. 12, no. 3.
Pearce, F. (1985a) 'Neo-structuralist Marxism on crime and law in Britain', *The Insurgent Sociologist*, vol. 13, nos 1–2.
Pearce, F. (1985b) review of Lukes and Scull (1983) in *International Journal of the Sociology of Law*, vol. 13, no. 2.
Pearce, F. (1986) 'Durkheim and the juridical relation', *Economy and Society*, vol. 15, no. 3. A summary and discussion of the significance of Durkheim's 'La Science positive de la morale en Allemagne', translated by Pearce in the same issue.
Pearce, F. (1987a) review of Hirst (1986), *Sociology*, 21(1).
Pearce, F. (1987b) 'Corporate crime', *Critical Social Policy*, 19.
Pearce, F. (1988) 'The struggle for Foucault', *International Journal of the Sociology of Law*, vol. 16, no. 2.
Pecheux, M. (1982) *Language, Semantics and Ideology*, London: Macmillan.
Pels, D. (1984) 'A fellow-traveller's dilemma: sociology and socialism in the writings of Durkheim', *Acta Politica*, 19, part 3.
Pepinsky, H. (1978) 'Reliance on formal written law, and freedom and social control in the United States and the People's Republic of China',

in C. E. Reasons and R. M. Rich (eds) (1978) *The Sociology of Law: A Conflict Perspective*, Toronto: Butterworths.

Phillips, U. (1918) *American Negro Slavery: A Survey of the Supply, Employment and Control of Negro Labor as Determined by the Plantation Regime*, New York: D. Appleton.

Pope, W. (1976) *Durkheim's Suicide: A Classic Analyzed*, Chicago: University of Chicago Press.

Portis, L. (1980) *Georges Sorel*, London: Pluto Press.

Poulantzas, N. (1978) *Political Power and Social Classes*, London: Verso Books.

Rabinow, P. (ed.) (1986) *The Foucault Reader*, Harmondsworth, Middx: Penguin.

Ranciere, J. (1971) 'The concept of "critique" and "the critique of political economy"', *Theoretical Practice*, no. 1.

Ranciere, J. (1974) 'Althusser's theory of ideology', *Radical Philosophy*, no. 7, spring.

Rattansi, A. (1985) 'End of an orthodoxy? The critique of sociology's view of Marx on class', *Sociological Review*, 33(4).

Reiman, J. (1979) *The Rich Get Richer: and the Poor Get Prison*, New York: Wiley.

Reiter, R. R. (ed.) (1975) *Towards an Anthropology of Women*, New York: Monthly Review Press.

Renner, K. (1949) *The Institutions of Private Property and their Social Functioning*, London: Routledge & Kegan Paul.

Rex, J. (1963) *Key Problems in Sociological Theory*, London: Routledge & Kegan Paul.

Richter, M. (1964) 'Durkheim's politics and political theory', in K. H. Wolff (ed.), *Essays on Sociology and Philosophy by Emile Durkheim et al.*, New York: Harper Torchbooks.

Roberts, S. (1979) *Order and Dispute: An Introduction to Legal Anthropology*, Harmondsworth, Middx: Penguin Books.

Rock, P. (1979) *The Making of Symbolic Interactionism*, London: Macmillan.

Rose, H. (1984) *Dialectic of Nihilism: Post-Structuralism and Law*, Oxford: Blackwell.

Rubin, G. (1975) 'The traffic in women: the political economy of sex', in R. R. Reiter (ed.), *Towards an Anthropology of Women*, New York: Monthly Review Press.

Runciman, W. G. (1978) *Max Weber: Selections in Translation*, Cambridge: Cambridge University Press.

Ruthven, M. (1978) *Torture: the Grand Conspiracy*, London: Weidenfeld & Nicolson.

Sahlins, M. (1972) *Stone Age Economics*, New York: Aldine.

Said, E. (1984) *The World, the Text and the Critic*, London: Faber and Faber.

Ste Croix, G. de (1981) *The Class Struggle in the Ancient Greek World*, London: Duckworth.

Ste Croix, G. de (1984) 'Class in Marx's conception of history, ancient and modern', *New Left Review*, no.146, July–August.

Sassoon, A. S. (1980) *Gramsci's Politics*, London: Croom Helm.

Sassoon, A. (1982) *Approaches to Gramsci*, London: Readers and Writers.

Savage, S. P. (1981) *The Theories of Talcott Parsons: The Social Relations of Action*, London: Macmillan.

Schatzman, M. (1976) *Soul Murder: Persecution in the Family*, Harmondsworth, Middx: Penguin Books.

Schmidt, A. (1971) *The Concept of Nature in Marx*, London: New Left Books.

Scholem, G. S. (1961) *Major Trends in Jewish Mysticism*, New York, Schocken Books.

Schwendinger, J. R. and H. (1983) *Rape and Inequality*, Beverly Hills, Calif.: Sage.

Scott, J. F. (1963) 'The changing foundations of the Parsonian action schema', *American Sociological Review*, 28.

Scraton, P. (1985) *The State of the Police*, London: Pluto.

Segal, C. M. and Stineback, D. C. (1977) *Puritans, Indians and Manifest Destiny*, New York: Putnam & Sons.

Selvin, H. (1965) 'Durkheim's *Suicide*: Further thoughts on a methodological classic', in R. A. Nisbet (ed.), *Emile Durkheim*, Englewood Cliffs, NJ: Prentice Hall.

Sennett, R. (1978) *The Fall of Public Man*, New York: Vintage Books.

Shaw, M. (1974) *Marxism versus Sociology*, London: Pluto Press.

Sim, J. (1982) 'Scarman: The police counter-attack', in M. Eve and D. Musson (eds) *The Socialist Register 1982*, London: Merlin.

Simon, W. and Gagnon, J. H. (1977) 'The anomie of affluence: a post-Mertonian conception', *American Journal of Sociology*, 82.

Sirianni, C. (1984) 'Justice and the division of labour: a reconsideration of Durkheim's *Division of Labour in Society*', *Sociological Review*, March.

Skillen, A. (1977) *Ruling Illusions: Philosophy and the Social Order*, Brighton, Sussex: Harvester Press.

Sklar, H. (ed.) (1980) *Trilateralism*, Boston: South End Press.

Smith, M. G. (1974) *Corporations and Society*, London: Duckworth.

Sorel, G. (1895a) 'Les Théories de M. Durkheim', *Le Devenir Social*, 1(1), April.

Sorel, G. (1895b) 'Théories pénales de M. Durkheim et Tarde', *Archivio di Psichiatria, Scienze Penali ed Antropologia*, 16.

Sorel, G. (1896) 'The socialist future of the syndicates', translated in J. L. Stanley (ed.) (1976) *From Georges Sorel*, Oxford: Oxford University Press.

Sorel, G. (1897) Preface to A. Labriola, *Essais sur la conception materialiste de l'histoire*.

Sorel, G. (1908 and 1941) *Reflections on Violence*, New York: Peter Smith.

Spitzer, S. (1975) 'Punishment and social organization: a study of

Durkheim's theory of penal evolution', *Law and Society Review*, 9.

Stampp, K. M. (1956) *The Peculiar Institution: Slavery in the Ante-Bellum South*, New York: Knopf and Vintage.

Stengel, E. (1973) *Suicide and Attempted Suicide*, Harmondsworth, Middx: Penguin Books.

Stevens, P. (1863) 'The punishment of convicts', in L. Blom-Cooper (ed.) *The Language of the Law*, London: Bodley Head.

Stone, D. (1983), 'The charismatic authority of Werner Erhard', in Wallis, 1983

Stone, G. P. and Farberman, H. A. (1967) 'On the edge of rapprochement. Was Durkheim moving toward the perspective of symbolic interaction?' *Sociological Quarterly*, 8.

Strawbridge, D. (1982) 'Althusser's theory of ideology and Durkheim's account of religion: an examination of some striking parallels', *Sociological Review*, 30.

Stuckey, S. (1971) 'Through the prisms of folklore: the Black ethos in slavery', in T. R. Frazier (ed.) *Underside of American History: Other Readings*, New York: Harcourt Brace Jovanovich.

Szasz, T. (1973) *The Manufacture of Madness*, London: Paladin Books.

Taylor, I. (1981) *Law and Order: Arguments for Socialism*, London: Macmillan.

Taylor, I., Walton, P. and Young, J. (1973) *The New Criminology*, London: Routledge & Kegan Paul.

Taylor, I., Walton, P. and Young, J. (eds) (1975) *Critical Criminology*, London: Routledge & Kegan Paul.

Taylor, S. (1982) *Durkheim and the Study of Suicide*, London: Hutchinson.

Theoharis, A. (1974) 'The rhetoric of politics: foreign policy, internal security, and domestic politics in the Truman era, 1945–50', in B. J. Bernstein (ed.) *Politics and Policies of the Truman Administration*, New York: New Viewpoints.

Therborn, G. (1980) *Science, Class and Society*, London: New Left Books and Verso Editions.

Thom, B. (1976) 'The unconscious structured as a language', *Economy and Society*, 5(4): 434–69.

Tiryakian, E. A. (1962) *Sociologism and Existentialism: Two Perspectives on the Individual and Society*, Englewood Cliffs, NJ: Prentice Hall.

Tiryakian, E. (1978) 'Emile Durkheim', in T. Bottomore and R. Nisbet (eds) *A History of Sociological Analysis*, London: Heinemann.

Tucker, R. (ed.) (1978) *The Marx–Engels Reader*, New York: Norton.

Turquet, P. (1975) 'Threats to identity in the large group', in L. Kreeger (ed.) *The Large Group: Dynamics and Therapy*, London: Constable.

Unger, R. M. (1976) *Law in Modern Society: Toward a Criticism of Social Theory*, London: Free Press.

van der Pijl, K. (1984) *The Making of an Atlantic Ruling Class*, London: Verso.

Vogt, P. (1983) 'Obligation and right; the Durkheimians and the sociology of law', in P. Besnard (ed.) *The Sociological Domain: The Durkheimians and the Founding of French Sociology*, Cambridge: Cambridge University Press.

Wallwork, E. (1973) *Durkheim, Morality and Milieu*, Cambridge, Mass.: Harvard University Press.

Warner, W. L. (1962) *American Life: Dream and reality*, Chicago: Phoenix Books, University of Chicago Press.

Weber, M. (1958) *From Max Weber: Essays in Sociology*, ed. by H. Gerth and C. W. Mills, New York: Oxford University Press.

Weber, M. (1949) *The Methodology of the Social Sciences*, New York: Free Press of Glencoe.

Weber, M.(1961) *General Economic History*, New York: Collier.

Weber, M. (1967) *Ancient Judaism*, New York: Free Press of Glencoe.

Weber, M. (1975) *Roscher and Knies: The Logical Problems of Historical Economics*, New York: Free Press of Glencoe. (translated by Guy Oakes)

Weber, M. (1976) *The Agrarian Sociology of Ancient Civilisations*, London: New Left Books.

Weber, M. (1978) *Economy and Society*, 2 vols, Berkeley: University of California Press.

Weisser, M. R. (1982) *Crime and Punishment in Early Modern Europe*, Hassocks, Sussex: Harvester Press.

White, H. (1978) review of Girard (1977). *Diacritics*,

Wiener, J. M. (1982) 'Max Weber's Marxism: theory and method in the agrarian sociology of ancient civilisations', *Theory and Society*, 11.

Wilden, A. (1972) *System and Structure*, London: Tavistock Publications.

Willeford, C. (1980) *Off the Wall*, Montclair: Pegasus Rex.

Willer, D. and Willer, J. (1973) *Systematic Empiricism: critique of a pseudo-science*, Englewood Cliffs, NJ: Prentice Hall.

Williams, E. (1968) *Beyond Belief: A Chronicle of Murder and its Detection*, London: World Books.

Williams, W. A. (1964) *The Great Evasion*, New York: Quadrangle Books.

Wilson, E. (1983) *What is to be done about Violence against Women?* Harmondsworth, Middx: Penguin Books.

Wolfe, A. (1973) *The Seamy Side of Democracy*, New York: David McKay.

Wolff, R. P. (1971) *The Rule of Law*, New York: Simon & Schuster.

Wolpe, H. (1968) 'A critical analysis of some aspects of charisma', *Sociological Review*, 16(3).

Wolpe, H. (1980) *The Articulation of Modes of Production: Essays from Economy and Society*, London: Routledge & Kegan Paul.

Wood, A. (1981) *Karl Marx*, London: Routledge & Kegan Paul.
Woodiwiss, A. (1985) 'A theoretical prologue to a socialist historiography of labour law: law, discourse and transpositioning', *International Journal of the Sociology of Law*, 13.
Woodiwiss, A. (1987a) 'The discourses of production (1): law, industrial relations and ideology', *Economy and Society*, 16(3).
Woodiwiss, A. (1987b) 'Against humanism: metatheory and the reconstruction of the concept of class' (cyclostyled).
Wright, E. O. (1979) *Class, Crisis and the State*, London: Verso.
Wrong, D. (1961) 'The over-socialized conception of man in modern society', *American Sociological Review*, 26(2), April.

Yaffe, M. (1981) 'The assessment and treatment of paedophilia', in B. Taylor (ed.) *Perspectives on Paedophilia*, London: Batsford Academic.
Yallop, D. (1981) *Deliver Us from Evil*, London: Macdonald Futura.
Young, J. (1971) *The Drugtakers*, London: Paladin Books.
Young, J. (1974) 'Drugs, deviance and mass media', in P. Rock and M. McIntosh (eds) *Deviance and Social Control*, London: Tavistock.
Young, J. (1975) 'Working-class criminology', in Taylor, Walton and Young 1975
Young, J. (1979) 'Left idealism, reformism and beyond: from new criminology to Marxism', in Fine *et al.*, *Capitalism and the Rule of Law: From deviancy theory to Marxism*, London: Hutchinson.

Zeitlin, I. (1981) *Ideology and the Development of Sociological Theory*, 2nd edn, Englewood Cliffs, NJ: Prentice Hall.
Zeldin, T. (1979) *France 1848–1945: Politics and Anger*, Oxford: Oxford University Press.
Zetterberg, H. L. (1968) 'The secret ranking', in M. Truzzi (ed.) *Sociology and Everyday Life*, Englewood Cliffs, NJ: Prentice Hall.
Zimbardo, P. (1971) 'The Psychological Power and Pathology of Imprisonment.' A statement prepared for the US House of Representatives Committee on the Judiciary (Subcommittee no. 3. Robert Kastenmeyer Chairman; hearings on prison reform). Unpublished paper, Stanford University.
Zimbardo, P. *et. al.* (1972) 'The psychology of imprisonment: privation, power and pathology', unpublished paper, Stanford University.
Zinn, H. (1968) *Disobedience and Democracy: Nine Fallacies on Law and Order*, New York: Vintage.

Index